The Guilded Pen

Fifth Edition — 2016

The Guilded Pen, Fifth Edition is a publication of the
San Diego Writers/Editors Guild
P. O. Box 881931
San Diego, CA 92168-1931
www.sdwritersguild.org

The Guilded Pen, Fifth Edition was printed by CreateSpace, an Amazon.com company, and is available at www.CreateSpace.com
Copies may also be ordered from our website: www.sdwritersguild.org

No part of this book may be reproduced or transmitted in any form without written permission from the publisher.

Marcia Buompensiero, Managing Editor
Ruth Leyse-Wallace, Editor
Simone Arias, Editor

"Ranch Hands & Cobras" was first published in *Dinner in Happy Valley, A Vietnam War Memoir*. Reprinted by permission of the author, Joseph Bonpensiero, (USAF, Lt. Col. Ret.)

"Good or Bad Luck" was first published in *Go West for Luck Go West for Love*. Reprinted by permission of the author, Mardie Schroeder.

"Occurrence at Dachau" was first published in Fate Magazine (2006) under the title "A Voice From the Other Side." Reprinted by permission of the author, Barbara McMikle.

Paperback price $15.00

Copyright © 2016 San Diego Writers/Editors Guild

All rights reserved.

ISBN: 13-9781534731509
ISBN-10: 1534731504

The Guilded Pen

Fifth Edition — 2016

An anthology of the
San Diego Writers/Editors Guild

Dedication

Rhoda Riddell

1920 – 2015

Rhoda (Fulton) Riddell was the founding mother of the San Diego Writers/Editors Guild.

She was born in Japan on October 28, 1920 to Robert and Karen Fulton, marking the start of an adventurous life. Her parents left Japan after the Great Kanto earthquake of 1923 and eventually settled in La Jolla. Rhoda graduated from La Jolla High in 1938 and then waited tables at her mother's local restaurant "Fulton's Green Dragon Inn." She also did some modeling and briefly attended UC Berkeley and secretarial school. Rhoda met an enlisted man in La Jolla and they went to Hawaii to be married — two weeks before the Japanese bombed Pearl Harbor. Rhoda told how she and her husband Robert were in bed when the Japanese attacked and how the Japanese were shooting at their get-away car. When the couple later divorced, Rhoda decided to travel the world with her two daughters, Laurie and Cecily.

Rhoda lived in nine countries and worked as a foreign war correspondent, had a radio show for armed forces, was a realtor in La Jolla and a travel writer and social director aboard a cruise ship in the Mediterranean. She loved to read and was a member of the Mensa Society.

Rhoda was known for her wit and, according to a close friend, was cheerful, funny and, above all, authentic. We are made richer by the struggles and labors of those who have carved the road before us.

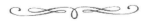

Table of Contents

Foreword – Kathi Diamant
Acknowledgements
About the San Diego Writers/Editors Guild
About the Contributors   287

Contributors	Title	Page
Amsden, Diana	Anastasia and Psychotherapists, 1962	187
	Monte Sol Police Chief Ismael Romero	279
Asher, Laurie	Pesky Little Critters	233
Barrons, William	San Diego at War!	77
Beeby, Gered	The Elements of Trust	67
Bonpensiero, Joe	Ranch Hands & Cobras	37
Buompensiero, Marcia	We'll Always Have Perris	159
Carleton, Lawrence Richard	One Night Only	165
Clement, Nancy	Summertime and the Livin' Is Easy	87
Converse, Al	A Rose for Mrs. Delahanty	43
Crothers, Barbara	Aurora Borealis — The Women — 1965	9
Crothers, Fred	Johnny the Choker Setter	101
Doublebower, Bob	A Walk in the Swamp	61
Eberhardt, Marty	Recipe for Calm	21
Edge, Chloe	Kip	171
Feldman, David	Russia Through Three Cameras	23
Hafner, Janet	The Unknown	111
	One Photograph — Many Memories	175
Harmon, Margaret	One Piece of Perfection	1
Hinaekian, Peggy	Looking for Rhett Butler	185
Huntington, Barbara Weeks	Gods and Genies	179
	House on Verdugo Road	95
	Season of the Witches	269
Huntsman, Harry	One Night	125
Janda, Anne	The Birthmark	105
	Skating	17
	Coffee	181
Joyce, P.K.	Home Sweet Home	259
Keeler, Emily	Vacation Questionnaire	263
Lederer, Richard	A Man of Fire-New Words	29
Leech, Tom	Quartets Abound	55
	What's More Awesome Than a Butterfly?	247

Contributors (cont'd)	Title	Page
Leyse-Wallace, Ruth	Sloppy Joe Summer	195
Mayfield, Donald	Retribution 1	45
	Retribution 2	51
	Rob Asked About Me?	75
McCullagh, Caroline	What I Remember About My Mother	191
McMikle, Barbara	Interlude on an Ancient Road	199
	Occurrence at Dachau	273
Naiman, Joe	A Benefit of Equal Treatment	91
Nelson, Carl	Stickup, U.S. Navy Style	57
Peterson, Richard	Gray Ladies	203
Posy, Norma	Coming Home	283
	Jelly Roll Blues	183
	Voyager Graveyard	137
Primiano, Frank	El Niño	249
	Easter	93
	Rituals	227
Raybold, Arthur	Dorothy Stang	277
	Green Flash	135
	Whistle While You Work	223
Roberts, Laura	Win, Lose, or 3-Day Novel!	215
Sandy, Muriel	Woman in the Hijab	141
Schroeder, Mardie	Good or Bad Luck	145
	So What's a John Wayne?	267
Warren, Sam	Zipolite — The Hippie Paradise	119
Winters, Gary	Chronicles of Drama Therapy	211
	The Fourth of July	153
	Tsunami	85
Yaros, Ken	Christmas Lights at Home	265
	Schwartz Nails It	97
	What Dentists Like	235
Yeaman, Sandra	To Sandy, From Henry	239
Zajac, Amy E.	Belly Up	131
	Swish	243
Zolfaghari, Val	Pythagorean Pursuit	133
	Story of a Drawing	253

Foreword

Kathi Diamant

"What is written is merely the ashes of our experience."
— Franz Kafka

This collection of short stories, poems and imaginative essays is the culmination of lifetimes of experience, of memory, of love. Of determination, perseverance and hard work. That you are holding this book in your hands in an essential final piece in the natural order of the writing process. By reading this book, you make the cycle—from germination of the idea to the writing, rewriting, editing, critiquing, copyediting, and so on until finally, publication—complete and whole. In exploring the prose and poetry within these pages, you will enter the writer's world and at least for a few pages, expand and enrich your own world. This is the promise of reading.

Most, if not all, writers start off as readers. The more we read, often, the more we are inspired to write, to tell our own stories, write our own histories, reveal our own truths. Ah, but then there is the writing. The actual putting pen to paper, or fingers to the keyboard. As anyone who has ever sat down with a bright and shining idea, a story, an unrealized reality, a dream, and tried to put it into words knows the immensity of that undertaking. The heartbreak. The frustration. The relief. The joy. The deeper you go in the process, the more you lose your way, and find yourself. But we writers are not alone. Although the act of writing is by necessity solitary, the writing world itself is brimming with help and support.

There are few professional communities with as much collegial advice and guidance as writing. There are myriad magazines, classes, books, meet-ups, blogs, websites and writing support groups. The writers in this anthology are members of the San Diego Writers/Editors Guild, a nonprofit organization which promotes, supports and encourages writing for youth and adults. Royalties from the sale of *The Guilded Pen* help fund the worthy endeavor of supporting San Diego writers, allowing for the fullness of their expression. In a vital way, this anthology promotes writers by presenting an opportunity for publication, a fine and noble achievement. It encourages reading, by offering the best efforts of our local writers, from bestselling authors to previously unpublished poets, and the opportunity to discover the many literary styles and subjects found in our own communities.

As a writer who learned to write because I had a story I had to tell, I know the long, unspeakable process of getting a manuscript ready for publication, even if it is just a few pages. I know how important it is to see one's work in print, the encouragement derived from a dream made real. My first book publication was an essay in an anthology, and it gave me the strength and certainty that I was on the right path.

To all the writers published here, thank you for sharing your talent, skill and hard work. To those seasoned pros, thank you for showing us why you are successful. To those published for the first time here, congratulations and well done! To the readers of this new fifth edition, know that in buying this book, you are actively supporting writers who may be your neighbors, colleagues, friends, and family. You are fulfilling the hope and promise of their labor by bearing witness. Bless you, dear reader.

Kathi Diamant is an author, writing instructor and coach, and above all, a reader.

Acknowledgements

The Guilded Pen, Fifth Edition owes its existence to the SDW/EG Board of Directors. Their dedication and foresight fostered the creation of a venue to showcase members' works and to carry on the mission to support the local writing arts.

Board of Directors 2016
Anne Janda, President
Robert Doublebower, Vice President
Ruth Leyse-Wallace, Immediate Past President
Laurie Asher, Secretary
Marcia Buompensiero, Treasurer
Richard Peterson, Membership Chair
Sandra Yeaman, Social Media Manager/Webmaster
Directors at Large:
Simone Arias
Gered Beeby
David Feldman
Mardie Schroeder
Val Zolfaghari

We are grateful to our editorial review panel who read, critiqued, and edited every submission. Special thanks and appreciation goes to Vincenzo Adragna, Laurie Asher, Gered Beeby, Anne Casey, Barbara Crothers, Robert Doublebower, Dave Feldman, , Joyce Kellawon, Richard Peterson, Sandra Yeaman, and Amy E. Zajac who contributed to the production and creation of the anthology.

The San Diego Writers/Editors Guild

Mission Statement: To Promote, Support, and Encourage the Writing Art for Adults and Youth

Founded in 1979, the Guild is believed to be the oldest writer organization in the region. The Guild is a 501(c) 3 non-profit organization. Monthly programs are planned to educate, entertain, and encourage communication among the members. A Board of Directors, elected by the members, directs and supports the program of work.

Benefits of membership include:

- Monthly Guild meetings
- Monthly Guild newsletter
- Periodic email newsletter
- Reduced fees for Guild-sponsored workshops
- Networking with other members
- Monthly Marketing Support Group
- Access to critique groups
- Listing in the annual directory
- Publishing in the annual *The Guilded Pen* anthology
- Manuscript Review Program
- Periodic presentation of awards: "The Rhoda Riddell Builders Award" — recognizing efforts to build/expand the Guild; "Special Achievements Awards" — for extraordinary service; and "The Odin Award" — to those who have been major stimulators of the writing arts in San Diego as evidenced by their body of published work.

Guild membership is open to all and guests are welcome to the meetings for a small fee. For a current list of meeting dates and speakers, go to: www.sdwritersguild.org

Draw your chair up close
      to the edge of the precipice
            and I'll tell you a story.

                      - F. Scott Fitzgerald

One Piece of Perfection

Margaret Harmon

An idealistic young architect named Zoe knew a hundred professionals who wanted to live downtown in a port city, but there was no chic housing downtown. She realized that if she designed a ten-story building of forty condominiums—architecturally striking and high-tech with green construction—she could establish herself as a design pioneer and help her friends live really well without destroying the earth.

"Put in $60,000 cash with a mortgage of $300,000," she said, "and you'll have a condo worth five times as much to you—you'll see—while reducing your carbon footprint five sizes."

She put her own life savings in first, and thirty-nine artists, attorneys, doctors, professors, and business owners paid $60,000 down and watched the building grow.

Choosing an award-winning contractor, and the very latest technology to make her building earthquake-safe, fireproof, termite-resistant, solar-powered, solar-tube-lit, and equipped with a wind-driven air conditioning system of her own invention, she built it eleven stories tall, to make room for a gym and eco-batteries on the ground floor. Underground parking provided two spots for each condo, plus twenty spaces for guests. A rain- and fog-catching system on the roof produced water pure enough to drink.

The condos were so eco-friendly, energy-efficient, and inexpensive to live in that Zoe called them "econdos." The building was so beautiful from every angle that she named it *Belle Maison*.

Owners met monthly for potluck suppers to learn about her inventions and bond with each other. They appreciated how cleverly she had positioned their building on the lot to give each condo a view of the bay, ocean, city skyline, or mountains. Every balcony had a solar barbeque to avoid charcoal's carcinogens. All window screens were magnetically charged to collect particles so air passing through them carried no pollen or soot.

The e-condos were identical inside because the prices were identical—and because Zoe designed the structure in precise geometric units that interlocked to provide absolute structural integrity. They were airy and sunlit, with a floor plan so functional that furniture and art settled in to express each owner's personality as though the spaces had been individually designed.

Belle Maison provided all the energy its residents used. The roof and south-facing wall were solar-tiled, and the gym's exercycles, treadmills, and weight machines turned electric generators. The elevator used electricity to ascend, but recharged its battery as it descended. Wind turbines on each corner of the building actually earned money for the owners. Their city was periodically buffeted by storms from the sea and, during severe winds, the wind turbines automatically adjusted to catch more wind and create more electricity. Turning the turbines dissipated the force of the wind, and the grateful city paid a small fee whenever wind speed rose above thirty knots.

Owners greeted each other in elevators and stairwells as partners sharing a whole greater than its forty parts. They had no power bills, low water bills, and air so clean they dusted their furniture only twice a year.

As word of Belle Maison's beauty and energy efficiency spread, international media lionized Zoe. After appearing on the covers of seventy-three magazines in sixteen countries, she sold her beloved e-condo to a red-haired interior designer living one floor above her and moved to Paris, where she was commissioned to design *Belles Maisons II et III*.

The e-condo owners lived Zoe's idealism and maintained their homes in perfect harmony . . . until a hairy-armed CEO in a west-facing e-condo tired of his ocean view because "at night a dark ocean is boring." Extending his balcony just three feet would give him the city skyline and lots of lights. He had the maintenance crew from his company push heavy-duty railing out three feet and add sturdy flooring.

When a writer who had turned her living room into her studio without changing any walls confronted the CEO about risking Belle Maison's structure by enlarging his balcony, he told her, "My e-condo is *my* e-condo" and slammed the door on her shoe.

A therapist with a mole on her lip tired of being perpetually cold. She called a builder to glass in her balcony so she could enjoy sun without wind. The builder suggested making it five feet longer and ten feet wider to create a solarium. The therapist bought furniture for her new room and began growing orchids.

But her solarium shaded the balconies below it, so a history professor extended his balcony ten feet, widened it fifteen feet, and planted palm trees in its corners. A ballerina kept her balcony small, but was angry. She had converted her living room into a ballet studio—with mirrored wall, barre, and hardwood floor—while maintaining Zoe's perfect design.

An attorney whose hobby was architecture sued the owners of the three extended balconies. "Belle Maison is a living work of life-sustaining art. Hodge-podging it destroys its value. We didn't buy concrete, steel, and glass; we bought a concept, design, and beauty that belong to all of us."

The judge decreed that, as a work of art as well as a life-sustaining home owned by all, Belle Maison could not have its balconies modified. But since the building was not designated as an historic landmark with preservation orders, he couldn't force the removal of what was already done. He could only stop further desecration of the exterior.

* * *

That winter a wine-connoisseur banker hired a specialist who combined hypersonic jack-hammering with concrete acid etching to secretly carve a walk-in wine cellar from the six-foot-thick concrete wall between his condo and the elevator shaft.

The operatic tenor next door found out and hired the specialist to excavate a soundproof practice studio from his wall of the elevator shaft.

An artist had two friends help him convert his e-condo into a loft space by stealthily removing all interior walls and suspending his bed from the ceiling. A harpist replaced her interior walls with glass bricks, for more light and brighter acoustics.

An English teacher had her out-of-work brother replace her e-condo's inside walls with bookcases accessible from both sides.

An orthopedic surgeon on the top floor planted fruit trees on the roof. Their fruit was delicious, but they shaded the solar panels and their leaves clogged the wind turbines and rainwater collector.

The red-haired interior designer who'd bought Zoe's e-condo one floor beneath hers hired a contractor to remove the floor/ceiling between the two living rooms to create a two-story Great Room with stained glass in all the windows. It took the contractor a year to blast, drill, and saw through four feet of concrete and rebar. When the ballerina said it was dangerous to tear out bearing walls and ceilings and floors, the interior designer said, "Mind your own business."

* * *

Three years later, a seismic tremor rattled the port city. Belle Maison residents didn't worry because Zoe had made their building earthquake-proof. But the tremor hit a frequency that made Belle Maison sway. Enlarged balconies exaggerated its sway and the trees extended its arc.

The trees slid off the roof. The heavy solarium and extended balconies yanked their e-condos from the building and flung them to the sidewalk. Appliances shot from holes in walls. Stained-glass windows popped out of the two-story great room bulging into the street. Glass bricks exploded into shards. Elevator cables snapped and the elevator free-fell into the parking garage as its shaft collapsed into the wine connoisseur's cellar and tenor's studio, crushing the artist's loft and English teacher's house of bookcases.

On the ninth floor, the writer who'd kept her e-condo walls as Zoe had designed them heard creaks and small explosions. She crouched behind her sturdy sofa, as advised by disaster survival manuals.

But she didn't need to. Her e-condo, a precise geometric unit of reinforced concrete and steel, rode down through Belle Maison like an elevator car, landing on the rubble of the condos weakened by their owners. So did the ballerina's and twenty-seven other e-condos remaining as Zoe had built them. Surrounded by the rubble of lesser-built neighbor buildings, twenty-nine e-condo cubes rested on eleven crushed like beer cans.

The ballerina and writer telephoned Zoe in Paris, and when she saw news footage of the disaster she returned immediately to Belle Maison with sketchbook and drawing pencils. The owners of the twenty-nine surviving econdos met with her to see if Belle Maison could be rebuilt.

Zoe opened the meeting with a smile. "A problem inspires its own solution."

An attorney sat forward. "Rebuilding is pointless if greedy people can destroy it again. We need tougher contracts."

A blonde biologist nodded. "Humans are acquisitive and competitive. Many animals are. But do humans lack a sense of 'enough'?"

A psychiatrist adjusted his glasses. "Some of us don't *get* the impact of our actions."

A museum director twisted her heavy bronze necklace. "Possessions express our personalities, but Belle Maison provides excellent space for self-expression."

An engineer cleared his throat. "G + I > W = Kablooey. If Greed plus Ignorance are greater than Wisdom, we'll destroy the planet and, of course, ourselves."

A statistician spoke from the back of the room. "Only 47.6 percent of humans are smart enough to appreciate Belle Maison, while just 18.4 percent have the self-discipline to sustain it."

"Eighteen percent!" Zoe's stomach dived under her belt buckle. "Only eighteen percent?"

Finally, the writer said, "*We* want Belle Maison. Let's rebuild it for us. When people see how well we're living, they'll build their own Belles Maisons everywhere."

* * *

All but two surviving owners voted to rebuild Belle Maison and sign a contract promising not to damage any safety or eco-features. The two dissidents cashed out their insurance settlements and moved away, and their e-condos were bought by a gentle pediatrician and a wise oceanographer.

Adding her European earnings to the remaining settlements, Zoe built thirty new e-condos in a ten-story building with a carbon-fiber elevator in a titanium shaft. Combining the space that had been the wine connoisseur's condo and the therapist's, she built a greenhouse where e-condo owners could grow organic vegetables year-round. The English teacher's e-condo was replaced by a library. The artist's loft became an art gallery. The tenor's condo was now a lovely, small theater.

She invented a movable wall to give owners greater design and function flexibility. Each living-room ceiling was now supported by a carbon-steel post to which she attached a wall that could swing ninety degrees to enlarge one room and shrink another.

For the new staircases, she created pressure-sensitive Piezoelectric steps so people recharged Belle Maison's batteries whenever they walked up or down stairs.

Each new e-condo was a precise geometric unit of concrete and steel, interlocking, balanced, divinely proportioned. Zoe rebuilt her original unit, replacing the space above it with an interfaith chapel/meditation room and labyrinth, in gratitude to all the owners who fulfilled themselves without endangering others.

She wrote a Construction Code and Owners' Manual explaining how every design and functional element interacted, and her attorney wrote a contract for owners promising to protect Belle Maison. Residents formed a Committee of Owners empowered to oversee changing anything bigger than a light bulb; the writer and ballerina co-chaired it.

Zoe watched happily as all the owners signed their final contract—until a software designer muttered and balked. When he finally signed the document, his hand shook, smearing his signature, and he growled as he left the room. Zoe followed him outside. "Why?" she asked.

The software designer glared. "Who *are* you people, to tell us how to live?"

Zoe kept her voice calm. "Why do you live in Belle Maison if you don't like it?"

"Changing a few things won't destroy it."

"Which few—solar panels and wind turbines? The bearing walls?" Zoe felt her cheeks redden.

"Well, but..."

"But what? Would you rather drive a car as big as a house, eat food so processed it has *no* expiration date, and *hide* from sun and wind instead of *using* them?"

"Never mind," he snapped. "I'll sell!"

Zoe reached out and shook his hand.

* * *

She ran alone on the beach to think. *Are we crazy to keep fighting for Belle Maison?*

The waves rushed toward her, hissing, flattening previous waves, gliding back to sea to rise again. She ran higher on the sand to keep her shoes dry, and watched the surf. New waves rose and rushed to shore, collapsed against the sand, and slid out to sea, where they swelled again and surged ashore.

Waves recycle each other! She laughed and slowed to a walk, dodging surf that kept chasing her shoes. "And you never quit!"

A flock of seabirds flew past her. They banked and turned, flashing gray-brown backs, then white bellies, and landed at the water's edge. Dainty birds stabbed short bills into the sand for shallow crustaceans. Birds with long bills plunged them into the sand up to their eyes and brought up deep prey. Swallows shaped like curved blades sliced the air above the kelp, capturing flies.

She watched a long time.

Those who fit the earth, thrive. And those who don't... die out.

"The eighteen percent." She inhaled enough ocean air to fill herself from her shoes to her sunglasses and walked home to Belle Maison.

Aurora Borealis
The Women – 1965

Barbara Crothers

A blinking red sign in the distance registered minus 56 degrees as I stepped off the plane in December 1964. I didn't know if it was night or day, only that it was dark. The vinyl covering of my new hairdryer shattered into a thousand tiny pieces as I stepped through the door of the plane into that cold world. My husband met me and our three kids at the airport and took us to a car driven by one of his friends. The kids sat in front where it was warm. There were two places we could see through the windshield where clear plastic ovals had been attached to it. All other windows were covered with ice, inside and out. Several miles down the highway I saw flames leaping into the air.

"Umm, must be another overheated furnace. Lots of homes burn down each winter." The driver had looked over his shoulder and spoke in my direction. I was shivering. My husband loosened his parka and took my feet out of my not-made-for-this-weather boots and placed one foot under each of his armpits to warm them.

We arrived at Eielson Air Force Base, about thirty-six miles outside Fairbanks, Alaska. Though my husband was an enlisted man, we were assigned a large housekeeping room in temporary officer's quarters until we could find an apartment. No base housing was available.

I was twenty-five-years old, married to a man in the Air Force, and mother of three small children.

We found a two-bedroom apartment in a barracks-style complex, with eight units to a building in Fairbanks. The two oldest children would attend first and third grades at Denali School, located three or four blocks from our new home. It was minus 46 degrees when we moved out of TOQ. Until the furniture arrived in late February, we slept on borrowed mattresses under borrowed blankets, used the footlocker for a table and read Dr. Seuss books aloud to each other. Only the upstairs windows were visible to us as we walked narrow paths with towering walls of snow where the sidewalks were cleared. My husband left before the children awoke and returned long after they were in bed, if he returned at all. On weekends, he played country-western music in the bars downtown and on the bases. Sometimes I joined him.

When the temperature fell below minus 50 degrees the children did not have to attend school. We were warned that a person can freeze to death in about ten minutes if not properly dressed.

By the end of March I could see the crossbars on top of the clotheslines in our front yard—and I could smell the rotting flesh of moose and caribou remains piled under them. During the long, dark days of winter there had been no need for the resident native family to discard the unwanted, less-tender portions of the large animals any further than the yard. They could stand outside the door of the building and hurl the unneeded portions onto the growing pile under the lines, out of the way.

Darkness hid them, sub-zero temperatures froze them and fresh snow soon covered them. The heads of two giant bull moose, with wide-flattened antlers, blank, staring eyes, and a white caribou head with antlers, jutted from the rapidly diminishing mound of snow under the lines. I learned that clothes could be hung out to dry on those lines for only two complete months of the year.

Snow and ice melted as the hours of sunlight grew longer. Legs, bare bones and entrails were exposed in the receding pile. Neighborhood dogs, barking, snapping and snarling, and an occasional black raven fought over the viscera and flesh. They ate meat left on the bones, then scattered and pulled the discarded mess into every yard of our apartments in F Building. As the heap dwindled, a cloying miasma hung over the neighborhood. One day two Inuit men, threatened by the management, piled the stinking mess into a battered blue `51 Chevy pickup and hauled it away.

I saw my patch of yard, without snow, for the first time about the middle of May, near the end of spring runoff. The walls of snow gone, and the air somewhat sweeter, I stepped out onto the porch. A native woman was bending over a small boy wiping his nose. She and several young people lived in the apartment next door.

"Yours?"

She motioned to the struggling child she held in a firm grip between her knees.

I studied her faintly oriental face as she straightened. "No, my son, Michael, is in the yard next door playing with Judy's little girl."

"My name is Gloria, F-4. We're neighbors." She released the child. He scampered away to find where the other children were playing.

"Nice to meet you, Gloria. I'm Barb. I live in F-5."

"It's nice to meet you, too, Barb. The men took the mess away. Sorry it took so long." She motioned to the place under the clotheslines.

"I've noticed your family. You really have your hands full with so many teenagers."

"Oh, they're not all mine. They are the high school students from our village. We are called Eskimo or Inuit."

Removing a bobbypin from her hair, she opened it with her ivory-colored, blunt teeth and replaced it, catching wisps of shoulder-length black and graying hair that had escaped its grasp.

"It was my turn to come into Fairbanks with them for the semester." She unbuttoned her sweater and leaned against the porch railing. "They go to school here. We have no high schools in our village on the tundra. We take turns, the women." Turning to look out over the yard, she moved with an easy, natural grace, like an animal. "Two of them, only, are mine. Lewis goes to school. Wanda stays home with me. She isn't right."

I had seen the beautiful, young girl walking outside each day. She was taller than her mother and carried herself erect. Her hair, long and black, reminded me of a wet seal. Its fiery, amber highlights glistened with sunlight. Sometimes I could see her leaning against our building on quiet mornings after the other children went to school. There, whether anyone was watching or not, she reached under her dress and touched her body with one hand and stroked her breasts with the other. Her sweet, innocent face and gentle eyes never showed an emotion.

"Your daughter is beautiful, Gloria."

"Yes, she doesn't look like the rest of us. She'll always be a child."

* * *

My clean sheets and pillowcases, hung by the corners with wooden pins, were flapping in the gentle spring breeze. I scrubbed and waxed the burgundy-colored asphalt tile floors in our apartment until I could see my entire length reflected. I forced open the windows and let the outside air come in. My running battle with the ever-present cockroaches seemed to be working, at least for the moment. Winter in this new state was too long, too dark, and too cold.

With my youngest son's hand in mine, we ran to the Kiwanis Park by the Chena River and watched birds and budding trees. A flock of tiny finches, red, yellow, green, swooped into the bare branches of the tree. We kept very still and watched them for a long time. We skipped, danced and shouted hellos to anybody and everybody, simply for the joy of shouting, dancing and skipping, drinking in great gulps of fresh, unused outside air. Occasionally, when the great paddle-wheel boat, Nenanah, was tied up there, we made up tales about its travels.

That first spring was when I discovered the old blue Dodge Sedan at the end of the parking lot, covered by a mountain of snow. That car became the binding element and key to adventure and freedom for all of the women and children in our neighborhood.

Gloria, my Inuit friend, and the children went back to their village on the tundra for the brief summer months. The village men took the mattresses, card table and chairs, their television set, the hides and sinew. Then Gloria and the young people climbed into the same truck that removed the collection of carrion from under the clotheslines.

"I'll be back in September. We'll have coffee. If I have any messages for you, you will hear them on KFQD."

Every day at 5:00 in the afternoon, virtually everyone in Alaska listened to KFQD radio. Weather reports, news, and messages from the villages were broadcast daily. Messages were also sent by the bush pilots to the villages regarding flights scheduled for pickup and delivery of passengers or supplies. The station was the main line of communication throughout the state. Life and death situations depended on the radio. There were no telephones in outlying areas and very few in the city of Fairbanks in those early days of Alaska's statehood.

"I'll see you then." I hugged my Inuit friend and waved to her until the truck turned the corner onto the Richardson Highway.

In September, Gloria moved back into the apartment next door. She brought the moose and caribou hides from last winter, now tanned and supple, and a few other hides to work on while the teenagers went to school.

"Hi, Gloria. It looks like you have been a very busy lady. That's quite a pile of furs there. What is your next step . . . looks like an awesome task?"

"Oh, it's not such a big deal." She flashed a modest smile, picked up some of the dried caribou sinew and put it in her mouth. "You just chew the sinew with your front teeth until it is soft and flat." She chewed the pieces, moving them slowly as she covered all the surfaces and began the process again. I could see that it would take much chewing to make those pieces soft enough to sew the hides together.

"Hey, Gloria, I brought coffee. If you'll show me where you keep your pot, I'll make it."

She gave me a small sauce pan. I filled it with water and a hand full of coffee grounds. I put the pan on the stove and turned on the electric burner.

"When an Inuit man wishes to divorce his wife, he knocks out her front teeth." Gloria smiled and flashed her teeth, ivory-colored, blunt and all still intact. "When an Inuit woman cannot make the sinew soft, she has no more worth. She has to leave the village. Some of them move to the city and become whores. What else is there for them to do?"

I had seen toothless Inuit women sitting in the bars and saloons where we entertained on weekends. I looked at Gloria's strong jaw line and the worn-down teeth. I thought about the hours she spent preparing the sinew with which she sewed the parkas. Survival of the village depended on its members staying warm through each long, dark winter. Therefore, her value as a woman depended on her teeth!

The water began to boil. I turned the burner down low. The rich aroma of fresh coffee filled the room. I took two mugs from the cupboard and poured a cup of cold water into the sauce pan to settle the grounds. Steam rose from the cups as I carried them to the card table.

Gloria walked over to the pile of soft, rich furs lying on the floor on a blanket. The moose hide was thick with long grayish-brown fur. It was large enough to cover a regular-size bed.

"This one will be for a man. I will sew some walrus ivory and beads on it and make a traditional Inuit pattern on the sleeves and around the bottom. I have some wolf fur to sew around the hood. Wolf fur does not freeze or become wet or covered with frost from a person's breath. I can sell it for about four hundred dollars. That will support my family for a long time."

She laid the fur down and came to the table. Sipping the coffee she obviously enjoyed, she continued telling me how the parkas were made. "The pieces for the parkas are cut from the smooth side of the hide with a single-edged razor blade, not the fur side, because I don't want to cut the fur. Not too long ago, we still used sharpened shells or bone knives to cut the hide. The fur overlaps the seams when the pieces are sewn together and make them wind and waterproof. Then I punch holes along the edges of the hide. I use a strong needle made of walrus ivory. It's old and belonged to my grandmother. I like to use it better than the steel ones. Those needles break sometimes."

I poured more coffee for each of us and drank in the story, the methods of survival and the warmth of this woman, so different yet so like me.

"The white caribou fur is for a woman's dress parka. I will decorate it with beads and ermine. It will be beautiful when it is finished. It will come down over the knees of whoever is wearing it. Her mukluks (waterproof boots made of animal skin) are usually up to the knees, so all the warmth stays inside. If she closes the hood and breathes into the parka, her own breath will keep her and a baby warm, if there is one inside the parka with her. I can sell it for about seven hundred dollars. I make good parkas with good furs." She wrinkled her nose. "Sometimes, when the hides aren't tanned just right they stink later. Mine never stink. I can sell them for more. I have a very good reputation."

"How can the villagers pay so much?"

"Oh, we provide for our village. We only *sell* them to outsiders."

* * *

One evening I went outdoors to look for the northern lights as I had many times. Usually they were bright and moving; however, this night they were brilliant—iridescent shafts of multicolored lights flowing across the sky. I called the inhabitants of my building out to look. The men stayed inside, but every woman came to see the enchantment of those Northern Lights and in the doing of it we each became aware of our own Aurora Borealis. Each bold, able, beautiful. Our eyes and hearts became aware of that shared truth within us. We talked, laughed and celebrated that awakening, that communion, that sole occasion we were all together once, dynamic and filled with that strength. The memory of that night still touches the corner of my heart where the spirit of my twenty-five-year-old self dwells.

Skating

Anne Janda

Death has always surrounded Lucy. Kittens die of distemper in the dark shadows under the porch. When there are too many feral cats to feed, her dad takes some of them in a sack to the creek at night and drowns them. During hunting season skinned rabbits and limp pheasants hang on the gate in the evening. Among them might be one of those her mother took in when it was orphaned by her dad's mower. He brings the frightened, furry babies home in his overall pocket and gives them to Lucy's mother. She keeps them in a cardboard box with a screen on top and feeds them water and lettuce until they are old enough to set free.

So when Lucy's dog, Blackie, stumbles up the porch steps and plops his haunch in front of her, limply wagging his black tail back and forth, expecting her to show him love, when his tongue hangs out the side of his mouth as though he's hot from chasing squirrels instead of worn out from trying to breathe, and he shifts his weight from his right leg to the left, and back again, Lucy knows he is dying in front of her. The effort to take short raspy breaths heaves his creamy chest in and out. His brown eyes—dull—no shine now, yellow moons hanging underneath, eagerly seek her affection… her usual attention.

She wants to run away from his death before it overtakes her. She wants to run away from the death she sees all around her. She sees it in him, in the dying leaves and the barren cornstalks in the fields beyond the creek. Even the sun is bleak in the face of winter. She tries to talk to her dog with her thoughts, *Get well, Blackie. Cough it up so you can breathe. Don't die.* She doesn't want to touch him. She doesn't want to catch what he has. She pats his head and feels the bumpy bones on the top of his gaunt skull. She is repulsed and pulls back. He wants more. He pursues her hand and tries to lick it.

Sometimes in winter a rabbit comes to the coal pile underneath the kitchen window and sits there in the snow. Her mother likes to say, "He's one of those I raised. He's come to say hello." Lucy's mother is happy when they come back. But in hunting season she fries up the rabbits for dinner. Lucy tries to forget seeing their bodies hanging on the gate stripped of skin and fur. She tries not to think about the ones who've come back to sit beside the coal pile to say hello to her mother. When Lucy eats the crispy, tasty, buckshot-riddled rabbit meat, it tastes good; just like her dad said it would. She wonders what the rabbit feels when the buckshot takes him down. Her dad says he doesn't feel anything.

Lucy believes that men have more to do with death than women do. Several times a year, her dad calls the "dead truck" to pick up a dead hog or sheep he's dragged from the fields. She's seen the maggots in their bellies. Then sometimes everything shifts and it's a woman's job. Every Saturday her mother takes a hatchet to a white feathery chicken or two. Lucy watches the body flopping around, the accusing eye in the severed head looking at her. Lucy covers her ears. Her mother says stop being silly. "You'll be doing this someday. "

"Not me, no I won't," her retort is strong and straight to the point, even though she doesn't say it out loud.

As Blackie sits in front of her, she thinks *I don't have time for this; I need to decide what I'm going to wear to the roller rink tomorrow night.* This thought is a trick she has for dispelling death. Lucy tells herself she will be happy. When her mother takes a nap on Sundays after working hard all week and enduring her father's abusive tirades, Lucy quietly opens the door and watches. When she can see that her mother is breathing, see that she hasn't died, she goes out into the sunlight. There she stays. Because she is young, she believes she will never be like her mother. She is the spring. Her mother is the winter.

Lucy tells Blackie to go away, and he turns obediently, slowly climbs back down the steps and heads to the back of the house. The next day, her mother comes upstairs to her bedroom. "Dad took Blackie to the vet today."

They sit together on Lucy's bed. She is still wondering what to wear to the roller rink. And, as usual, she's irritated that her mother avoids looking her in the eyes. She gets impatient as her mother looks down, not saying anything.

Why can't she just say what comes next?

"He isn't coming home. They put him to sleep. Doc South said his lungs were filled with some kind of fungus, something he ate here on the farm, and there wasn't anything they could do."

"What kind of fungus? Can we catch what he had?"

"No, I don't think so. Doc South would've told dad if we could. If you don't feel like going skating I'm sure the girls will understand."

"Why wouldn't I want to go?" she asks as she walks toward her closet. Lucy has decided to wear her short black skirt with her creamy sweater.

That night, she wonders why the older boy who always wears a white shirt and a dreamy scent of shaving lotion doesn't ask her for a couple's skate under the turning ball of mirrors. As usual the mirrors transform the wooden floor into a galaxy of starlight. She sees an image of Blackie in the magical mirage. For an instant she remembers the way he looked at her during the sunset. She doesn't even wonder why she is void of feeling anything at all.

Recipe for Calm

Marty Eberhardt

People say she's welcoming,
Once called a "coffee person,
Fresh, warm, strong
In a deep, wide cup."
But one who matters
Wishes she were another person
Entirely.
She edits her words,
Suppresses her preferences,
Compliments when just
Modicum to praise.
Still she is mocked.
Yes, so unfair
But absurd to complain.
She's no Syrian refugee,
No Guatemalan mother
In a town of drugstores.
Still, a betrayal
Burns orange, black-edged,
Deep inside her gut though
Compelled to breathe kindness.
Older than her offender

Woman of patience
Perched on sandbar
Plunging to indignity?

Russia Through Three Cameras

Dave Feldman

After our trip to Russia was over, I admitted that taking three cameras on our tour was a mistake.

I carried an 8mm movie camera and a German box camera, and Betty handled the 35mm Canon. Two days in, Betty said, "I've had it with the cameras." That left me to manage all three. I saw most of the country through one lens or another. I must say that Betty held any two cameras while I shot pictures with the third.

That was August of 1964, with the Communists still clearly in control.

We flew out of Frankfurt, Germany, thirty-three of us on a guided tour, with a first stop in Budapest, Hungary. We were expecting wine and song, but the gaiety seemed gone. Even the champagne at our first dinner proved as flat as the looks on the faces of our tired waitresses. So much for communism.

But never mind that. Buda sat on one side of the Danube, Pest on the other. We got to see both sides, along with fashionable shops (by their standards), graceful gardens, and several of the museums.

For our departure breakfast, handed to us at 4 a.m., we each got a box lunch with a hard-boiled egg, a greasy ham sandwich and, perhaps for dessert, a green bell pepper. All were to be devoured on the plane.

Moscow awaited. We were dog-tired on arrival, and wanted only a hotel bed, but the bus driver, following orders, insisted on giving us a guided tour of the city. To him, the highlight seemed to be the sight of the Moscow River, complete with boats, as seen from a speeding bus.

He became the first of many local guides to proudly proclaim about the "Great October Revolution." After hearing so many "Great October Revolutions," a guy in the back of our bus suggested just shortening it to the initials, "G.O.R." It didn't work.

Our digs were in the towering Leningradskaya Hotel. Betty

and I were lodged on the 17th floor. With two elevators, and one of them often not operating, getting everyone down to dinner proved a challenge. Our tours ended at 6:15, with dinner scheduled for 6:30. We tried the down stairways, but a burly Russian woman sat at a desk, on guard. No, the doors to the stairs were locked.

"What if there's a fire," Betty asked.

"We don't have fires," the guard replied.

She was susceptible to a small bribe, however. Perhaps a trade would be a better word than bribe. We offered two ballpoint pens for the poster of the Bolshoi Ballet on the wall behind her. Agreed. We had stocked up on ballpoint pens, as well as bubble gum. A man's white business shirt would bring even more loot. The most prized American creation of all: Levi's. I wished I had brought some.

With security more than tight, we felt as if we were being watched by someone. An older woman reported that her false teeth were missing from her luggage. They certainly were: An older man, who resided three rooms away, found them in his luggage and returned them to her. We had all been away for the afternoon, so someone (the KGB?) must have invaded the woman's luggage and forgotten which room the dentures belonged in.

Olga, our guide, could have been mistaken at first glance for an NFL ball carrier, but she had much more class than that. In fact, she had translated J.D. Salinger's *Catcher in the Rye* for Russian readers. She stayed with us for nearly the entire trip—and we wondered if she might defect to the West when we crossed the border into Germany. After all, she had admitted publicly that she hated Russian toilet paper.

She gave us more wandering room than we expected. Betty and I wanted to visit the Pushkin Museum in Moscow.

"Take this piece of paper," Olga said, writing out the directions in Russian. "Go down to the subway station, take the train going to the right, and show this paper to anyone on the train. They'll direct you."

We boarded the train, showed the paper around, and a young lady said, "I'll take you there," in English. She got us off the train, up to the street, then walked two blocks to the Pushkin. Though she went out of her way, she wouldn't take money, just thanks. The Pushkin's artworks were splendid, and the mosaics in the spotless Moscow subway stations were nearly as artistic.

* * *

Leningrad (now St. Petersburg) came next. The overnight train left Moscow at midnight. Betty and I and two tour friends, Roman and DeDe, decided to team up for the trip. One benefit: Roman had brought along, and hidden, a can of forbidden Coca-Cola. My mouth twitched at the thought of a few drops of the ambrosia.

I started the night off in usual poor fashion. Roman had some vodka, so we bought tomato juice at a kiosk near the train station. The tomato juice turned out to be bad, so I looked around for a place to dump the contents, keeping the bottle for use as a glass. I bent over, poured the tomato juice out onto the railroad tracks, and managed to spill some on a pair of highly polished shoes. I looked up to apologize. The owner of the shoes was the train conductor, and she was not amused. (I pretended not to be amused myself.)

When we got to our assigned berths on the train, we found that, somehow, Roman and I were billeted in one little cabin with two Russian men, and Betty and DeDe were booked next door, along with two very pleased young Russian men. They were so pleased about the ladies that they had already stripped down to their undershirts.

Roman and I went searching for Olga, with no luck. When we returned, Betty and DeDe had solved the situation, using bubble gum and two ballpoint pens to work a trade, and our women were back with us.

Leningrad, called the Venice of the North for its many canals, could not have been prettier. The colors on the onion-domed buildings were brighter than we had expected.

Again I managed to mess up. Searching for a men's room, I got lost in the Hermitage, the famous Leningrad museum. I stumbled upon our tour group just as it left. The evening worked out better. We sat in our hotel room and savored the many small bottles of liquors that tour members had smuggled in. Unfortunately, the Coca-Cola did not appear. I would have to wait.

The return overnight trip to Moscow went smoothly, with no young men coveting our ladies. In Moscow, we enjoyed the usual tourist attractions: Red Square, complete with Lenin's Tomb (he looked yellow and waxy). And we found the G.U.M. Department Store to be a collection of small stalls selling items for tourists and residents alike. We took home a three-stringed balalaika.

At our Moscow Hotel, and elsewhere in Russia, we Americans were always served the same dinner: breaded veal cutlets, mashed potatoes, green peas and carrots. Betty and I attempted to eat at the table for the French tourists, assuming it had much tastier fare, but we were rebuffed.

I still have photos of the Russian version of a soft-drink machine. We inserted a few coins, held a tin cup under the spigot, and waited for a not-very-appetizing drink. I found it to be light on fizziness, and light on sweetness. And I hoped the germs on the tin cup, attached by chain to the spigot, were not interested in Americans.

It came time for the bus ride back to Germany. A long bus ride. A friend described the landscape as the world's longest airplane runway — 700 miles or more — totally flat. We crammed into the bus, Olga still smiling and with us, for the drive to Minsk and Warsaw and Prague.

Minsk offered a wreath-laying ceremony at a military monument. In Warsaw, as elsewhere, the demand for American dollars on the black market stayed high. Ducking down an alley, I exchanged fifty dollars worth of my bills for a whole lot of Polish zlotys. I might still be in prison if I'd been caught.

We found the Polish men and women to be the happiest of the people we saw in the Iron Curtain countries. We had a sign on the windshield of our bus that said U.S.A., and the people throughout Poland would wave and smile at us.

* * *

Czechoslovakia proved quietly beautiful. But at the border

with Germany, guards armed with machine guns marched along on catwalks, making sure that only Americans could cross. Other guards carefully scrutinized our passports. Once our bus drove into Germany, we broke into applause. Olga stayed behind, waving goodbye. We missed Olga, who had shared her expertise, her kindness, and her vodka with us.

Roman, the owner of the smuggled Coca-Cola, brought out the can and offered me a sip.

"No," I said, because I was angry with him. "Why didn't you open it up before? Now I'm in a land where I can get all the Cokes I want."

As for the three cameras, two of them stayed home on the rest of our trips.

A Man of Fire-New Words

Richard Lederer

What do these six sentences have in common?:

Has Will a peer, I ask me.
I swear he's like a lamp.
We all make his praise.
Wise male. Ah, I sparkle!
Hear me, as I will speak.
Ah, I speak a swell rime.

Each is an anagram that uses all the letters in the name *William Shakespeare* and captures a luminous truth: Peerless Will Shakespeare shines through the centuries and inspires our praise.

Little information about William Shakespeare's personal life is available, but from municipal records we can deduce that he was born in the English village of Stratford-upon-Avon, in the county of Warwickshire, on April 23, 1564, and that after having retired to his home town around 1611, he died there on April 23, 1616.

Shakespeare's plays, which he wrote in London between approximately 1590 and 1613, have been in almost-constant production since their creation. Because the playwright dealt with universal truths and conflicts in human nature, his tragedies, comedies, and history plays continue to draw audiences from all walks of life, just as they did in their own day. Time has proven the truth of what Shakespeare's contemporary, Ben Jonson, said of him: "He was not of an age, but for all time."

An often-neglected aspect of William Shakespeare's genius is that his words, as well as his works, were not just of an age, but for all time. He was, quite simply, the greatest word-maker who ever lived. Ongoing research demonstrates that there are 20,138 lemmata (dictionary headwords) in Shakespeare's published works. That figure represents approximately forty percent of the total recorded for the English language up to the year 1623 — and

Shakespeare could not have owned any dictionary in which he could have looked up these words! For purposes of comparison bear in mind that the written vocabulary of Homer totals approximately nine thousand words, that of the King James Bible eight thousand, and that of John Milton ten thousand.

Of the 20,138 basewords that Shakespeare employs in his plays, sonnets, and other poems, his is the first known use of over 1,700 of them. The most verbally innovative of our authors and our all-time champion neologizer, Shakespeare made up more than 8.5 percent of his written vocabulary. Reading his works is like witnessing the birth of language itself.

"I pitied thee,/Took pains to make thee speak," says Prospero to Caliban in *The Tempest*. "I endow'd thy purposes/With words that made them known." Shakespeare is our Prospero; he dressed our thoughts with words and teemed our tongue with phrases. Without him, our "native English" would be, as Thomas Mowbray says in *Richard II*:

an unstringed viol or a harp,
Or like a cunning instrument cas'd up —
Or being open, put into his hands
That knows no touch to tune the harmony.

Consider the following list of fifty representative words that, as far as we can tell, Shakespeare was the first to use in writing. So great is his influence on his native tongue that we find it hard to imagine a time when these words did not exist:

accommodation	*dwindle*	*misplaced*
aerial	*eventful*	*monumental*
apostrophe	*fitful*	*obscene*
assassination	*frugal*	*pedant*
auspicious	*generous*	*perusal*
baseless	*gloomy*	*pious*
bedroom	*gnarled*	*premediated*
bump	*hurry*	*radiance*
castigate	*impartial*	*reliance*
clangor	*indistinguishable*	*road*
countless	*invulnerable*	*sanctimonious*

courtship
critic (and critical)
dexterously
dishearten
dislocate
lapse
laughable
lonely
majestic
seamy
sneak
sportive
submerge
useless

Now add to these individual words Shakespeare's daring originality with compounds. He created such splendid audacities as *proud-pied April, heaven-kissing hill,* and *world-without-end hour,* and he bequeathed to the English language such now-familiar double plays as *barefaced, civil tongue, cold comfort, eyesore, faint-hearted, fancy-free, foregone conclusion, father Time, foul play* (and *fair play*), *green-eyed, half-cocked, heartsick, high time, hot-blooded, itching palm, lackluster, laughing-stock, leapfrog, lie low, long-haired, love affair, ministering angel, pitched battle, primrose path, sea change, short shrift, snow-white, stony-hearted, tongue-tied, towering passion,* and *yeoman's service*. The striking compound that Shakespeare fashioned to describe Don Adriano de Armado in *Love's Labour's Lost* is an appropriate epithet for the playwright himself: "a man of fire-new words."

Orson Welles once quipped, "Now we sit through Shakespeare in order to recognize the quotations." Unrivaled in so many other ways in matters verbal, Shakespeare is unequaled as a phrasemaker. "All for one, one for all," and "not a creature was stirring, not even a mouse," respectively wrote Alexandre Dumas in *The Three Musketeers* and Clement Clark Moore in *The Night Before Christmas*. But Shakespeare said them first – "One for all, or all for one we gage" in *The Rape of Lucrece* and "not a mouse stirring" in *Hamlet*.

A student who attended a performance of *Hamlet* came away complaining that the play "was nothing more than a bunch of cliches." The reason for this common reaction is that so many of the memorable expressions in *Hamlet* have become proverbial. In that one play alone were born *brevity is the soul of wit, there's the rub, to thine own self be true, it smells to heaven, the very witching time of night, the primrose path, though this be madness, yet there is method in it, dog will have his day, the apparel oft proclaims the man, neither a borrower nor a lender be, frailty, thy name is woman, something is rotten in the state of Denmark, more honored in the breach than the observance, hoist with his own petard, piece of work, the lady doth protest too much, to be or not to be, sweets for the sweet, the be-all and end-all, to the manner born,* and *more in sorrow than in anger.*

Cudgel your brain, and you can append a sample of everyday, idiomatic phrases from other Shakespearean plays: If you knit your brow and wish that this disquisition would vanish into thin air because it is Greek to you, you are, to give the devil his due, quoting William Shakespeare in all his infinite variety. If you point the finger at strange bedfellows and blinking idiots, you are converting Shakespeare's coinages into currency. If you have seen better days in your salad days, when you wore your heart on your sleeve and had a spotless reputation, you are, whether you know it or not, going from Bard to verse. If you break the ice with one fell swoop, if you never stand on ceremonies, if you play it fast and loose until the crack of doom, if you paint the lily, if you hope for a plague on both houses, if you are more sinned against than sinning because you have been eaten out of house and home by your own flesh and blood (the most unkindest cut of all), if you haven't slept a wink and are breathing your last because you're in a pickle, if you carry within you the milk of human kindness and a heart of gold (even though you know that all that glisters is not gold), if you laugh yourself into stitches at too much of a good thing, if you make a virtue of necessity, if you know that the course of true love never did run smooth, if you kill with kindness, and if you won't budge an inch — why, if the truth be told and the truth will out, what the dickens, in a word, right on!, be that as it may, the game is up — you are, as luck would have it, standing on that tower of strength of phrasemakers, William Shakespeare.

Shakespeare lurks in the most astonishing places. Some assert that the Porter's speech in act 2, scene 3 of *Macbeth* is the source of the modern knock-knock joke: "Knock, knock, knock. Who's there I' th' name of Beelzebub? . . . Knock, knock. Who's there in th' other devil's name? . . . Knock, knock, knock. Who's there? Never at quiet!" And, if you look hard, you can find Shakespeare peeking out even from the pages of the Bible.

The most famous of all biblical translations is the King James Version, the brainchild of James I, who fancied himself a scholar and theologian. The king decided to assure his immortality by sponsoring a new Bible worthy of the splendor of his kingdom. To this end, James appointed a commission of fifty-four learned clerical and lay scholars, divided into three groups in Cambridge, Westminster, and Oxford. Three years of loving labor, 1608- 1611, produced what John Livingston Lowes called "the noblest monument of English prose." Few readers would dissent from that verdict.

Among the many wonders of the King James Bible is that it stands as one of the few great accomplishments achieved by a committee. At the same time, some commentators have wondered why William Shakespeare was apparently not included among the fifty-four translators chosen. After all, Shakespeare had already written *Macbeth* in honor of King James (who also fancied himself an expert on witchcraft), and what better committee member could one ask for to work with the greatest collection of religious literature of all ages than the age's greatest poet?

But an intriguing peculiarity in the King James Bible indicates that Shakespeare was *not* entirely absent from the monumental project. No one knows who made the astonishing discovery or how on earth he or she did it.

In 1610, the year of the most intensive work on the translation, Shakespeare was forty-six years old. Given this clue, we turn to the Forty-sixth Psalm as it appears in the King James Bible. Count down to the forty-sixth word from the beginning and then count up to the forty-sixth word from the end, excluding the cadential *Selah*:

> *God is our refuge and strength, a very present help in trouble.*
> *Therefore will not we fear, though the earth be removed,*
> *and though the mountains be carried into the midst of the sea;*
> *Though the waters thereof roar and be troubled,*
> *though the mountains shake with the swelling thereof. Selah.*
> *There is a river, the streams whereof shall make glad the city of God,*
> *the holy place of the tabernacle of the Most High.*
> *God is in the midst of her; she shall not be moved:*
> *God shall help her, and that right early.*
> *The heathen raged, the kingdoms were moved:*

he uttered his voice, the earth melted.
The Lord of hosts is with us; the God of Jacob is our refuge. Selah.
Come, behold the works of the Lord,
what desolations he hath made on earth;
He maketh wars to cease unto the end of the earth;
he breaketh the bow, and cutteth the spear in sunder;
he burneth the chariot in the fire.
Be still, and know that I am God:
I will be exalted among the heathen, I will be exalted in the earth.
The Lord of hosts is with us; the God of Jacob is our refuge. Selah.

If you counted accurately, your finger eventually lit upon the two words *shake* and *spear*. Shakespeare. Whether or not he created the majesty of the forty-sixth psalm, he is in it. Whether the embedded *shake spear* is a purposeful plant or the product of happy chance, the name of the world's most famous poet reposes cunningly in the text of the world's most famous translation.

Shakespeare also hides in many works of modern literature. He was a busy and prolific writer who, in twenty-five years, turned out thirty-seven long plays and co-authored several others, yet he still found time to provide titles for their books to generations of authors who return again and again to the well of his felicitous phrasing.

Take John Green's immensely popular teen novel *The Fault in Our Stars*, which has recently transmogrified into an immensely profitable movie. The title echoes Cassius's speech in *Julius Caesar* to his co-conspirator: "The fault, dear Brutus, is not in our stars,/But in ourselves, that we are underlings."

From that same play have been lifted the titles of Robert Frederick Forsyth's *The Dogs of War*, James Barrie's *Dear Brutus*, John Gunther's *Taken at the Flood*, Barry Sadler's *Cry Havoc*, R. Lance Hill's *The Evil That Men Do*, H. Hall's *The Valiant* and David Halberstam's *Noblest Roman*.

Take *Macbeth*, for another example. Near the end of the play, Macbeth expresses his darkening vision of life: "It is a tale/Told by an idiot, full of sound and fury,/Signifying nothing." Centuries later, William Faulkner purloined a phrase from that speech for his novel *The Sound and the Fury*, which is indeed told by an idiot, Benjy Compson. Earlier in the play one of the witches chants, "By the pricking of my thumbs,/Something wicked this way comes." Agatha Christie plucked the first line and Ray Bradbury the second as titles of their bestsellers. Other steals from just the one play *Macbeth* include Robert Frost's "Out, Out – ," Rose Macaulay's *Told by an Idiot*, Ellis Middleton's *Vaulting Ambition*, Adrienne Rich's *Of Woman Born*, Ngaio Marsh's *Light Thickens*, Anne Sexton's *All My Pretty Ones*, Alistair MacLean's *The Way to Dusty Death*, Edward G. Robinson's *All My Yesterdays*, Philip Barry's *Tomorrow and Tomorrow*, Malcolm Evans's *Signifying Nothing*, and John Steinbeck's *The Moon is Down*.

From two other high school favorites, *Hamlet* and *Romeo and Juliet*, we get A. G. MacDonnell's *How like an Angel*, Rex Stout's *How like a God*, Joyce Martins' *Rosemary for Remembrance*, Robert B. Parker's *Perchance to Dream*, Arthur Schnitzler's *Undiscovered Country*, Ernest Hebert's *A Little More than Kin*, Edith Wharton's *The Glimpses of the Moon*, Philip K. Dick's *Time Out of Joint*, Ogden Nash's *The Primrose Path*, Richard Yates's *A Special Providence*, Frederic Manning's *Her Privates, We*, Tom Stoppard's *Rosencrantz and Guildenstern Are Dead*, Louis Auchincloss's *The Indifferent Children*, Maxwell Anderson's *Both Your Houses*, Eric Knight's *This Above All*, Dorothy Parker's *Not So Deep as a Well*, Ford Madox Ford's *It Was the Nightingale*, Frederick Reynolds's *Fortune's Fool*, and Henry Wade's *No Friendly Drop*.

Add to these Aldous Huxley's *Brave New World* (*The Tempest*); W. Somerset Maugham's *Cakes and Ale* (*Twelfth Night*), John Steinbeck's *The Winter of Our Discontent* (*Richard III*), and dozens of other bardic titles, and it becomes evident that William Shakespeare was one of the most generous souls who ever set quill to parchment. Although he himself was never granted a title, he freely granted titles to others.

The etymologist Ernest Weekley said of Shakespeare, "His contribution to our phraseology is ten times greater than that of any writer to any language in the history of the world." At the end of Sonnet 18, the Bard himself wrote, "So long as men can breathe and eyes can see,/So long lives this and this gives life to thee." 2016 commemorates the 400th year since his death, yet he still gives life to us. If Shakespeare had not lived and written with such a loving ear for the music of our language, our English tongue would be immeasurably the poorer. No day goes by that we do not speak and hear and read and write his living Will.

Ranch Hands & Cobras

Joe Bonpensiero

"Remember, captain, keep your eyes sharp for snakes—cobras. They hide in the grass along the paths. It's breeding season." These parting words came from my guide, Charlie, as he pulled the jeep up to what would be my hooch. Then, bam! A boyhood memory flashed—Tarzan battling an eight-foot python in the steaming jungle—eight-year-old me guzzling a Coke, eyes glued to the movie screen in the opulent Casino Theater, mesmerized and scared shitless. Slithering fear sliced through my conscience. Snakes? Shit!

Eyes darting from side to side, I moved up the path toward the Quonset hut entrance. At the outer courtyard security wall a naked, hairless body sprawled on a deck chair temporarily blinded me. He wore nothing but a loincloth, sunglasses, and a cowboy hat. He was trying for a tan—but he looked like a beached whale heading toward lobster red.

"I heerd'ja coming," said the blob.

"Howdy stranger," I said in my best Texan. "How's the tan coming?"

"You a wise-guy or just the FNG (funny new guy) we've been waiting for?" he said, rolling over. His front was a shock—blinding corpse-white.

"Been working on my tan for a month now. Wha'cha, think?"

"Work harder. You're almost pussycat pink."

That got a hat rise and nod in my direction. "You're a wiseguy. By the way, did I tell you we don't have any spare rooms at the ranch?"

"No, but I'm the FNG—the new aircraft maintenance puke. I have a room or you don't get the airsheens to fly, Bud."

"Hell, they don't fly for crap now," he said.

"Really, then you need me!"

"Hey, you'll find your lucky Ranch Hand welcome gift in your room. It's just a few feet down the dayroom hallway on the right. You'll see the door marked with an 'A' — you'll love it."

"Why is that?"

"Because it's right across from Horndog's room."

"Is that good?"

"Wait and see."

I was already eighteen hours in this hole and this guy's palaver was getting to me.

"Thanks, I'm bushed. After the toilet-flight special to Nam and the stage-ride from Cam Ranh Bay, I really need some sleep. By the way, what's your handle?"

"Call me Cowboy," the bleached whale said.

"Sounds good, *Caboy*. Call me Bomb Dispenser."

"Bomb Dispenser?"

"How in hell did — ?"

"Long story. My father is Sicilian. And my surname is difficult for you military white guys to pronounce. Ergo, 'Bomb Dispenser' — I'm okay with it."

"Gotcha, Bomber," he said.

Wow! Now it's 'Bomber' — just when I was getting used to 'Bomb Dispenser' here comes another one.

"Hey, Caboy, any truth to the rumor about snakes around here?"

He chuckled. "Hell no! You must 'a been talking to some enlisted swine."

"Well, the driver did mention--."

"Screw him. That snake is all BS. Haven't you heard not to pay attention to the enlisted swine? Most are drugged up and crazy as hell."

I let out a mental sigh of relief. "Well, thanks, I appreciate the straight word, lieutenant."

"How did you know my rank?"

"You're a simple pilot. You've got your bright shiny silver bar on your frigg'n cowboy hat. Duh!"

I couldn't wait to get away from this loony-toon's space and turned toward the hooch. I pulled the door open and a blast of cold air met me. Thrilled to be out of the sweltering heat, I dropped my duffel and suveyed the room. A typical horny guys living like college pukes frat house, the walls were plastered with *Playboy* and *Hustler* magazine centerfolds. Center attraction was a picture of Trish Nixon in her wedding dress. The photo was cut in half, then pasted onto the sumptuous body of some babe — naked, of course. The President would not be pleased, but Trish never looked better.

There were a couple of couches, a few easy chairs, and a TV placed high on one wall. On another wall was a well-stocked bar, decorated with an AK-47, a bandolier of munitions and a gook helmet. On both sides of the AK, two 30-inch machetes crossed. *Interesting Deco.*

I swept the room and noticed the "Honor Bar" sign near the glasses above the refrigerator. Starving after 16 hours without sleep, I decided to take a few minutes to relax. After removing my shirt and really cooling down, I opened the fridge and found some bananas, sliced pineapple and limes. Hell, the guys had all the fixings including mix. *The almost tropics of Nam might not be so bad for grub.*

I made a tall Beefeater gin and tonic and snuggled into a comfy chair. I ate a banana, followed that with a piece of pineapple and gulped down a couple of shots of my drink. I was feeling refreshed in no time.

I was thinking this was definitely a good start to my tour in Nam; however, the stiff one knocked me on my butt. I dozed off. Minutes later, I was startled awake by the A/C kicking in and noticed the empty glass on the coffee table.

Hell, I need a nap — in a real bed!

I grabbed my shirt, duffel bag and stuffed my mouth with pineapple as I headed down the hall to my room. I didn't have to go far because someone put a big "A" on the door like a welcome sign. I pushed right in. The ambient glow from the hall slightly brightened an otherwise pitch-black room — about eight by eight with a shadow of sparse furniture. A chest of drawers stood off to one side. I thought my eyes played tricks on me. I froze and locked my stare on a shadowy object on the wall near the chest. It quickly morphed into several shapes that scampered up the wall.

What the hell? Was I seeing things?

I didn't even want to guess what they were — roaches, spiders, lizards, whatever! Then my gaze shifted to the top of the chest. *Were my eyes playing tricks on me after the booze? What the hell was it?*

Could it be? No frigg'n way.

My exhausted eyes bored holes in the object that perched on top of the dresser. I hoisted my duffel in front of me and slowly slinked toward the door.

Holy Hell! A frigg'n snake!

My mind lost it. *Damned Cowboy! I 'm going to kill that schmuck.*

I kept eye contact with the coiled cobra, which was poised to strike.

At the doorway, I found the switch plate and flipped the switch while flinging myself backwards through the door. Out the door, I dropped my duffel and charged down the hall. At the bar, I grabbed a machete. Now armed, I spun around and headed back down the hallway.

I stopped short at the door, figuring the snake probably slithered down to the floor — waiting for me.

The room was bathed in light — but I didn't see the snake. The machete poised, I was ready to strike — quick and deadly — no screwing around. It was quiet. Deadly quiet.

Slowly, I peered around the door's edge.

There he was! Staring from at me from the dresser with those cold, black deadly eyes, jaw open, dripping venom, his head and body coiled in the strike position.

I took aim and swung. The machete made full contact with the bastard, decapitating him six inches below the top of his head. His head flew across the room and landed on the mattress. Momentary relief flooded me. I stared at the severed head. But something was off.

There was no movement. No slithering. No blood.

Then, it hit me. I'd been had. The brotherhood of Ranch Hands had gotten me. *The sonofabitch was stuffed.*

I vowed to get even. *Was it Caboy who came up with the novel idea to literally scare the hell outta me?* If so, it worked. My pants were wet — and not just from sweat.

I moved the snake parts around with the edge of the machete blade, then grabbed the snake near its neck where my slice severed it in half. I took both parts of the snake and placed them on the bar and the machete on its mount.

I took a long, hot shower and felt revitalized. I owed myself another drink before getting some sleep.

At 1700 (5 p.m.) I turned on the room's light switch and took stock of my crib. On one side was a bed mattress mounted on a wooden frame sitting about three feet above the floor. Directly across was another mattress where the snake's head ended up. A wall-mounted air conditioner perched about twelve inches above the head of the bed. I flipped on the A/C. It cranked, making all the blaring and whirring sounds. A working system, no less, as cool air blasted from the vents. Do tell.

My first day in Vietnam and my encounter with the cobra should have been a forewarning of unknown things to come. In truth, the only snakes I saw during my tour were stuffed; or, if alive, slithered in glass containers awaiting their turn to be served up — a selected delicacy in a Saigon or Taipei restaurant. Truth is, snakes aside, there was much more to fear in Vietnam than the animals, unless you consider man an animal. Well, just maybe?

A Rose for Mrs. Delahanty

Al Converse

He always wanted to jump up and shake the old bag. Mrs. Delahanty always called him out in class. "Your spelling is atrocious, Murphy."

Or, "You need to work on your grammar."

Well, he always did the assignments. She should have been content with that. She returned all his papers with a C. What was her problem?

That's not to say she didn't ridicule every kid in the place. She did. She was one sorry, mean, dried-up old prune. Most of the students hated her.

This time she just threw his paper on the desk and said, "That's terrible. You just have to take more time with your work and pay attention to detail."

Blah, blah, blah.

Murphy's thoughts turned to the girl in the desk in front of his. She danced her leg up, down, up, down, in the aisle. His eyes followed along the limb up to a short skirt that rose on her creamy thighs with each movement.

He jerked his head back to look at the old goat. She hammered on someone else, another guy, her bitching about spelling. Then she hesitated, a slight falter, and steadied herself with her hand on a desk.

Christ. Is she having an attack or something?

She stood up straight as if to reaffirm her vitality, but her grimace betrayed her. No one but Murphy noticed. Stiffening her back, she walked to her desk. Her matronly dress, dark blue and buttoned up to her neck enveloped her like a nun's habit. She wore a small cameo around her neck on a silver chain and on her feet were heavy-looking black shoes with thick raised heels.

She must be a frustrated old maid.

The spring of 1961 gripped Murphy in the throes of serious senioritis at his New England high school. He waited for the class to clear out after the bell and approached her desk bent on complaining about her attitude, something he had never done before.

Hell, someone should tell her off. I'll graduate soon, so who gives a shit if I offend her.

In strode the vice principal, a man about Delahanty's age. "How are you doing today, Edna?" he said.

He spotted Murphy. "Are you waiting to see Mrs. Delahanty young man?" he said in his official voice.

Mrs. Delahanty addressed Murphy, "It will have to wait until tomorrow Mr. Murphy. I am feeling ill right now."

"Why not take a sick day tomorrow, Edna," the vice principal said, forgetting his official tone.

He turned to Murphy. "Can I help you, Murphy?"

"Yes, I wanted to complain to her about her attitude."

"Well, now. A student complaining about a teacher's attitude, that's a switch. What do you know about a proper attitude for a teacher?"

Higgins, another one of those adults who thinks he knows everything and looks down on kids.

"Do you know anything at all about Mrs. Delahanty, Mr. Murphy?"

The lecture came. "Mrs. Delahanty's husband has been an invalid since six months after they were married in 1917. He was a Canadian who went off to fight the Germans in the Great War. Mustard gas at the battle of Ypres nearly killed him. She's cared for him ever since. They can't have children. She works hard on her lessons and spends all her free time with him."

The next day, there was a single red rose on Mrs. Delahanty's desk when she arrived. Murphy sat quietly at his desk.

Retribution I:
The Mouth of the Klamath, 1952

Don Mayfield

"Gwen," a fisherman shouted to Mom from the bank, "Carl took a hook past the barb. It's going to be a tough one."

It had to happen. Actually, it happened every day on the line. I had hoped it wouldn't happen to Dad, but Mom knew it would.

"Donnie, get the needle-nosed pliers and some towels."

Needle-nosed pliers? In the tackle box. Towels? Not a chance. The only thing Mom had was a rag that I bloodied from yesterday's salmon catch when Dad had snagged, not hooked, a Chinook in the forward part of the body and wrestled it ashore. A snagged salmon, always bloody, was an embarrassment. It only took a barb to "snag." But took a skillfully wrought jig to "hook" into the fish's mouth.

When snagged, the fish's blood streamed from gills to tail. I washed it off in an eddy just up from the line of about thirty-five salmon fishermen they called Death Row. When Dad hauled the salmon near shore, he had little room for control. He had to break away and weave upstream through the line of men.

The general rule for landing a Chinook at the mouth of the Klamath River in fishing season? Once hooked into the fish, get enough space to control it, then move back away from the river. The heartbeat of Death Row had to pound again so that everyone might have a fair chance to catch more.

Mom had now dammed the bleeding. Dad leaned back to let gravity keep the blood in his body.

Earlier, Dad said there was a guy on Death Row who moved too quickly through the thin line of casters.

"He's gonna sure as hell hook someone," Dad had said. "Look for a watchman's cap. Like mine, but red."

No sooner than that, a man with a red cap pushed his way into the small crowd around my bleeding father.

"Sorry 'bout that. First time I snagged a caster."

I got up to see the man who hooked my father. I gawked too long for Red Cap.

"Wadda ya standin' around for, boy? I got fish to catch and only a month to catch 'em. Ha! Ha!"

"Let him be. He's my son. You been haulin' pretty fast down the line. Maybe that's why your hook ended up in the wrong place."

"The name's Kurt. I move with the line."

For Dad, Red Cap was too quick and sloppy. He was new to Death Row, the 60-yard line of fishermen who cast one-pound weighted salmon lures into the swift-moving stream. Red Cap, all geared up with a ten-foot fiberglass rod, thirty-pound monofilament line and a new Mitchell spinning reel, had it all. The new Mitchell spinning reel had caught on. The company claimed no backlashes, no sitting on the bank untangling your line while everyone else cast out and reeled in.

Despite arriving after 8 o'clock, late for these fishermen, Red Cap had a clean morning and had observed the understood agreements:

One: When you hook a Chinook, set it.

Two: Yell "Fish on!"

Three: Reel in; avoid all fishing lines. Treat each as a potential mess.

Four: Weave through the cast lines. Some lines will have crossed over; others you will have floated under. Expect the casters to back off and allow you to squeeze through.

But Dad noticed Red Cap had cast too fast and hadn't yet found a rhythm. When he hooked in once and wove down the line, he yelled "Fish on!" then stumbled and fell to the shore.

At that, a neighboring caster announced "Well, we had a fish on. Now we have a man off! Ha!" Red Cap looked around to find errant stares, deflected them, nodded apologies, then left.

"Speed kills, Kurt," Dad said, but he knew immediately the words had pricked Red Cap.

Kurt's eyes perked up. "Yeah, well, draggin' your ass ain't good, either, Mister."

"Draggin' my. . . ?" Dad's eyes narrowed.

"Carl," Mom interrupted, "you have to hold that rag tighter.

Blood's runnin' down your face."

Dad's need to stop the bleeding and fix his nose replaced his urgency to defend his manhood. No room for pride here. Most line fishermen had suffered the "Satan's Tail," as they called the barbed treble hook, but all knew it was as inevitable as the tide.

Nose wounds were not bad, even though they bled inside and bled out. Scalp wounds bled bad, but you could push on them and they would stop. Most lucked out when Satan's Tail imbedded in their shirt or pants, sometimes their rubber waist boots. Mouth wounds were probably the worst and usually needed a doctor. Crescent City, about twenty-five miles north on 101, had one.

Like the nose, the mouth bled on both sides, but the nose gristle was tough to tear. Those treble hooks that barbed into cheeks often tore. A torn cheek always looked bad. They said it always looked worse than it really was, but I did not believe that attempt to cover the pain.

The sheer numbers of men, close to forty now, shoulder to shoulder, hurling lead into the stream, made the Row a hazardous place. Every day, August through September, thirty to sixty men stood there crunched into a forty-five yard span. With barely enough room to raise their arms and brandish their twelve-foot bamboo poles, the men twisted their shoulders and hove one-pound jigs fifteen yards into the current. They cast by shifting their upper body weight forward and snapping the tips of their rods, sending the projectile flying fast over water, then in.

Most often the jig landed safely; sometimes it did not.

The jig held a one-pound, four-cornered lead weight, a true friend of pain, especially when it hit soft flesh at 30 mph. Two feet below the lead was wired a big man's treble hook wrapped with stainless steel wire on which were three tantalizing glass salmon eggs, and a large thumb-sized, polished brass spoon.

One of the treble hook barbs had bit into Dad's nose.

Casting the lure was straightforward, not shy, but bold, swift and succinct. The tricky part? The initial thrust of the obelisk lead weight followed by the spinner and Satan's Tail. The caster placed the rod tip at the precise coordinate, just off perpendicular, with the jig as still as the dawn's early light. Then he zipped back the tip of the rod, launched the one-pound weight forward at a 15-

degree angle above the horizon, barely missing the face of a fellow angler. The cast trajectory might very well land where intended.

But, if the caster had skipped his cup of java, or dreamed about hot blackberry pie from the Yurok pie shack down the beach, or had argued with his wife or slapped his kid and cast errantly, well, Satan's Tail might get embed in a shirt, a boot, or, possibly, human flesh of man, woman or child. From time to time jigs landed in the row of Yurok skiffs, called Suicide Row. Just twenty yards offshore and loaded with anglers, the Yuroks tied their skiffs and anchored them against the river mouth stream.

Once in a great while, shore casters snagged a Yurok guide or one of his clients. Often that brought a painful world of Yurok justice.

I understood the Death Row on shore. I understood the ghoulish humor. James Cagney movies made Death Row easy to take. Give our punishment system to a Hollywood director and he will minimize it. Alcatraz's Death Row becomes entertainment. Make criminals amicable, Death Row becomes palatable.

Suicide Row had a darker meaning.

Suicide Row was a line of coupled skiffs, fifteen or so in each line, strung across the mouth of the river. Twenty yards beyond Death Row swayed Suicide Row, where Yurok fishing guides captained the skiffs.

As they faced each swift-turning tide, the Yuroks tempted tragedy. Careless rowing and capsized boats led to death at sea. Few Yurok skiffs went awry, but there were some that ended in pain or death. Typically, the skiff ended in the ocean upside down or "turtled," as they would say.

"Oh, shit," Dad squawked, now resting on the shore with a bandaged nose. "Red Cap cast a sinker into a skiff. Looks like he hit a Yurok full on."

There was no telling the damage done by a one-pound lead weight with sharp corners, propelled through the air at 30 miles an hour. Would it bring a brain concussion or brain hemorrhage? Both were possible when lead met flesh, with no hospital closer than Crescent City.

Once around the fire pit at the Yurok pie shack, I heard two Yuroks grousing: "I think most of the casters understand the danger; but the new ones to the river? If they had seen Sparrowhawk take a sinker in the temple, that would cure 'em. He was a bloody mess and didn't handle it so good. They had to take him out for that one."

Lead weights landing in their skiffs was serious business for the Yurok.

And, now, early Friday afternoon, late August, 1952, one of their own began rowing furiously to shore to both quiet the pain from a hit and to administer Yurok justice.

There are few known rules about retribution at the mouth of the Klamath. It was still the Wild West, especially on the reservation. No Fish and Game officer asked about fishing licenses. No signs declared Civil Code violations. So, once the wounded Yurok landed ashore, no one knew what would happen next.

"Bear is after Red Cap." said Dad.

Jesus.

Dad, on his feet already: "See? What'd I tell you? Red Cap was too fast, too sloppy."

"Is that another Yurok breaking the Row?" someone chimed in.

"Yea, that's Chinook-in-the-Morning. They don't come any bigger. They'll probably herd Red Cap to the back of the pie shack."

By this time, five Yurok women from the shack had wandered out.

Bear landed the skiff just below Death Row and headed toward Red Cap.

It happened fast.

Within seconds, six more Yuroks landed and headed up the bank. The Yurok women had now formed a line, loose but definite.

A few white folks, younger ones who watched all of this, had quick-stepped toward the pie shack. A young mother with her toddler turned back when her husband shouted out.

Red Cap disappeared behind the Yurok women who, just seconds before, were cooking hot, sweet, gooey blackberry pies, encrusted in thick buttery crusts.

Through all of this, the fishermen on Death Row continued to cast their lines against the tide.

A few white kids looked over to the pie shack, then turned to their moms and pointed.

No one heard fists and steel-toed boots slam into flesh behind the shack.

Those who were close, especially the Yurok women, might have described the sounds as ocean waves thudding against the beach.

Retribution II:
The Steelhead, Mako Shark of Inland Streams

Don Mayfield

I was glad that I had Keds. They had soles that grabbed the mossy rocks, just enough. I was knee-deep at the top of the riffle, now more a sudsed-up washboard than a glassy summer stream. The river got foamy at low water, especially when the rocks lay an inch under the top. I could see pockets where Steelhead trout might hide.

I had a couple of bites--hard to tell in a riffle because the sinker careened from stone to stone on the way down, then got caught on sharp-edged granite when I reeled back. The sinker might pin itself between the close-jammed rocks or the hook might bite into stone.

I now stood on a clean-cut, submerged stump and balanced myself against the current, which pushed incessantly.

I didn't see it coming.

The Steelhead smashed into my lure with the ferocity of a bulldog on a bone. The lazy flutter of the polished brass spinner against sunlight had teased him into an orgasm. Snagged by my vicious, barbed treble hook, he tore out of the stream. His furious, but magnificent, lunge arched him back onto the water surface with the concussion a fat boy makes when belly flopping on flat water.

Ca-Whoop.

Slipping off the stump into waist-deep turbulence, I snapped out of reverie into reflex. The temperature change lightning-shocked me and water poured into my pants, planting me into slush, just below the stump.

I thought to myself: *He owned the river, but I had the weight. He had the speed, but I had the line, the swivel, the barbed treble hook, the "fluorescent, sex-hormone-filled, natural, straight from the uterus," salmon egg.*

I might have panicked, except for my Keds, which were acting like duck feet. I squatted to gain leverage, then pushed against the stump for support. Thank God, I hadn't gone under, but the current persisted and pushed, pushed, pushed.

How could I reach firm riverbed where I could get solid anchor and haul in this peripatetic monster? Any move through this on-rush felt like my fist pushing through molasses. And there was no branch to brace myself against.

Then I slipped to one knee. Pain soared through my thigh. I jacked up my torso to block the current. I was quarterback on a demolished football team holding back one ton of linemen, each determined to crush me against the goalpost.

Then gravity released my feet.

I tumbled back, managed to teeter on one knee, while the Steelhead dragged *me* against the current.

If I am tired, he must be exhausted. A one-hundred-pound boy against a trout?

The odds seemed too great.

Suddenly, I fell again, this time I gulped water, spat, then choked. My butt bounced on bottom rocks.

My God, this thing is dragging me downstream!

He had vacated the current, arched toward shore and hauled ass to the big hole under the oak tree. He sought relief, and I knew then that I had him. I would soon secure my feet, yank him into submission, land him without net and hike back to the camp, triumphant.

I got my footing, jammed my legs into the silt and heaved back.

Only to feel . . . nothing.

He was gone, as quickly as he had come, sending me back, unable to stand in salute to his escape.

It was over. It was all over.

Quartets Abound

Tom Leech

Back in school was this singer crew,
They warbled fun tunes when cool kids met,
Harmony was their amazing style,
Calling themselves a barbershop quartet.

It was fun listening to those singers,
We joined right in hearing those voices soar,
They made me think about other teams,
How many were around in groups of four?

On Sunday morning in Bible class,
As we learned life's lessons hither and yon,
We heard much from a heavenly four,
With stories from Matthew, Mark, Luke & John.

In history class, or was it in Lit?
We found enforcers who waved heavy whips,
Conquest, War, Famine & Death,
Four Horsemen of the Apocalypse.

We'd tune up our radio volume,
Swaying with our Moms and Pops,
Quartets singing current hot hits,
Four Aces, Four Freshmen, even Four Tops.

One time on that Ed Sullivan show,
He introduced a group called the Fab Four,
They also went by a different name,
The Beatles' success was soon to soar.

Another group of four were women,
They got many laughs on their TV show,
Known as Estelle, Betty, Bea, & Rue,
Those goofy Golden Girls made chuckles flow.

To see four famous leaders
And revive historical lore,
George, Tom, Abe and Teddy,
Carved high on rocks of Mt. Rushmore.

In life some go solo and that's okay,
And plenty of pairs also do quite well,
Trios galore help us hum and pray,
But memorable foursomes ring the bell.

Stickup, U.S. Navy Style

Carl Nelson

On November 12, 1974, we departed Auckland for American Samoa, an island group in the south central Pacific about 1,600 miles northeast of New Zealand. We were to stop only long enough to take on sufficient fuel to make it to Hawaii, where we would refuel again before going on to our home port of San Diego.

At the time, I was in command of a frigate named after my Annapolis classmate Wilmer Cook, an attack pilot who had been shot down and killed over North Vietnam. The Cook had been detached from Squadron Nine with the USS Hammond, another frigate, and because I was a few numbers senior, I was in command of the two-ship division until we returned to the States.

On arrival at Pago Pago, the capital of the islands, the captain of the Hammond and I were invited to join the governor, an American political appointee, and his wife for cocktails at their home high on the hill overlooking the fuel pier.

We arrived exactly at the appointed hour and were ushered into a cozy room with a balcony protected by an awning from the evening sun. An elderly Samoan asked, "Would you gentlemen like a drink?" As I remember, sea captains were drinking martinis at the time and we were soon rewarded with tall-stemmed glasses of the world's finest.

When the governor and his wife, a much-younger attractive blonde, entered, they invited us to join them on the balcony in chairs that I suspect were leftovers from the very first governor who, back then, was an American naval officer. The chairs were as rickety as the pier lying in our view about 300 feet below. Our ships were moored there, making preparations to take on fuel from the considerable supplies held in reserve on the island just for such purposes. The pier had been built sometime after 1900 when the U.S. Navy administered the islands. Sailors of that time had built it in the crater of an extinct volcano.

Our view of a blue South Pacific stretched under a red twilight sky fading behind dark green hills with winding dirt roads, right out of Michener's *Tales of the South Pacific*. Tuna boats floated in silence as they sailed back from an idyllic day of ocean fishing.

"Welcome to Samoa, gentlemen." He raised his glass skyward.

"Thank you, governor." Our martini glasses matched theirs.

The small talk began with a question from his wife. "How do you like our island?"

"Haven't been here long enough to find out, ma'am."

"Do you know much about it?"

"Not really."

"The people are lovely, mostly Polynesian, about fifty thousand of them," she said.

"Village life is very simple, based on a social system headed by matais, or chiefs. We're still learning about them ourselves, but they seem to be happy and congenial. There are actually seven islands in a chain, names like Ofu and Ta'u. Tutuila is the name of this island."

"Very interesting. How long have you been here, governor?"

"About a year. We'll return to the States next year. Where are you boys coming from?"

"Australia, sir, with a stop in New Zealand," I responded.

"How wonderful. How did you like Australia?" she asked.

"The trip was a blast. Everyone enjoyed the people of those countries."

"Too bad about the oil embargo," the governor said.

"Yes, it is," I answered.

"Oh, you've heard that we can't give you any fuel."

I looked quizzically at the skipper of the Hammond. I thought the governor was pulling our leg. "You're kidding."

"Well, no. As you probably have learned, the embargo's been imposed on America and the Netherlands by the Organization of the Petroleum Exporting Countries—OPEC. United States oil reserves are being rationed, no exceptions. Apparently the Arab members of OPEC are getting even because the United States supported Israel in the Yom Kippur War. The embargo is causing significant shortages. Of course, Americans are very upset with a government that permits petro-blackmail."

"Do you really mean you can't give us fuel?"

"Sorry. All reserves have been frozen."

"But," the governor's wife added, "it will give you and your crew plenty of time to see our island."

"When will you be able to release oil?"

"That's undetermined right now," the governor said.

My mind spun through the scenario. *Here we are with two crews away from their families for seven months and for lack of oil get stuck on this godforsaken place? Nothing to do but wait? This might be their paradise, but not for our sailors. Bad deal!*

It was by my third martini that I came to the conclusion that if OPEC could use blackmail, so could I. That's when I asked the governor what he would do if we pulled a stickup and made him give us oil. But the governor was either not a good drinker or did not interpret my remark as a joke because his face transformed from one of good humor to a serious reflection of fear.

I looked at my companion and shrugged to give the message that, although I had said it, I didn't really mean it.

"What if, Mister Governor of American Samoa, what if I said to you, 'This is a stickup!' Then ordered my ships to point their five-inch guns at your beautiful mansion? Then would you give us enough fuel to get our sailors back to the States?"

The governor frowned, then picked up the telephone and said to the operator, "Get me the most senior naval officer in the Pacific Ocean."

He then sat back and sipped his drink. He had called my bluff.

Almost instantaneously, the phone rang. The governor picked it up and said a few words; listened; then handed it to me.

"One minute for the admiral, sir," said an aide. Then he added by the way of gratuitous advice, "By the way, commander, the admiral is very busy hosting a party for dignitaries."

There was a pause. Then I heard, "Captain, what's this about sticking up the governor of Samoa for fuel?"

"Ah, ah, sir …"

"Well? I'm waiting."

"Ah, sir, admiral…. Well, we need enough oil for two destroyers. We need to get our sailors back home."

"Where's home?"

"San Diego, sir."

"How long have they been out here?"

"Seven months, sir. Since the spring of 1973."

"Seven months? Let me talk to the governor."

The governor's conversation was rather lengthy, but when he hung up the phone he said, "The admiral gave me the okay. We can fill you up."

I didn't say anything, but thought, *trump on trump.*

After fueling all night, our ships were under way on time early next morning. As we were getting under way, one sailor said to me, "Sure glad we're out of this place, skipper. Can't wait to get home to the wife and kids."

I said to myself, *There are stickups that send you to prison, and there are those that don't. I doubt this will be the last stickup for the U.S. Navy.*

A Walk in the Swamp

Bob Doublebower

Elsie would have sworn she heard the crack of a rifle somewhere behind her, but you know how that still, humid air intensifies sound, just like smells. She bent at the waist, and ran faster than she had ever run.

The errand on which they had sent her—"you…go fetch that!"—had taken her within 20 feet of the field border to get to the tool bin. That border was mostly thick briars along here, couldn't get through them, but she kept her eye on it just the same as she shambled ahead, looking for any break. Then, there it was. The dry summer had thinned out the bushes along a short section here. She'd been thinking about this for the whole six years she had been here, and she didn't have to think anymore. *The boss, some 100 yards away, could see her if he was looking*. Elsie glanced in his direction. He wasn't. Years of longing, years of hard field labor, and years of desperation swept her through that small window in the brambles. She was bent at the waist and running faster than she had ever run.

For six long years she'd looked at that distant, low treeline as the "other" life. She imagined it, with all the bright polish of imagination, to be like her life growing up, back across the ocean when there was no cotton in her life. Elsie hated cotton. Now even more.

It was that treeline on which she fixed her sights. It lay probably six miles away, maybe less, but Elsie had no way of knowing that. In her former line of work, field trips, at least the kind you came back from, were rare. She was running faster than she had ever run. The ground between was a mix of flat land and bush-growth—good for running, she was glad to find out, but bad for not being seen. She hadn't heard the dogs yet. Maybe she hadn't been missed yet. But they would come, and she had no plan for that except distance. It occurred to her that the chase may be brief and half-hearted. She was, after all, just a woman, but she'd cost some money, to be sure. In that treeline she hoped there would be water. Water confused the dogs, every time.

Oh, there would be water.

Elsie had been running hard for about a half hour. The sun above her had barely moved in the sky. She hadn't gotten to choose her time of day. Had she, this, mid-afternoon, would not have been it. Sweat sluiced off her body, hardly slowed by the recut grain sack she wore cinched at the waist. It wasn't time to be thirsty yet, but that, too, would come. Her legs were on fire. She lifted her head to coax in more air. That helped not at all, so her body, all by itself, found a compromise between covering ground and breathing. She was strong, her legs particularly, and they complained to no end, but they carried on.

The treeline looked closer now, maybe half as far away.

Then, damn it, there was that sound — the clamor of the dogs being roused. It would take a little more time to leash them up and head out, but instinctively Elsie picked up the pace and bent again low at the waist. The air felt like running through gauze, but the ground stayed sure underfoot. Stopping was all Elsie could think of now. *Just sit down, just for a minute.... Just for a minute. They're far away. Just stop for a minute... Is getting caught really worse than this? You could say you got lost. They'd understand. Maybe just a whipping.... Anything to stop this running...running.*

Big Ed, the boss hound, gave a long tenor howl, and hearing that stopped this kind of thinking in its tracks. Elsie kept running, faster than she had ever run. The "other" life lay just ahead.

In another 15 minutes, the firm ground began to give way a little. The plants got taller and closer together. Elsie could always smell water, and she knew it lay straight ahead. She had to dodge sapling bunches and it slowed her considerably, but, without half realizing it, she soon stood in ankle-deep water. She rose to full height and looked about.

A great, black swamp spread out before her eyes, from her left all the way to her right. Sunset wouldn't be long, and what sunlight remained slanted in low from the west like sabers, sharp and pointed, illuminating patches of dense undergrowth surrounded by black water. These patches were the rises of land not yet decayed. Their edges frayed into something between hard sand and black, loose mud. A fetid smell arose from the footholes in which Elsie stood. Everywhere there was deadfall. Tree trunks lay horizontally, skewed without regard for paths or clearings. Turned-up rootballs, their dry halves standing in stark contrast to their submerged and rotting lower halves, stood sentinel at water's edge. Most were hollowed out, offering a lightless den for who-knew-what. The air was suffocating. Beyond the dying streaks of sunlight, it was already dark in here. The water reminded Elsie of the black glass they'd sometimes kick up plowing. Even in low light, the water surface gave off an iridescence that betrayed the tiniest movement, like the huge dragonflies that landed and sent off ripples from each tiny foot, or the vague vee from something swimming beneath. What trees were still between birth and death stood straight and spindly, with feathery crowns, and from their thin branches suspended moss of untold age; in some places, from lower branches, even touching the ground. Animal sounds crackled all around her – birds above, no doubt the ones she'd heard from a distance all those years, and rustles in the bushes, both large and small, and sometimes a splash. Sometimes a big splash. Elsie didn't know what lived in here.

    She had, for the moment, forgotten about Big Ed and company. She stumbled forward. She'd never learned to swim, but splashed off anyway to one of the clumps of dry land that looked big enough to support a trail. She had to keep moving.

    She found a path, of sorts, barely the width of her foot, but it promised direction. She raced along it as best she could. Every hundred yards or so, it would dip and be cut by a wide channel of the ever-present black glass water. Elsie had to ford these, luckily few deeper than her chest. She had to keep a sharp eye out to either side for whatever made that big splash. The bottom was a primordial ooze that sucked at her feet. Every step was a struggle. This one time, as she crawled up on a bank, something sharp punctured her ankle. Elsie shrieked, not caring who might be in earshot. She yanked back her leg and grabbed at the pain. Blood ran between her fingers. She squeezed harder and after a while the throbbing eased. She lay like that for the better part of an hour, and by now it was full dark. Moving ahead seemed like a bad idea. There'd been no sounds of dogs nor man, so she'd rest here till first light. Fatigue beat fear this time.

And now it was time to be thirsty. She abhorred the idea of drinking the still, shiny water — people got badly sick — which abutted where she lie. Her ankle screamed at the idea of walking, so on hands and knees, Elsie crept along the decomposing bank until she found a small animal dam over which the water fell for a few inches. It made the water look cleaner. She drank her fill and rolled onto her back. She slept a profound sleep, in which she saw herself both as a pale spirit, floating free, and a trudging form sinking ever deeper into the ground, and these were in fitful conflict. So sound was her sleep and so mesmerizing were these images that the variety of animals that crawled over her and around her that night went unnoticed.

With the sabers of sunlight now coming from the other side, Elsie roused herself. Her ankle could bear her weight, but looked hellish. The puncture oozed milky pus, and for an inch all around, it raged red and swollen. Pain be damned, Elsie set out. Mid-morning brought on the heat of the day, and a dull upset had started in her gut. Food, she thought. It had been a full day, and her body needed food. Foraging here was much different from foraging in the work fields. There, wild onions and mushrooms and dandelions grew scattered about. Here she found only fiddleheads and skunk cabbage. Elsie settled on the latter, they were everywhere, and chewed down the stinking root and stems until she retched.

As always, her salvation would be found in movement. The "other" life must be out here somewhere. She kept to the tiny trails across dry land and through swamp water. That night she found a clearing, but the pain in her lower half kept boiling up. She clenched her knees to her chest as much as her ankle would allow. Next morning, Elsie felt empty and weak. Her face and head felt hot and her one eye was partially shut. She fought to stand and found her ankle all but useless. Attempts to bear her weight produced bolts of pain that challenged her consciousness. Elsie yanked a good-sized stick from a nearby canebreak and, with that as a crutch, left the clearing.

Again in the late morning heat, Elsie stumbled along trail after trail. The fording interludes were becoming welcome. The water cooled her fever, and she'd given up on abstaining from drinking still water. She drank whenever she wanted. Once, as she rested by a bank, the images of the pale spirit and the sinking form returned. They shouted at each other back and forth. Elsie couldn't make out what was being said, but the pale spirit appeared to be gaining strength. Then they faded.

More walking. More skunk cabbage. More retching. By afternoon, her lower leg had swollen, and her stomach was feeling the full effects of whatever that still water bore. She drank but still felt thirsty to her core. Couldn't be much further to the "other" life.

As the sun again showed itself in the West, the fever had Elsie hallucinating that she lived in a great manor house, and was walking from room to room. Finally, in her mind, she came to a bedroom, and a bed piled high with downy green covers. She hallucinated that she threw herself on that pile when, at last, she lay herself down on the overgrown path. In this, her sickest hour, she did not feel alone. The pale spirit had returned. The sinking form was nowhere to be seen. Elsie blinked, and broke a faint smile. The pale spirit gently took Elsie's hand, and together they flew from the cursed swamp. She was free.

The Elements of Trust
A Leadership Ideal

Gered Beeby

At Issue

Who do you trust ... and why?

These often become questions for anyone who is placed in a position of responsibility, or indeed, of trust. At a subliminal level, one could say it's the gut level where we usually arrive at a decision about another's trustworthiness. Is it possible we can gauge this elusive concept of trust in a more structured way? There is no known diagnostic evaluation that can quantify trust.

Tests such as the MMPI (Minnesota Multiphasic Personality Inventory) are used in some critical industries for screening. Primary intent of such testing is to ferret out those with psychopathic disorders. Numerous other psychology-based categorization methods attempt to classify personality types. These typically derive from the theories of Carl Jung; one of these is the Myers-Briggs classification index.

Clinical methods in a laboratory setting are all but non-existent. Chemical analyses of body tissues, whether solid or liquid, cannot distinguish traits that may guide research into the concept of trustworthiness. No examination of the human genome has yet to discover the "Trust Gene."

Thought Process

We are left with an ocean of perceptions when it comes to judging whether or not we place our faith in another person. Many simply rely on experience, instinct, or just plain seat-of-the-pants reasoning. This may work. Often leaders in many fields succeed in making sound decisions even when all facts are not available. This essay hopes to provide a framework of understanding. What is really going on in the vague, sometimes shadowy, and decidedly fuzzy logic involved in assessing human trust?

Most would agree that trust must show some element of strength. This gets revealed in any number of ways. Resolution, determined effort toward a goal, and just plain guts help explain this quality. The armed forces have evolved numerous ways to measure strength, not only of its people, but also its systems. Success and advancement often come to those who demonstrate repeatedly this most fundamental skill.

But the slings and arrows of hard experience can evoke yet another elemental concept. Strength alone is not enough. A necessary second dimension is needed to form a clearer, more complete picture. Discussion of this trait may not set well with some. This second concept lies imbedded in a fundamental denial. This is an important attribute, in effect a kind of anti-factor. For want of more polite language, that term equates to a lack of political motivation. Or this could be the lack of outside agenda, or by any other name that de-emphasizes self-interest and ego. At its worst, this trait could be summarized as naked ambition.

Officially, even unofficially, the armed forces creed in the United States denies such separate motives. On the other hand, there are legitimate allowances for professional goals. Hopes for advancement generally are healthy. But for trust at any level, whether in military service or in a private business or in other sectors of government or wherever, we may find that talking the talk is one thing, walking the walk is another.

A Trust Matrix

Applying a quasi-technical approach to these two fundamental motives, one can envision a kind of X-Y matrix. Strength, resolve, courage forms the X-axis, in both positive and negative directions from the origin. Noble thoughts and actions proceed positively to the right. Not-so-forthright motives, knavish behavior, and ultimately just plain cowardice, retreat to the left.

Now superimpose the other factor. The Y-axis corresponds to someone's integrity in relation to some alternative, even ulterior motives. Proceeding upwards from the origin on this axis is not good. At the farthest reaches one finds the truly ruthless and too-often criminal. But a downwards progression from the origin, away from the temptations of power and avarice, is a welcome start for trustworthiness.

Some may view this directional orientation as counter intuitive. After all, is upward not always better? Not in this philosophy. Often we hear from various public officials how humbled they feel when placed in their positions of authority. As citizens we can only hope that most of these assertions are actually true.

Four neat and very elementary quadrants form this Trust Matrix. In essence this coordinate system presents a framework for viewing other people, a guide for ethical thought. We can tour this landscape one quadrant at a time.

Reviewing the Quadrants

The Lower Left encompasses those who are hopelessly weak with no drive for power. For the most part they are never truly reliable, but otherwise remain harmless. Positions of responsibility might be forced upon them, but they would not actively seek them. They know their limitations. President Theodore Roosevelt spoke of such persons as "… those cold and timid souls who know neither victory nor defeat."

Proceeding to the Upper Left creates a substantially different picture. The Upper Left types are weak, yet grasping. They combine the worst attributes for any sense of trust. Overall, they hold the greatest potential for betrayal—the ultimate sinners. Cassius did indeed have that lean and hungry look, as observed by Julius Caesar. But Cassius lacked strength. He needed Brutus, and the rest is history. Delving further into Shakespeare we find the fictional Iago, the secret nemesis to Othello. By all indications Iago had no redeeming qualities. But as counterpoint to his master we get introduced to another zone of the Matrix.

Othello was in many ways heroic. Upper Right ideologies typically generate bold action. They harbor decisive opinions; then act on them. On the downside they can also merge this strength with ruthlessness and the will to get ahead. Often power-hungry, they let their careers transcend their dues to humanity. In total contrast to the Lower Lefts, they follow no proper limits. Could Desdemona ever have guessed the heights of her husband's hubris?

Some may question at this point whether anyone can ever trust anybody. Three out of the four matrix zones are shaded when it comes to extending trust. Others may also wonder if the matrix presents little more than moral leadership through the lens of a philosophic dental exam. The last quadrant may help.

The Lower Right sector is populated by those with both resolve and endurance. But here, these strengths are tempered with faith that value-added derives from a reliance on others. When in a leadership position, power is used sparingly. To gain support and trust, leaders with this ideology subordinate their individual will. Lower Rights can be relied upon to place duty ahead of ego and opportunism. Even more so, they will put their duty ahead of their fear.

Variations on the Theme

Humans are a diverse and often unpredictable lot. Whatever traits that generate respect and loyalty for one could readily breed distrust and contempt in another. Some may argue that all persons inhabit all the trust matrix sectors at one time or another. Such a theory would state that residence stay-time may vary, quadrant to quadrant. But an extension of the idea would allow predominance in one quadrant. To a limited extent this author agrees.

Transitions may occur, but only in certain ways. This Matrix concept allows someone to shift their ideology, but only across one axis. One example could be someone with an Upper Right ideology who decides their personal ambitions must be subordinated to the greater good. Taking the other direction, an Upper Right persona may lose their courage. They could morph into an Upper Left institutional hack. And thereby accumulate the attendant ills of one who strives for position, but who fundamentally lacks the guts to act, and in short, to do the job. Similar relocations can be postulated from any of the other groups.

At this point some limits must be imposed. "No matter how hard you try, you can't straighten a pretzel," observed Linus in the Peanuts comic strip. A single boundary-to-boundary movement is okay – one time. Attempting a transit across two axes, in effect moving across the center 0 – 0 origin, corner-to-corner is beyond scope. An Upper Left knave could never be fully trustworthy as someone in the Lower Right. The two are congenital opposites.

Current History

Early in 2002, the author published a thriller-spy novel in which one of the protagonists ponders the question of trust. His concerns were whether the main character in the story could be trusted with much of anything. The Trust Matrix as described in this paper was first presented in that book.

In more recent times a group called Culture University created its versions of trust matrixes. Culture University presents self-help ideas for organizations, in particular those whose culture seems to have strayed into distrust and dysfunction. Diagrams espoused by Culture University also shows X-Y coordinates, but their presentation only show the Upper Right or positive-positive region. Axes differ both in labels and in concepts. Saying versus Doing distinguishes one of these.

Formats such as these form the core for inspirational talks about organizational norms. Merits of a fully trustworthy environment are proposed at length. No arguments here. They do not, however, examine what intrinsic characteristics exist within people when deciding individual trustworthiness. Further to the point, they do not tread into the darker regions where trust may not be achieved. This is understandable. Why would a positive motivational presentation want to grapple with the negative?

This existence of other "trust" matrixes is noted for factual clarity. Confusion should be avoided between this essay's version and those in the Culture University or others that may exist. One similarity is noted. Classification into definable quadrants, thus four and only four as a consequence, seems a common thread among psychological analyses in Western thought. We seem to relish that comfort zone of analytical precision first formulated by French philosopher René Descartes in the 17th century.

The Real World

Theories and opinions can be elegant, even persuasive, but as the saying goes, how do they play in Peoria? A refinement on this theme is stated in a quote found at a major military evaluation command. *One Test Is Worth a Thousand Expert Opinions.*

Given the wide range of behaviors and attitudes, some may wonder what can be said, or done, about this question of trust. In most situations, whether in business or in life, people need to work together. This is especially true even when ultimate trust, the province of the Lower Rights, cannot always be found. Our reactions must be tailored to a variety of situations. Ways to suitable resolutions frequently are not obvious. When trust may be found in an individual, there is no guarantee they may be likeable. As part of human nature we tend to gravitate toward those whose values seem similar to our own. Proceed with a bit of caution: Pleasant does not always guarantee reliable.

This thesis suggests guidelines about the gritty reality of people and groups. Skills associated with these issues may not always be available or even definable. When applying a model such as this Trust Matrix, a heretofore unknown person cannot be categorized immediately. Assignment of their Trust must start at the 0 – 0 origin. Only after observation can we migrate into whatever quadrant applies to them. And as said before, much too often the convenience of personal reliance is neither available nor essential. We must work around any number of limitations, not wait for perfection, but cope with reality, and lead. And do so without coercion, gamesmanship, or guile.

Numerous treatises have sought answers to such questions. Those in authority typically do the best they can. As with any number of elusive concepts, leadership success defies measurable attributes. Opinions may vary, but those who are successful at it often do not display a common, visible trait. As stated earlier about the genetics of trust itself, there is no "Leadership Gene" either.

Questions are posed at a several points in this essay. The trust concept with its many ramifications as elaborated above may be useful for some, for others not so much. For the most part these ideas offer a way of addressing the topic. Here is a final question that some may derive from this review.

When all is said and done: How trustworthy am I?

Rob Asked About Me?

Don Mayfield

Are you kidding? Pompadour Rob?

That pompadour was a masterpiece. I oughta know. My dad gave me a butch.

You might say Rob was *suave*. That is a French word and it fit.

In the band he played lead trumpet. I played second. He always got the solos and I think I know why.

Rob's trumpet was a Selmer, made in Paris. The bell on the trumpet was hand scrolled. The filigree looked like it came from a book in a Paris bookstall where, when you opened it, the title page jumped out with a crazy design of loopdeloops.

That was *suave*, just like Rob.

The trumpeters who played Selmers were world-class, meaning "accepted by the French:" Louis Armstrong, Old School; Harry James, Swing School; and Miles Davis, Cool School—all played Selmers.

First thing he said when we sat down in the first trumpet section was, "When my mom and I lived in L.A., I took lessons from the first chair of the Los Angeles Philharmonic."

The best I could come up with was, "Oh yeah, my teacher is Mr. Dahlgren. He taught me since fourth grade and taught me to triple tongue—not just double. And he plays at the best club in town, the Chi-Chi. You know, where their sign shows a girl with no shirt and little titties."

"My mom says the Chi-Chi is a strip joint."

"It's not," I said, louder. "They do burlesque where girls dance and comics tell jokes about tits and ass, which my mom thinks is stupid."

I was pissed because I had to say all that stuff. But Rob couldn't argue with that, so he shut up.

I'm glad I didn't tell Rob they called Mr. Dahlgren "Mr. Bump n' Grind."

San Diego at War!

William Barrons

Being born on the coldest day of the year in 1926, in the coldest spot in Michigan, it is no wonder that I appreciate the balmy climate of San Diego. Here, "A discouraging word seldom is heard and the sky is not cloudy all day."

I joined the United States Marine Corps fifteen months after the Pearl Harbor disaster brought the United States to war. That was in February of 1943, and it meant I had to give up the privileges of being the oldest boy on our little family farm in the northern wilds of Michigan.

Doggone it, my younger brothers would have the undoubted pleasure of chopping the firewood, pumping the water from way down deep in the ground, and, as well, spading and hoeing the seemingly endless acres of mom's garden as I had done since the age of ten.

San Diego, I found, was to be my place in the sun.

In June of 1943, the Marine DI's (those initials stood for Devil's Instruments, not Drill Instructors, no matter what they said); those DI's cussed up a storm as they met us terrified teenagers at the Santa Fe Railroad Station here. That place, like all railroad stations of the day in our nation, was busy with wartime traffic.

Although I had been sworn in as a Marine four months before, I finally was to be taught *how to be a Marine* in the Recruit Depot here. I shall not dwell on that "exhilarating" boot camp experience. But it's interesting to note that the Marine's rifle range was at Camp Matthews, where now stands the University of California at San Diego campus and the VA Medical Center. Only recently have the WWII Quonset Huts been torn down there, that we used back then.

At the Recruit Depot was a "grinder" parade ground where our Devil's Instrument Corporal Lassiter taught us close-order drill…*seemingly endlessly*. Tragically, next to that grinder was the end of a runway where Consolidated Aircraft's giant B-24 Liberator bombers would take off—if they cleared the chain-link fence. Often, the wartime lady pilots flying them didn't get their planes quite in the air and that fence and that grinder were full of patches.

When my platoon spent two weeks at Camp Matthews learning how to shoot our Garand M-1 rifles, a giant B-24 bomber — with fuel tanks full — crashed into the recruit's mess hall, killing a lot of young Marines at dinner time. That awful slaughter was never reported in the newspapers because of wartime censorship.

Amazingly to me, in those eight summer weeks of Boot Camp, not a drop of rain fell!

My recruit platoon and I were in the movie "*Gung Ho!*" starring Randolph Scott. He often flubbed his lines so it took the entire day to get his speech to us "Marine Raider volunteers" on film. We actually weren't volunteers at all; the entire platoon was ordered to sit there and listen while the noted actor tried to get his speech rightly done and "in the can."

Of course I had no major part in that movie.

In another movie, called "*To the Shores of Tripoli*" starring John Payne, I was among a few hundred marching in a parade on the Depot for that film.

After I graduated as a Private First Class from MCRD, I was trucked to MCAS, Miramar. There I waited "in transit" for assignment to the Marine Corps Administration School, then housed at the Naval Training Center. That former base is now the commercialized "Liberty Station."

While waiting there at Miramar, we had lots of infantry training on the "boondocks," watching intently for rattlesnakes.

On that same training ground is now established the beautiful Miramar National Military Cemetery. That is where I am to be interred someday. *But being merely ninety, I am definitely in no very big rush to get there! I'm aiming now for the century mark!*

The Miramar cemetery is an extension of the Rosecrans National Cemetery.

Taking a bus from Miramar "on liberty" to downtown San Diego was a really big treat. There was then an especially busy USO club for service guys. The USO at that time asked pretty girls to volunteer to dance with us lonely fellows. Although it seemed there were about ten thousand guys in San Diego to every girl in residence, I got extremely fortunate and began dating a gal from the USO who was a looker and a terrific dancer.

That lovely gal and her younger sister were wonderful acrobats. In addition to the young lady entertaining me with her dancing and loving company, the two agile sisters "entertained the troops" with their demonstrations of acrobatics in USO shows.

She lived in the Kensington neighborhood. Her dad told me he purchased their lovely Spanish-style house for $6,000 in 1932. The Great Depression was fully upon the nation at that time. Today, I'm sure that house is worth at least $600,000! That's an increase of one hundred times for that little piece of pretty real estate! We can expect there have been lots of "updates" to that property since then.

My girlfriend's dad worked as a machinist at Consolidated Aircraft during the war, turning out various parts for those huge B-24 Liberator bombers.

Those people were so very nice to me. They drove their daughter and me way out east to see the great piles of boulders called mountains. I found East County to have fantastic terrain with all that cactus, sagebrush, sand and *billions of rocks.*

While spending sixteen weeks of schooling at NTC, I took a streetcar from Gate 3 on Rosecrans Street all the way to Adams Avenue in Kensington for a great big nickel price!

That streetcar line went up Park Boulevard past the Naval Hospital, which was then on the west side of Florida Canyon. Today, the new Naval Hospital is down in that canyon. On seemingly every day, I could see, from the streetcar, hundreds of servicemen recovering from wartime wounds, lying about on the grass to soak up the healing sun.

That trip took me past the San Diego Zoo also. Even then it was a world-famous institution. When a couple of years later I got home on furlough, I mentioned that zoo to my mother in Michigan. She was aghast that I had simply passed by the zoo again and again without going in! I told her, of course, that I was a whole lot more interested in two-legged pretty girls rather than the four-legged creatures housed there. Hey! I was seventeen and full of romantic vigor!

I tell you, downtown Broadway seemed to be a sea of white hats every night! Sailors came ashore on "Liberty Boats" to the Broadway pier from the hordes of warships in San Diego. You could almost hop, skip and jump across the bay on them then, the ships were so thick there. Sailor boys wore their white uniforms and walked along, looking for something exciting to do.

San Diego Bay was truly a wondrous sight during the war. You could see those huge aircraft carriers, and battleships with their nine sixteen-inch guns—and hundreds of anti-aircraft guns and all those ships. Visible were heavy cruisers, cruisers and light cruisers. Destroyers, destroyer-escorts and sub-chasers were anchored there. There were transports, freighters and oil tankers there too. Also, of course, our gallant and extremely effective submarines had a base in the bay at Ballast Point. Those submarines proved to be more devastating to enemy shipping than the efforts of all other warships combined.

The drinking age of twenty-one was strictly enforced in San Diego, except on military installations where a lad even of only seventeen could buy a couple of beers. Even if we weren't man enough to drink alcohol ashore, we were manly enough to fight for our country.

All of the armed services were well-represented in San Diego during that war.

The U. S. Army Air Corps had Rockwell Field on North Island, where young officers were taught to fly the powerful, twin engine, twin boom P-38 fighter planes. They could be seen flitting about and training in the sky every day.

As we student Marines in my class stared bug-eyed, a P-38 fighter plane nearly came crashing through our schoolroom window at NTC one day. Instead, it barely missed the top of our school and crashed into the hillside across Rosecrans Street from us, while missing three houses there. That fighter pilot was killed in the crash.

Of course, North Island was also a Naval Air Station, where Navy and Marine officers learned to fly an assortment of Wildcat, Hellcat and Corsair fighter planes as well as larger ones.

Aircraft carriers, then as now, docked at North Island.

The U.S. Army also manned anti-aircraft batteries here and

there all around San Diego and beyond. They also maintained at the ready huge coastal guns against the possibility of the enemy attempting an assault on our favorite part of planet earth. The Army also had a base at Fort Rosecrans on Point Loma.

Those many anti-aircraft batteries scattered about the town made everyone very much aware that we were indeed at war. When they practiced with those booming cannons, we were further reminded of the situation whereby the enemy might at any time attack us here. Even here in beautiful San Diego!

The Consolidated Aircraft Company, next to Lindbergh Field, was busy building thousands of warplanes. That vital facility was camouflaged by having—over the factory and a lot of Pacific Coast Highway—an amazing assortment of cardboard houses and phony palm trees. It was weird to ride a streetcar under that camouflage netting canopy, which would hopefully confuse enemy bombers aiming their bombs.

At that time, we saw Consolidated Aircraft's PBY two-engine and four-engine flying boats taking off from and setting down on the sparkling blue waters of San Diego Bay. How they found room to skim along the water and reach into the sky with so many ships anchored there, I will never know. Those flying boats barely cleared our Marine Corps Administration school building day after day, while struggling into the blue above.

The Thirty-Second Street Naval Station had only a few piers on which to tie up warships then. So that is why so many warships were mostly crowded into and anchored in the Bay.

The U. S. Marine Corps then had, besides the Miramar Marine Corps Air Station, a nearby armored tank and mortar training facility called Camp Elliott. Also, there was the gigantic ground-fighting Marine base of Camp Pendleton, established in 1942.

The U. S. Navy had a lot of schools besides the Recruit Training Camps on their Naval Training Center.

No way can I ever forget leaving San Diego for the war in the Pacific.

A few thousand Marines like myself were trucked to the North Island Naval Air Station. There, we were to embark on the brand-new giant aircraft carrier *Hornet*. It had been commissioned to replace the aircraft carrier by the same name sunk in the wonderfully decisive Battle of Midway. That happened to be a major turning point in the war. The Japanese Navy had suffered grievous losses, especially since American aircraft had sunk four of their few carriers in that battle.

Aircraft carriers, I must mention, were the true "battleships" of that war and most certainly are today. The nine sixteen-inch guns of a thick-steeled battleship then could reach out as far as twenty miles — and not necessarily with accuracy. The more or less *one hundred* aircraft on a *real battleship* could and did absolutely devastate the enemy on land, on the sea, and in the air for a *thousand miles* in every direction.

Anyway, my last hours of my last day in San Diego for a long time, were spent hauling crates of apples onto the *Hornet*. When I got aboard as the vessel was casting off, I could not find a single place on the hangar deck to lie down. Luckily I met a friend from my hometown who was a crewman on the ship. He said, "Hey Bill, there's a pile of cargo nets on a shelf under the flight deck by the bow of our ship. So you can make a 'nest' for yourself outside of the ship."

I did just that and spent the voyage to Hawaii bedded there through several days in a tremendous hurricane. Thereby I breathed fresh air while a thousand or more replacement servicemen on the hangar deck, in transit to Pearl Harbor, suffered in the stink of endless vomit!

After fourteen months in the always-hot and humid Marshall Islands, I returned to my favorite place on this earth, good old San Diego.

I clambered aboard a ship over there in the Marshall Islands to come home on April 12, 1945. That happened to be when the news hit us with a shock that our commander in chief, President Franklin Delano Roosevelt, had died.

The small and so-called "Jeep Carrier" I returned to San Diego on docked at North Island, where I had embarked from. To our utter astonishment, we saw on the docks pretty girls in Marine Corps uniforms! They were lady Marines! That had to be the beginning of really big changes to our Corps and to our world!

There was a wonderfully happy reunion with the Kensington girlfriend I had left behind when I went off to war. But after celebrating my return to the ever-so-beautiful girl in this ever-so-beautiful town, I was granted a furlough to see my family in Michigan.

Unfortunately for me, I was to report back for duty after that family reunion, not to my beloved city, but to Cherry Point, North Carolina. The major general commanding base at that time needed my abilities on his staff, it seemed, and so I spent the rest of the war in that job.

I didn't get back to this fabulous climate to live out the rest of my life until 1972!

Tsunami

Gary Winters

I felt something crack when I first saw her

like a dormant volcano waking up

no lightning strike splitting the azure skies

but a faint fissure in my calm sea bed

only a hint of what was yet to come

a force of nature not playing around

swelling and spreading exponentially

raging out of season from murky depths

unstoppable as it swept me along

toward a jagged coast of jutting granite

eyes lasering through the howling darkness

confronting the night and all its demons

no surrender or strategic retreat

poet warrior charges into abyss.

Summertime and the Livin' Is Easy

Nancy Clement

I was so looking forward to the summer of 2015. Then an envelope arrived in the mail; it was an invitation to my high school reunion. How could that be happening again, so fast? It wasn't a decade or even a half-decade celebration. It was a totally random year, because the high school was so small that the organizers decided to invite people who graduated in the '50s and the '60s. I graduated from Hot Springs High School in Truth or Consequences, New Mexico, in 1967, and here I thought I had two more years to get into shape. Nope, I had less than two months.

Stress set in ... how was I going to lose 40 pounds in two months, have a firm, hard body in that time without losing my mind or a major body part? I stewed over this and then realized it is not going to happen, so I had better make the best of it. Besides, I can still wear the same earrings I wore in high school.

Maybe I could find fabulous outfits to wear. Well, that didn't turn out as planned. I tried on those cute, skimpy sundresses that I used to wear in high school ... but they didn't look cute and adorable on me. If I had a teenaged granddaughter, I could imagine her saying, "You can't leave the house looking like that, what would the fashion police say?" In fact, as I tried dresses on, I had to laugh and realized wearing them in public would cause that same reaction from others.

So I lowered my expectations, settled on a couple of color-coordinated outfits, and realized that while I am fluffy and well-fed, I'm still above ground, and that's something to be thankful for. Besides, I was able to keep my sanity intact.

Okay, so I was not going to wear the same size I did when I was in high school, nor was I going to wear an eye popping outfit. But I could still look forward to a fun time, right?

Then another thought filled me with anxiety: what if someone says "Hello, Nancy," and I don't recognize that person? Then what do I do? It happened to me before at a class reunion, and now, since more years have passed, I'm even more likely not to remember someone. I just hope I'd be standing close enough to read their name tag, so I could at least pretend I recognized them. Then I heard of a trick, "Ask the stranger in front of you what their last name is." When asked for their last name, people instinctively give their first name as well. Problem solved. Now I could relax and look forward to connecting with old friends and classmates.

Another stressful thought occurred. "What will I say after I say hello, how are you?" Friends who have attended their class reunions say many of their classmates are retired and obsessed with talking about their grandkids. While I adore my grandkids, I try not to bore others with photos and stories about them, even though they are fabulous. Paraphrasing Winston Churchill, when asked if he had seen photos of a person's grandkids, he replied, "No, and I thank you."

So if the conversation stalled, I could ask, "So what do you do for fun?" If the answer to that question was, "I play with my grandkids," I'd quickly and graciously end the conversation and move on to chat with another person.

Finally, the big day, well actually big night, arrived. We had a meet-and-greet scheduled at the new, beautiful golf course. Summer evenings in TorC (Truth or Consequences), pronounced TORK, are wonderful ... first a gorgeous sunset colors the sky, then the temperature drops to the high '70s, and a slight but cool breeze perfumes the air with the desert smells of creosote. As the skies darken, the stars pop out and begin twinkling, and the bats fly their zigzag pattern searching for and eating bugs, reminding me of why New Mexico is the Land of Enchantment. Our class reunion was so relaxing and it brought back memories of summers I enjoyed when I was growing up in a small town named after a TV show.

Everyone was warm, friendly, and gracious towards one another. All high school cliques dropped away, and we were able to enjoy greeting one another and sharing stories of times past. I've heard it said that the older we get, the more we embellish stories of how good we all were when we were younger. I think those are called tall tales, and many were told that night.

Eddie, one of our classmates, apologized to my friend, Janet, and me and told us how guilty he felt about scaring the wits out of us years ago. One evening he took us to the wooded area around the Rio Grande River and in his most solemn voice told us about La Llorona. She's a ghost who roams at night looking for the children she drowned in a fit of rage when she found out her husband had been unfaithful. She's seeking revenge by looking for teenagers she can throw into the river to drown.

You know when she's around because you can hear her moaning. We heard that sound because he had gone earlier to place coke bottles strategically so the wind whistled in them. It sounds silly now, but Janet was spending the night at my house and both of us were so scared we stayed up all night, being vigilant in case she had followed us home. We accepted his apology and had a good laugh about it. To this day, the legend of La Llorona lives on. I read in the *New Mexico* magazine that the story is still frightening teenagers. I guess some things never change.

It was a lovely stroll down memory for me, and I was so relieved that no one threatened to show me pictures of their grandkids. Plus, the mosquitoes were a no-show because the truck filled with mosquito killer had been driving up and down the streets spraying bug poison. It worked, and since I was only at the golf course for an evening, I didn't need to worry whether or not that was going to ruin my health. So it truly was "summertime and the livin' *was* easy." And I had followed Erma Bombeck's advice: "Never show up at a high school reunion pregnant. They'll think that's all you've done since you graduated."

It was a magical evening.

A Benefit of Equal Treatment

Joe Naiman

Most of my high school graduating class, including the entirety of our 30-year reunion committee, turned 50 during 2014. A few of the ladies had 50th birthday parties.

Mary and Renee both turned 50 in August 2014. Mary was the first to send invitations to her birthday party. Her birthday was on a Wednesday that year, and instead of holding the party on her actual birthday she had the party on the previous Sunday.

That particular Sunday was August 24. Mary is not a professional sportswriter who covers horse racing, so I can't fault her for not being aware that August 24 was the day of the Pacific Classic at the Del Mar Thoroughbred Club. I am a professional sportswriter who covers horse racing, so I had no option other than to send my regrets.

Renee's birthday was on a Monday in 2014, and she chose to have her party on the previous Saturday. It wasn't on the same day as the most prestigious race of the Del Mar meet, but I had a decision to make. I was concerned about the impact if I attended Renee's party but not Mary's. Mary deserves to be treated equally to Renee, and with neither holding their party on their actual birthday it would have been an injustice to Mary if I had attended Renee's party. I explained the situation to Renee, who understood my decision.

The Del Mar Thoroughbred Club press box has extra programs, so when I was there for the Pacific Classic and the other August 24 races I took one for Mary so that she'd at least have a souvenir from the reason I was unable to attend her party. Since I had vowed to treat Mary and Renee equally, I also took one for Renee.

Shared Belief won the Pacific Classic that year. The press conference took place after the race. I explained to winning jockey Mike Smith and to winning trainer Jerry Hollendorfer that I gave up a birthday party for the Pacific Classic, and both were willing to autograph each of the extra programs I had.

I didn't see either Renee or Mary until after the end of that summer's Del Mar meet. On the final day of the meet a horse named *Reneesgotzip* won a stakes race. This time the occasion called for getting appropriate memorabilia to Renee while giving equal treatment to Mary. Peter Miller trained *Reneesgotzip*, and when he was in the paddocks for a subsequent race I asked him to autograph the two extra programs I had obtained. He willingly signed both programs. When I saw Mary and Renee after the meet concluded I provided them with the autographed programs from the Pacific Classic and the autographed programs from Closing Day when *Reneesgotzip* won her stakes race.

The stakes races on Closing Day also included the Del Mar Futurity. That was won by *American Pharoah*, who became a first-time winner. Eight months after the Del Mar Futurity race *American Pharoah* won the Kentucky Derby, and five weeks after that he became the first horse in 37 years to win the Triple Crown.

In my attempt to treat Renee and Mary equally, they now both had programs that included *American Pharoah's* first winning race.

Easter

Frank Primiano

"Damn son of a bitch," came spilling from my mouth before I could catch myself. I don't like to swear in front of Eddy, bad example and all. But that damn, er, darn, rabbit was eating the leaves from my potato plants. And I like fresh-from-the-garden new potatoes.

"Grandpa, you have to watch your mouth. You know I'm still an impressionable child." Eddy's lips and eyes smiled as he let out a quiet, "Heh, heh."

"You won't tell your mom, will you?"

"Naw. She doesn't have to know."

"You're a good kid."

Eddy picked up a golf ball-sized stone. He said, "Here, let me solve your problem," and wound up like a pitcher. He let fly, right at the little cottontail, and missed. But the animal got the message. It took off.

"I hate to do that," he said. "It could have been the Easter Bunny loading up before his big day next weekend."

I watched the little rodent bastard scamper into the bushes lining the yard before I said, "Uh, Eddy, there's something I have to tell you."

"What?"

"You're too old to keep believing that."

"Believing what?"

"About the Easter Bunny."

"What about the Easter Bunny?"

"That there is one."

"What do you mean?"

"There is no Easter Bunny."

"No Easter bunny?"

"That's right."

Eddy looked at me in silence, frowning. His eyes faded into a blank stare. He said, "You mean that all the cocoa powder I leave out the night before Easter is wasted?"

"Not really. Your mom pours it back into the canister before you wake up."

"The Easter Bunny doesn't eat the cocoa?"

"Nope."

"Then who makes all those tiny, squishy, bitter-tasting, chocolate-colored jelly beans I find sprinkled on the lawn on Easter morning?"

House on Verdugo Road

Barbara Weeks Huntington

In the twilight, the house hunkered dark behind the deodar trees. Brown pine needles crunched under our feet and hung in the cobwebs that were barely visible in the sickly porch light. The house on Verdugo Road in La Canada wasn't elegant like ones we couldn't afford to rent in South Pasadena, and certainly not homey like the Altadena tract house we had shared with the roses when we were a happy family of four.

No, as we drove up in the battered Nash Rambler, our final load of furniture in the trailer behind, the house appeared as an old lady who had finally given up. She stood there, a small frame house with a strange dowager's hump of a room as a second floor, hands on hips in her old slippers and bathrobe, shrugging off our attempt to make her a home. She was beyond that. And so was my mom.

Brother Bill and I unpacked the car and then, alone, I carried my pajama dog up the complaining stairs to that hump that would be my room. It squatted over the living room, kitchen, two bedrooms, and the moldy bathroom that would require navigating back down those stairs in the middle of the night if I forgot and drank too much water before going to bed. From one of the two windows, I could look down into the weedy backyard with green pools of mosquito larvae in a caved-in fishpond.

My other window of this remnant of another time stared at a busy intersection. The deodars and maple trees shut out some of the apartment neighbors, but afforded a clear view of the ambulances and cop cars that arrived for the way-too-numerous accidents below.

That room became the nightmare central of my anxious adolescence, the place I awoke to screeches and crashes followed by red lights flashing against my wall, thunder, lightning, rain, wind thumping branches against the wall, cats howling, and a sense of cold, smooth malevolent creatures crawling between my stuffed dog and my nightgown.

I dreamed of rattlesnakes, but it wasn't nightmares that fueled my greatest fears of that house on Verdugo Road. No, they arose from the very real sound of my brother's scream, the long chorus of horns, the screech of brakes, the banging of the wood and screen door, and looking out my window to see my brother walking my nightgowned mother through the now-stopped traffic and wondering when she would try again.

We didn't stay in the house long after that. I couldn't sleep, and my parents decided to try again in another house in the next town over, La Crescenta. A few months later, a Crescenta Valley High classmate said she knew of our strange little house in La Canada. She told me about Rattlesnake James, who killed his wife by putting rattlesnakes in her bed and then dumping her body in the pond behind the house, but that's another story…

Schwartz Nails It

Ken Yaros

Schwartz and Cohen grew up in the same apartment house in the Bronx, dated the same girls, and attended NYU together. But that's when their close relationship ended. Cohen, being the studious one, became a rabbi. Schwartz chose business. Thirty years passed, each had married and raised families. After the children were married off, the two reconnected and agreed to meet for chess Sunday afternoons.

They'd convene at Central Park in the parking lot. Cohen drove his older white Toyota compact and parked next to Schwartz's fire-engine-red Cadillac convertible. Cohen could hardly take his eyes off it.

The game offered a good opportunity to talk about family, reminisce, and boast about their accomplishments.

Cohen headed one of the largest Jewish congregations in New York and officiated at many bar mitzvahs and weddings for some of society's most notable families. He went on to describe some of his congregants and why they were so important.

Schwartz would listen, smile politely, nod his approval, but say little. One afternoon, Cohen asked him why he was so quiet. "You weren't like that growing up."

"Well, to tell you the truth, I find most people are pretty ordinary," Schwartz said. "Presidents, kings, billionaires, they're all the same once you get to know them."

"Ha! Now that's the Schwartz I remember, always the big shot." Cohen reached across the board. "You're now in check, and we both know you're full of you know what, right?"

"Cohen, believe me, my business takes me all over the place. I figure that I've met just about everyone at some point. There's hardly anybody of importance I don't know."

"Tell you what, big pants. Next Sunday I'll come up with someone you don't know, and I'll bring a crisp fifty-dollar bill to back it up. You game?"

"Sure, sure, if it will make you happy."

***

Next Sunday arrived and Cohen couldn't wait. As soon as they sat down, he placed the fifty on the table and says, "Obama."

Schwartz looked at the bill and shook his head. "Sure you want to do this? I really don't want to take your money."

"Take it or admit I win," Cohen says with a smile.

"Okay, have it your way, but the fact is I've known Barack since he was a teenager in Honolulu, living with his grandmother who ran a bank we did business with."

"Schwartz, you are so full of it—"

"Cohen, come to my office tomorrow morning, and I'll prove it."

The next morning the two of them sat in Schwartz's office while the businessman placed a call to the president.

"Hello, Barack, Bernie Schwartz here. I just wanted to call to thank you for the wonderful donation you made to my favorite charity and to introduce you to my special friend, Rabbi Cohen from New York City."

Cohen, dumbfounded, sunk into his chair, stood and left.

"Are we still on for chess, Sunday?" Schwartz asked.

"Sure, why not?"

***

Sunday, Cohen showed up just in time to see Schwartz reach across the board and place the fifty-dollar bill next to his queen.

"What's this?" Cohen said.

"I can't take your money. We're friends, take it."

"No, you won it fair, you keep it."

"If you insist."

"But I want a chance to win it back, okay?"

"Sure, sure, Cohen, whatever you say."

"I've been thinking all week of someone you don't know. Queen Elizabeth."

"Cohen, please don't make a fool of yourself," Schwartz said.

"Here is two hundred to back me up," Cohen said.

"Listen here, I've had dealings with the royal family for years. I know Elizabeth quite well."

"Then prove it."

"That's going to be a little harder; you know she almost never takes calls. But if you're willing to come to England with me, I can prove that we know each other."

* * *

The next week they flew to London and presented themselves at the royal quarters in Buckingham Palace. Moments later, a matronly woman greeted them and smiled when she saw Schwartz.

"Mr. Schwartz, what a pleasant surprise. What brings you to London? Come on in and we will arrange for tea. You know Phillip really misses playing polo with you."

Cohen could hardly believe his eyes, but there was no mistaking what he heard. They were both silent during the flight home.

The following Sunday, Cohen was a no-show for chess, so Schwartz called him the next day.

"Cohen, I feel awful. I couldn't sleep all night. My wife says I should give you back the money and be finished with it."

"I know, I feel bad too, but you know if there is one thing that drives me crazy as a rabbi, it's a braggart."

"I know, and you are right of course, but the plain truth is that I do know everyone," Schwartz said. "I wouldn't tell a lie, especially to my best friend."

"Schwartz, there are over four billion people on this earth, and I did think of one you couldn't possibly know. He grew up in South America and is now the Pope. I say that one thousand dollars proves you are nothing to him."

"Cohen, don't do it, please. I'm asking as your friend."

"Too late, I've already sent it to your office. It's time you learned a lesson."

"Well, Cohen, this is a tough one, I admit. You see, the pope doesn't take phone calls and private audiences are booked months ahead. But I have an idea. Every week he comes out on the balcony to bless the faithful. What if I could stand there next to him, would that be acceptable?"

They agreed, and the next week they left for Rome.

***

A massive crowd gathered in the piazza in front of Saint Peter's one morning. Schwartz beckoned Cohen good-bye and disappeared into the crowd.

At noon, the doors to the balcony were flung open and out stepped Schwartz, who walked right up to the railing to wave to Cohen.

To his horror, he watched as Cohen collapsed to the street.

"Oh my God, Cohen. I'll be right there!"

Schwartz rushed back to him and held him gently in his arms.

"Cohen, Cohen, are you okay?"

"Yes, okay. I'll be fine in a minute."

"What happened?"

"Well—after you disappeared into the crowd, I got to thinking. After all this, maybe you did know the Pope. Then, after the doors swung open, you waved. That's when the nun standing next to me from a remote village in Africa began shouting, 'What the heck is Schwartz doing up there with the Pope?' I couldn't take it anymore!"

Johnny the Choker Setter

Fred Crothers

Johnny was a young guy who frequented my tavern, Freddie's Bungalow, in Carson, Washington. He had a baby face, big blue eyes, curly blond hair, and an easy smile. He looked so young that I carded him the first time he strode into the tavern. I liked him right away, a well-mannered, congenial young guy with an excellent sense of humor. Johnny was a heap of fun and provided me with insight into his workday world as a Carson logger.

Most loggers wore the same general outfit to work; black *stagged pants* (roughly cut off with frayed edges that tore easily rather than snag up on tree limbs or low lying brush), a cotton blue-lined, long-sleeve shirt and wide black suspenders with brass clips. He wore tall black leather boots generally referred to as *corked* boots (caulked with rows of sharp steel points set in the soles for maximum traction).

His boots were laced up with rawhide laces in a series of brass hooks. On his head, he wore a large, round aluminum hat with webbing inside that completed his macho workday outfit. The loggers usually showered and changed into casual clothes when visiting the tavern. (Corks were expressly forbidden in the tavern because the savage little points chewed up wooden floors, or, in my place, red carpet.)

He worked in the woods as a choker setter and had a reputation for being a hard worker. Choker setters were almost always young guys who ran, jumped and easily trod the *bucked* (limbs cut off) trees. They needed a critical eye and fast hands to wrap the cable (called turns) around several large logs, locking the ends of the cable with a bell housing, and get clear so the logs could be lifted or dragged to a clearing by the *yarder*, the man who operates the winch that hauls everything into the main landing site by winding up the cables on huge spools. He is in charge of the logs, which are stacked at the site for loading and hauling by log trucks. Choker setting is a particularly dangerous job, owing to the risk of being maimed or killed by falling trees, lashed or cut in twain by broken cables, or falling headlong into a morass of downed logs and limbs.

It was always an exciting night at the tavern when a chosen few of the local loggers were able to hire on with one of the Alaskan logging camps. These jobs were hugely rewarding in terms of excitement, adventure and a hefty pay increase. Naturally, not everyone was eligible for these jobs; it required a letter of recommendation from his crew chief, several years of experience in a number of related tasks, and an intense physical exam from a doctor. We were always eager to hear any news about our guys and how they were faring in Alaska.

Sure enough, it wasn't long before Johnny got the call too and made arrangements to fly to Alaska. Not only was this a huge adventure for Johnny, but also his first flight in an airplane. He was hired as a choker setter for a large-scale logging company owned by the Seventh-day Adventist Church. This outfit had some pretty strict rules and regulations. Johnny liked the company, his job and his logging crew, but hated all the rules. He missed drinking and having fun times with his Carson friends.

We didn't hear much about Johnny for several months, and then one of his friends brought us the news. He was critically injured on the job and confined to a hospital bed somewhere near Ketchikan. We never really got the scoop on the accident, but we heard he wasn't responding well to various performance tests he was given in the hospital. The story, currently circulating at the time, indicated he would soon be released with lingering mental issues and might never work in the woods again.

Johnny came home a few months later and we all treated him gently and didn't ask a lot of questions. It was obvious that he'd cut way back on his drinking and sat very quiet for the most part.

A month or so later, I said, "Hey, Johnny, what really happened up there in Alaska? All we heard is that you had one hell of an accident and spent a lot of time in the hospital."

He said, "I was standing on a stump near the landing site, minding my own business, taking a break and smoking some grass. I wasn't paying close attention and sure enough I got hit in the head by the haulback, which knocked me clear off the stump.

If I hadn't been wearing my hard hat it would have been church!"

"So how are you doing now?"

"Fine, but I had to cut down on my drinking while I'm taking all this pain medication."

"You still got your wits about you after taking such a jolt?"

"Oh, I'm doing all right."

"We heard you didn't respond well to any of the performance tests they gave you in the hospital and suspected that you would be kind of drifty after the accident."

Johnny said, "I got a big chunk of dough from their insurance company and a monthly check for the rest of my days, based on those tests. I did suffer some bad injuries and was in a coma for a week or so, but they sewed me up and I'm fine now."

I said, "What about all those tests and negative reports we heard about?"

"Well, the truth is I never could read or write, or spell my own name. That's why I couldn't answer their questions or make heads or tails out of all their stupid charts."

I loved his answer, simple and honest, and we both had a good laugh about it. They hadn't even considered the fact that he couldn't read or write. They just assumed that he had lost his marbles.

The Birthmark

Anne Janda

When she was pregnant with me, mother was sickly throughout the nine months, and during that ordeal she became convinced that I wouldn't be quite right. She had proof of her prediction when the red spot on my forehead, dismissed by the nurse as a bit of blood, turned out to be a rosy, bumpy birthmark eventually as thick and large as a quarter. She thought it might suggest some deeper brain abnormality and worried that men would be repulsed by it when I was of marriageable age.

In my mother's opinion, the only suitable future for a young woman was to marry well. Her mother told her to marry my father because his family owned a farm and she had herself married my grandfather for the same reason. Mother wanted to give me every advantage to carry on this womanly tradition. She must have known about Aylar's repulsion of his wife Georgiana's birthmark in Hawthorne's famous story, *The Birthmark*. Unlike dad, who majored in agriculture, mother was an English major in college.

I was very young when she told me we were going to the city.

She said, "Men won't like your birthmark when you're older so we have to fix it now."

This was very confusing to me. Why should I care what men thought of me when I was older. She had to resort to bribery to convince me that this was a good thing.

"Afterward you can pick out anything you want from the gift shop."

I rarely went shopping outside a Sears catalogue, so I rode in the back seat of our Buick for the sixty miles to Carew Tower in downtown Cincinnati, dreading the unknown but sure of the fabulous reward. It would be like Christmas. She did admit my forehead might hurt, but not for long.

I saw the gift shop on the way to the elevator. From the corridor I could see the shelves filled with dolls and plush bears and silver hand mirrors, and sachets and perfume bottles. Thrilled with excitement, I went with my parents in the elevator up to the medical offices. And then I remembered to be scared.

When we were shown into the doctors' examining room there were three men in white coats waiting for us with tense smiles on their faces. They directed me to a small bed built into the wall. The area above it was lit and they told me to lie still. I was really scared now but I told myself whatever they did would end and then I could go to the gift shop.

Across the room, dad looked uncomfortable in his rumpled city suit, wanting a smoke. Mother stood beside him, timidly smiling at the doctors. Neither of them touched me or reassured me. They seemed unsure themselves and that wasn't giving me confidence. The doctors took measurements of my birthmark and my head and discussed among themselves whether I was too young for this, but decided to go ahead.

One held my feet, another my arms and the third held my head. The cold carbon dioxide felt like an ice burn on my forehead, and then when it was over it felt numb. They explained what would happen next. They said it would swell and become painful and to call them if the pain didn't eventually subside. During the numb stage, I knew it would all be worth it when I got to the gift shop.

Either dad didn't know about my deal with mother or he was too worried about the crops to care. He was in a hurry to get back to the farm. He told mother he would go get the car and bring it around in front. Mother and I went to the shop, but she left me on my own so she could stand outside the door to watch for our blue Buick through the larger glass doors across the lobby.

Inside the shop, I wasn't tall enough to reach the first shelf or to see all those marvels on the several glass shelves above unless I stood in the back of the shop. Mother kept telling me to hurry up. I panicked because there were so many beautiful things and I needed time to choose. My birthmark began to throb with pain.

Looking up at the first shelf, I fell in love with the music boxes. There was one with a canary in a cage spinning around as the music played. I could see that the dolls wore velvet dresses, and unlike me they had flawless faces with clear, beautiful skin. There were sachets filled with exotic scents, and plush teddy bears wearing satin bows, and there were silver compacts, and porcelain rose soap dishes and bags of marbles and tiny trucks for boys.

"Dad is getting the car. Hurry up. We have to go," Mother demanded, still standing outside the gift shop door.

I felt sick to my stomach with panic and the pain from my forehead. I was pretty sure I wouldn't get another chance to have something from the shop. My panic triggered another anxiety: I was worried that I'd ask for something too expensive. It came to me how I had once, without knowing it, made mother very angry. We were in a dress shop and I wanted a dress with a red strawberry embroidered on it. I loved the red strawberry. Mother reluctantly said "Yes," making me as happy as I would be today if I could have one of those bears or one of the music boxes.

But when we got to the car with the dress in a bag, she grabbed me, pinched my face up to hers and shouted that it was too expensive. She screamed at me that I had embarrassed her by asking for it. She hissed that she had to buy the dress; otherwise the clerk would think she didn't have the money. I should always follow her lead. I should always do what she did.

But now she wasn't beside me to tell me what was too expensive and what wasn't. She was too busy worrying about dad and making him angry at her if we were late to the car when he drove up. My dad's words cut like knives when he was angry. His words and the way he spit them out made you believe he had never loved you and never would and that you weren't worth much at all.

I thought I was supposed to know what was too expensive, and what was not in the same way I was supposed to know the strawberry dress cost too much. I wanted the canary music box but I was sure it was too expensive—the canary cage was painted gold and I longed for one of the bears, but they were probably expensive too. I didn't want to be shaken and screamed at, especially not now with my forehead on fire.

"Dad has the car in front. We have to go!" mother yelled from the door.

The clerk saw my panic. Near her cash register was a miniature tea set—not for a child—but for a doll. The tiny tea pot and cups and saucers were blue with white painted flowers. She quickly grabbed it and held it up, "Would you like this?" I couldn't say "No." I couldn't say that I really wanted a music box or a bear. The pain on my forehead was exploding, but I was sure it didn't earn me the right to ask for something expensive. The canary box was playing and the music was magical. But I nodded yes that I wanted the tea set because it seemed to me that it was so small it couldn't be too expensive, so it was the tea set or nothing.

I looked longingly over at the shelves with the beautiful dolls and music boxes and felt tears roll down my cheeks. The pain on my forehead was punishing now. I just wanted to lie down somewhere. I just wanted the pain to stop.

The clerk nervously looked at my swelling birthmark covered loosely with gauze, and said cheerily, "Now you'll be just like Alice in Wonderland having tea."

I stared at her. I didn't know who Alice in Wonderland was. The clerk's smile faded. But then she perked up. "Would you like this gift-wrapped?"

"No," my mother said as she came to the counter, jerked open her handbag, and paid the woman. She pulled me out to the car. My dad was angry that he had to wait for us with city traffic all around him and cars honking their horns. "What took you so long?"

I lay on the back seat of the car tightly holding the tea set. While my father harangued her, mother threw me guilty looks from the front seat. I lie there in the back silently angry with helpless tears in my eyes. I wanted to scream at her. "You lied to me. I didn't have time to choose anything I wanted from the gift shop. And I love my birthmark. It reminds me that I was born in May when spring explodes overnight into green trees and lavender flowers. If God created me like you say, then God created my birthmark too. It's a badge of my creation."

She was pleased when, after several more excruciating treatments, the strawberry color was made a pale pink and, after swelling out to the size of an apricot each time, it finally shrunk below its original size and could at last be covered with thin hair bangs. I wasn't allowed to go to the gift shop again; dad said it took too much time.

Sometimes my friends would ask when they saw the pale

round oddity, "What is that?" And I would say "It's my birthmark." And I would feel sorry for them that they didn't have one.

The Unknown

Janet Hafner

Waiting to return an item to my local outdoor store, I glanced at the rack of brochures to my left. One called out, "Port Hardy — ripe with outdoor adventures." I wondered if sixty was too old for a wildlife adventure. No, definitely not.

I had no idea where Port Hardy was, nor did I know what wildlife adventures they spoke of, but it didn't matter. Glowing sunsets, mink scurrying along logs in rain forests, and splashing Orcas that frolicked with their young beamed off the brochure into my mind. The words, "Kayak with us for eight days from island to island. Experience the best the Northwest Passage has to offer," caused my limbs to vibrate. The brochure went home with me.

* * *

After two phone calls, I had the price, a list of the equipment I needed, the departure date and, most importantly, specifics about how physically fit I had to be.

"I'm going on a trip," I gleefully announced to my sons. This must be how someone feels when they win the lottery.

"Going to see your brother in New York?" my oldest son, Marc, asked.

"Not exactly. I'm going to kayak for eight days off the tip of Vancouver Island in British Columbia."

Heads turned. With stupefied looks and curled-up noses, the chorus sang in unison, "Reeeeally?"

"Mom, you don't know anything about kayaking," Chris said, and with his next breath added, "You know you're not thirty any more."

I squared my shoulders and watched them trying to change my mind. My youngest made the last attempt, "You love New York. Go there, please."

I felt my cheeks color. With eyebrows raised, I said, "I know how happy you all are for me."

***

San Diego to Seattle, on to Vancouver, then Port Hardy and finally the dock, the beach and far-away water. I stood with my watertight bag filled with a bathing suit, change of dry clothes, water shoes and waterproof jacket. I looked out beyond a deep expanse of dark matter. At some distant point, water met this unknown substance. What was that between me and the water? Surely not a sandy beach.

My kayak mates were six men and two women, ranging in age from eighteen to me at sixty. Jake and Stan, two tall, muscular, beautifully tanned youngsters with wild sun-streaked hair, announced themselves as our leaders to the unknown.

Jake said, "Tents, kayaks, sleeping bags, water and food — which we'll prepare — are all waiting. All you guys have to do is paddle." Ah huh . . . exactly how far? A safety lecture and a 'how-to-handle-a-kayak' session poured into all the free space in my brain.

"Okay, are we ready?" Stan, the second guide, was grinning at us. His eyes sized us up. In two steps, his tall figure stood at my side. His smile poured over me. I relaxed. Then, all six feet of him leaned forward until his blue eyes stared into mine.

"And how about you — are *you* ready?"

"Absolutely." My head bobbed up and down.

"Okay, let's hit it," he sang.

"Yeah," sang the chorus. As I looked around at our group, my stomach flipped. Jake and Stan were the only fit ones, but what we lacked in fitness, we certainly made up for with eagerness and commitment.

"What you're standing in front of . . . is your best friend. It can save you. Get to know it really well." Stan walked around his kayak. His hand caressed its side. What I saw before me was, indeed, a man and his best friend.

I made friends with my kayak. I climbed in and out on dry land. We examined the footrests, the wobbly seat, a splash cover. All good. I can do this. Of course, standing inside a kayak on firm ground is a little misleading. It was nothing like the real thing that

I soon discovered.

"Get your water shoes on. Got to load the week's supplies into the dry storage wells, then we'll be ready to get to the water," Stan barked. With the kayaks packed, we picked a partner and carried the kayaks out to the water.

Port Hardy is famous for tides that move the water in and out by hundreds of feet. The tide was out. My kayak-carrying partner was a man in his forties. The look of his portly shape told me he loved beer. Above the belly were broad shoulders that would be a plus carrying a fully stocked kayak.

We carried one kayak to the dark stuff, stepped in the muck and sank to our ankles. We wobbled, we squished, we trudged forward ever mindful that the water was far off. The further I pushed forward, the deeper I sank until my knees were deprived of sunlight. "Should we put it down and rest?" I shouted.

"Not such a good idea," came Marty's reply. We forced ourselves through the sludge—stepping, sinking, struggling to pull our feet out of the muck. The suction held us tightly and then let go. My foot flew up, flinging black mud in my face.

At last, we were at the water. The kayak danced and bobbed, happy to be where it belonged. Frigid Northwest water washed away the slime. We dropped a mini-anchor, took a couple of deep breaths and headed back to do it all again.

The command came, "Get in your . . . " Jake paused long enough to see if one of us would call this means of transportation by any other name, like boat or canoe. We all shouted, "Kayak." We passed the first test.

I threw the top half of my body over the side of the kayak, my rump sticking up in the air like a whale's tale, and then, as if by some miracle, I was in it, exhausted but . . . in it. When does the fun begin?

Jake whistled three times and shouted, "Let's paddle."

* * *

Energy and enthusiasm traveled from the bottom of my feet, pressed hard against the foot rests in my kayak, into my bottom, cold from water left on the seat. From there it flowed up my spine, where it branched out into my arms and finally into the paddles.

Paddling is a blend of art and science. The effortless strokes of our leaders propelled them forward. They skimmed the water. They understood the science part and as I watched they transformed science into art. It was beautiful. When they tire, I bet it won't look so pretty.

Awkward and tense were the trademarks of those of us who were inexperienced. Our paddles dipped either too far or not far enough into the mirror-like icy waters. Water ran down my paddle and, without stopping, continued in mini-streams down my arm and ended in my armpit, then trickled down my side.

We tried to keep up with Jake's style. A couple of strokes and a long smooth glide . . . we paddled and paddled and . . . paddled . . . no gliding. We found ourselves far behind.

"Follow me," came the voice from far up front. Jake was paddling from the center of the channel to a spot that was about fifty feet from shore. "Link up. Watch your fingers." We formed a cluster. Smiles had faded, minds held one thought, someone murmured, "Thank God we stopped."

"How's it going? Drink some water. You all did pretty good, but if we're going to make it to our island for overnight, we've got to pick up the pace." No reply. My heart thumped against my chest. That was . . . full speed. Are you kidding me?

Our other water-god, Stan, picked up his paddle. "Look, it's a pull and push motion that makes it work. It's the rhythm. As the right hand pushes forward, the left hand pulls the paddle alongside the kayak. Like this." In the space of one blink, he left the pack, positioned himself fifty feet away and demonstrated what he expected us to do.

Jake sang, "Got it?" A couple of us nodded timidly. "Let's give it a try."

Our watercrafts jostled for position, paddles poked and pushed as we tried to get away from the group. A new mantra emerged. Push and pull . . . push and pull. My right side was definitely stronger than my left side. Even it out, I hummed. The superior leaders paddled left, right, left, right. You couldn't miss the cadence. My rhythm was left, right, left, left, left. I needed three lefts to make up for the powerful right.

We struggled, no doubt about it, but we were getting faster. Not pretty, but with a mission in mind, we paddled to the island arriving in time to pull our best friends onto the beach.

"About ten miles, not bad, now get everything out of the drywells before we lose the light." Jake unloaded his cooking gear and supplies for the evening meal, set up the kitchen and, with water starting to boil, was well on his way to preparing dinner.

"Pick a spot to set up your tents. Two to a tent. Get your sleeping bags set up and everything ready for an early morning."

"What's for dinner?" asked Jonathan, a tall young man whose body stuck out of his kayak like a periscope. An empty belly made him circle the cook like a vulture.

"Did I mention that our meals are vegetarian?"

"It didn't say that in the brochure. You're kidding," another kayaker griped.

"Wait till you taste it." Jake laughed.

My stomach didn't care. It would chow down on cardboard if it had to. All I wanted was to fill my clamoring empty belly. That evening we sat around the fire eating something that was really delicious. Vegetarian cooking is really tasty. Talk focused on paddling and most answers came down to, "It'll get better with each day." Exhausted arms and full bellies crawled into sleeping bags.

***

Barely light. "Come and get it," Stan intoned. A hot nut, grain and dried fruit cooked cereal and campfire coffee satisfied us. All was going well until we noticed that our means of transportation were sitting on land, not water. The fluctuating tides would follow us from island to island. We packed up camp, squished and sank in the muck until we got the kayaks to the water. If the coffee didn't wake us up, the frigid water did. We were off.

With each day, distance increased because the prediction, "It'll get better with each day" came true. The art of gliding was mastered. When he wasn't paddling, Jake was a botanist. Lichen, moss, nurse logs, fern were words that glided off his tongue. The brochure said mink scampered along logs—they did. We watched.

"Each island we visit is a primitive island," Jake said. "What you'll be walking on will feel like a giant sponge. It's been growing for centuries just like the nurse logs." We beached our craft and walked — with soft steps — to the interior of the island. The canopy overhead gave it an eerie feeling like some fantasy movie. Exposed tree roots formed tunnels. Jake explained how years before, seeds had fallen onto a felled tree. Seeds received nourishment and roots grew around the fallen tree. After many years, the log rotted away, but the roots remained, holding up the trees that became the canopy overhead. And . . . it was all lush emerald green. By day five, we were tired, and disappointed that what we had really come to see, the orcas, hadn't materialized. The straits are famous for pods of orcas. We teased Jake and Stan about advertising and not producing.

"We only have three days left — when are you going to cue the orcas?" one of the group shouted.

"Do we get a refund if no orcas show?" the tall Texan called. We laughed, they laughed, but no killer whales surfaced.

* * *

It was our last day. It was misty. Morning was just getting started. We paddled on a clear sheet of glass. Our paddles no longer slapped the water as if to wake it up. We dipped our paddles delicately without a sound. Because we had used most of the water we carried, the kayaks sat lightly in the water. Paddle, paddle, glide.

Jake yelled, "Look left, over near the shore." A mama orca and her calf were playing, breaching high out of the water. The pod of kayaks moved swiftly to get a closer look. When he yelled, I was adjusting my gloves, so I was left in the middle of the strait. Stan's kayak came up behind me.

He yelled, "Look down the strait. Get your paddles out of the water."

I squinted far beyond the bow of my "best friend." I lifted my paddles out of the water. My eyes focused straight ahead at a gigantic submarine and a smaller sub coming directly at me. My heart pounded in my ears, my breathing a runaway horse. They weren't veering off to one side or the other. They were lined up with me. Stan called to me, "Janet, don't do anything. Sit perfectly still." I wondered why I wasn't paddling at top speed out of the way. I wondered what would happen if he surfaced under my kayak. I wondered which way I would dive and subsequently die. I watched. They dove . . . they surfaced. They dove . . . they surfaced. One, two, three, four, I counted to ten and counted again. Just when I thought my heart couldn't beat any more — they dove - ten, eleven, twelve, thirteen. Up they came, twenty-five feet directly behind me. They continued their journey without ever looking back.

A roar of cheers and yells from my fellow paddlers rang across the strait. Then, I closed my eyes and bowed my head. They circled around me making whooping sounds. Jake raised his arms; quiet returned. With eyebrows raised and lips that touched his ears, he said, "We said we'd give you orcas. We keep our promises."

Zipolite — The Hippie Paradise

Sam Warren

On the Oaxacan Riviera

As a writer who has never had a best seller, I didn't salt enough money into my retirement nest egg to survive in San Diego with its high cost of living. Then a friend told me about this hippy beach town in the southern Mexican state of Oaxaca. That's how I came to live over a thousand miles away in the sleepy Mexican beach town of Zipolite. It isn't the end of the world, and they have WiFi so I can still communicate with friends with email and Skype.

The nearest Walmart and gas station are over 45 minutes away by a colectivo or camioneta. A colectivo is a taxi in which the driver crowds as many people into his vehicle as he can. He only charges a few pesos per person. A camioneta is a tarp-covered pickup truck with benches in the back. It is cheaper than a colectivo but not as comfortable. A joke goes, "How many passengers can fit in a camioneta?" The answer is, "*Uno mas*," or "One more."

In the 1960s and 1970s, counterculture hippies began to congregate here, in part due to the beach's isolated nature. At the time, there was little law enforcement, and drug use became common. In the 1970s and 1980s, the beach gained a reputation in Mexico and among foreign travelers as a free-love paradise. Zipolite evolved by word of mouth into an offbeat place with middle-class Mexicans, retired ex-patriots, people with alternate lifestyles, and liberal tourists who come from all over the world.

When I first arrived I rented a small, three-bedroom house a half block from the beach. That was over a year ago, and I'm still there. My rent is only 3,000 pesos per month plus utilities, which at the current exchange rate is about $180. As it gets hot in the off season, most of the houses have large, covered patios where residents do most of their living. Sitting on the patio, one can catch the breeze from the ocean. The only rooms in my house with doors are the bedrooms and bathrooms. The bedrooms are the only doors than can be locked, but luckily the crime rate is low here. The bathroom, as in most of the local homes, has only cold water, which sometimes heats up in the sun.

My kitchen is on the patio and my combination kitchen sink and laundry is outside. I have to do my laundry by hand as I don't have a machine yet. I think of the pictures I've seen of native women washing clothes on rocks in rivers and can relate to them. On the negative side, with no walls, one has to sweep and dust a lot, especially when it is windy.

There isn't much privacy as I can wave to my neighbors as they walk by. Lisa, my neighbor's dog, comes by every day for her belly rub. The house came with a house cat, who keeps pestering me by rubbing against my leg and meowing. If this cat was a woman, she would be a stalker. I thought that if I didn't feed her, she would go away. Not only did she not go away, she dropped a load of kittens in my storage room.

I now have a cat and her family of kittens to feed. I also have to keep the neighbor's dogs from eating their food. And there's the chicken who comes by to peck at my kitchen floor for any food that has been dropped.

One day during a rainstorm, as I worked on my computer on the patio, I had this feeling I was being watched. I looked down and found a small land crab looking up at me. I also saw a number of these land crabs walking sideways across my patio. Later, I found out that when it rains, the crabs come out of their holes in the ground to keep from drowning. I was told that the locals gather and eat them. However, I don't see that there is enough meat on them to make it worthwhile.

While there are drawbacks to my modest house, the sound of pounding surf 24/7 isn't one of them. Some people in the U.S. who have trouble sleeping buy white-sound generators to help them sleep.

My days have settled into a pattern. I spend the morning writing and usually take a break to get a little exercise by walking down the beach. I cross the road near my house and follow the path to the beach. During the off-season there are not as many people on the beach as there are in high season. Most beachgoers are local kids playing in the surf, some tourists and a few ex-pats. The waves on this beach come in rather high. Being originally from Kansas, I'm used to my water being flat, and I am not used to battling waves. So I stay on dry land.

About midway down the beach, I see a large hill with a thatched building on top. It is the bar/restaurant Vista del Amor. It overlooks the *Playas del Amor* on the other side of the hill. *Playas del Amor* (Lover's Beach) is a small, secluded beach with the only access being to climb up a path over the hill, past the bar, and down the other side. As with many of the local establishments, the bar is usually closed during the off-season.

As I stand on the patio behind the bar. I can see a couple swimming nude in the small beach cove below. The waves are much more manageable and I have swum here in the past. Looking in the other direction. I see the entire Zipolite beach stretched out to another large hill in the distance. This is the best 360-degree view in all of Zipolite. I discovered that there are images of Zipolite on YouTube where some intrepid photographer shot a video of this view. I almost envision travel agents worldwide hawking it as tourist getaway. I hope not.

All along the beach you see establishments. Some are permanent structures and others are just thatched buildings. Many are in bad shape due to the *mar de fondo* – ocean wave. The structures have not been rebuilt yet from the unusually high tide that washed many of them to near destruction only a couple of years ago.

Most of the businesses are not open during the low season as many of the owners take a long vacation at this time. The ones that are open cater mostly to the locals and the ex-patriots, who actually prefer the off-season with its tranquility and lack of crowds. The prices, which can double or triple during the high season, are much friendlier now.

One can rent a dormitory or pitch a tent for less than $5 a day, or rent a cabana without an inside shower for about $10, or $15 a day for an indoor bathroom. A room in one of the finer hotels with inside bathroom, air conditioning, hot water, TV, and a nearby swimming pool goes for about $40 a night. There are no high-rise hotels here and the tallest buildings are only three stories high.

As I continue my walk west along the beach, it is a hot day, in the high 90s. I stop in at the Colibri, a beach bar with some cabanas for rent. It is owned by Kevin, an ex-pat and his wife, Jilda, a Mexican citizen. He had to rebuild the bar after the *mar de fondo*. He still has a lot of work to do. In the past, he had to rebuild after two hurricanes, but he says it's worth it. He says he isn't rich but makes enough during the high season to weather the problems with the weather. Plus, he loves beer, and owning his own bar enables him to drink at wholesale prices.

Kevin told me that once about three in the morning, he saw a female turtle the size of a human come ashore and bury her eggs in the sand. The next day he dug up the eggs and took them to the Turtle Museum in the nearby town of Mazunte, where they hatched them and released them into the wild. Before it became illegal, locals would harvest the eggs to eat or sell.

I ran into Austin, one of my friends from a small town in Nevada. He had a construction business back home but likes Zipolite so much that when his father died and left him two houses in Arizona, he rented them out and hasn't been back since. He bought some land and built his own house in Zipolite. The street he built on is an arroyo. An *arroyo* is a stream that is only full of water when it rains. So during rainy season, his street is a part-time river and floods his house once a year. But that doesn't bother him. When it floods, he just stays at one of the local cabanas until the water goes down.

I left Austin to his work and continued my beach walk. I passed one of the local Indians pushing a wheelbarrow full of coconuts. He was selling them on the beach, cutting off the top and sticking a straw inside for the coconut milk. For a bit extra, he will pour in a generous helping of locally made mescal. There is all kinds of stuff that is sold on the beach including pastries, hammocks, peanuts, Havana cigars, blankets, fresh fish, even plastic chairs. One youth from Sweden buys pastries from a local bakery and sells them on the beach so he can afford to stay here.

Moving on down the beach, I passed some establishments in need of repair and I came to a place named "A Nice Place on the Beach." Their motto is, "This is the place where you come to do nothing." It is a bar and restaurant that also rents out cabanas. One of the few Americans here is Amanda, the manager, who also teaches English in the local school. She brought me an ice-cold Corona with a slice of lime without my asking. Beer is the lifeblood of Zipolite. The number of bars located on the beach is testament to that.

Most are built on the sand and don't have floors. Employees and customers are usually barefooted and shirtless. Although some of the small children walk around nude, most of the establishments prefer their clients to have at least shorts or swimsuits on. I've observed that Europeans and visitors from Commonwealth countries are not as dismayed by nudism as Americans are. As a matter of fact, there are not all that many Americans who visit here. It is lucky for me that English is an international language. A monolingual here is called a "*Norte Americano.*"

I talked with Gabby, a retired business lady from Canada. She works a few hours a day on the computer, taking care of the books and the online reservations. She does not get paid, but receives a free room and two meals a day. She got the job from a website that finds places where people can trade room and board for a few hours of work a day. One is not allowed to get paid, and it sounds like a great way to travel and learn the culture of a country.

I finished my Corona, thanked Amanda and continued down the beach, heading for the center of the town. Along the way, I passed a number of more-upscale establishments. In addition to having tables on the beach, they also have regular floors. Almost every place has hammocks. At the far end of the beach, I came to the Nude Hotel. In spite of its name, no one inside is nude. It is owned by a German.

The Nude Hotel is only one of two places that has an ATM machine—both of which work only part of the time. Unlike Tijuana, where you can pay in dollars, only pesos are spoken in Zipolite. If you want to exchange dollars or have money wired to you, you have to take a 45-minute trip to a nearby town where there is an ATM. As there are no banks in Zipolite, you can have a fist full of 500-peso bills and be the poorest person in town because, it's difficult to buy anything with bills of that size.

The street in front of the bars and *posadas* (hostels) is the *Roca Blanca*, the main street of Zipolite. It is named after the large white rock nearby in the ocean. The rock is white because of all the bird droppings. As it was getting dark, I left the restaurant for the street on the other side of the hotel. Many of the restaurants have tables that they set up in the evenings on the street. This is not a problem, as there are more taxis here than personal cars. There are a number of good Italian restaurants here, and there are more pizzas sold than tacos.

Evenings, a few young international artisans set up tables on the street to sell handmade jewelry and other handcrafts. They will multiply during the high season. I stopped by a small market to shop for tomorrow's meal before I headed home. There are only small stores in Zipolite. For anything major, one must go to one of the larger towns.

Heading back, I passed by the small shop on the corner that sells artisan mescal made in the nearby mountain towns. Did you know that all tequila is mescal, but not all mescal is tequila? Like tequila, mescal is distilled from the agave plant. There are over 30 agave species, but only one, the Weber Blue Agave, is made into tequila, and is located only around the town of Tequila. Tequila is cooked in stainless steel vats, while mescal is cooked underground using volcanic rocks and burning oak. Mescal, with its rich smoky flavor, is starting to gain in popularity.

Driving down the highway near where I live, one sees a number of roadside stands selling artisan mescal. They are of different strengths and flavors. Some have agave worms or scorpions inside. The poison from the scorpions is rumored to add to the strength of the mescal. Some are mild, and others will knock your socks off. You can just buy a shot, a liter in a used water or Coke bottle, or bring your own container.

After another day in paradise, I hit the road to my house and menagerie. Some may yearn for the big city, but the tranquil beauty of Zipolite and its laid-back residents is the life.

One Night

Harry Huntsman

In March 1963 I had been pastor of the Dominguez Community Methodist Church, outside Long Beach, California, three years and eight months. I was making my last pastoral call of the evening.

"You should let me give you a gun," eighty-one-year-old George Dodge said from his hospital bed. George was an atheist, but Mrs. Dodge was active in my church. They lived across the street from the parsonage, at an intersection with no stop signs. For months, all the neighbors had heard the squealing tires that blackened the streets all directions from the intersection, and the crash of bags of bottles tossed onto the sidewalks and streets night and day as drug addicts, on orders of their dealers sought to intimidate my wife and me. I thanked Mr. Dodge for his concern. It wasn't the first time this kindly neighbor had urged me to arm myself.

I stepped out the hospital door and looked around. A big prison-tattooed stranger sat on a bench. He glanced at me and stood. I looked under my car for any sign of a bomb, then got in from the passenger side, just in case someone waited to run me over as I entered the driver side. I heard the roar of a motorcycle as soon as I turned on my headlights. At every intersection on the way home I heard the revving of his motorcycle engine.

As I put the key in the parsonage door, my wife, Ollie, opened it. She was pale and trembling. "The Pastor-Parish committee is waiting for you at the church." I looked at my watch. "An unscheduled meeting at nine o'clock at night?" That committee had only met three times in almost four years.

"Marlina was here about an hour ago. I don't think she was alone. Marlina said, 'We will be back.'"

Seven of the nine members of the pastor parish committee had been supportive of my ministry. The other two had frequent complaints, but worked hard for the thirty-four-year-old church, and each year had reluctantly voted to request I be reappointed as pastor. During my tenure, the church had become self-sustaining, previously supported in part by the board of missions. The congregation built and mostly paid for a long-needed education building and the church's first kitchen. Attendance had doubled and the income tripled.

I sat in the only vacant chair in the circle of committee members. Chairman Paul Henderson was clearly upset. He looked at Buck Scougle, my most vocal critic, and said, "Buck."

Scougle began. "At six o'clock this evening this committee met at my home with six women from the community, our neighbors, who are very upset with you."

"Who are they?" I asked.

"We can't tell you that. It was a confidential meeting," Buck said.

I forced myself to keep quiet.

"They say you are causing innocent people to be arrested," Buck said.

Dorothy Haney the local Realtor was clearly angry. "Your newspaper articles about the drug problem might lower the sale value of our homes," she said.

Chairman Henderson said, "Reverend Huntsman, I don't like this. But I don't go to church to argue. This committee has voted unanimously to ask that you be transferred at Annual Conference."

I looked around the circle. Stony faces. "I need the names of those women," I said.

"Absolutely not," Buck Scougle yelled. "They are our neighbors. We have to live with them. Our kids grew up with their kids. Went to elementary school together. They rode the bus together to Banning high school." I thought of what the vice-principal of the high school had said a few weeks earlier. "Dominguez has some of the best people in the world, living next door to some of the world's worst people, and they don't know it."

"The police will want the names of the women you met with," I said. "This changes everything, Buck. When court opens in the morning, a judge will issue an order. At least the police will get the names." I stood to leave.

"All right!" Buck said. He took a list from his coat pocket and handed it to me. The only name I recognized was Marlina, the beauty who had tried to seduce me, the oldest Mafia trick to silence someone. Failing that, she had, for three months, tried to run over me with her car. Sheriff's detectives said that automobile-pedestrian "accident" was the main method of execution by organized crime in Los Angeles County.

Later, the police told me that the six women who met with my church committee were wives and/or mothers of drug dealers.

Back at home, I had barely hugged and kissed Ollie when the doorbell rang. As I turned to the door Ollie said, "Be careful."

Marlina stood under the bright porch light I had installed on police advice.

"Come in, Marlina." I stepped back, holding the door open.

"No!" Her voice broke as she took a step backward and glanced toward the street.

Her car was at the curb. A man I had never seen sat in the passenger seat. He pointed a .45 caliber semi-automatic pistol at us. The gun looked like the one I had worn as an armed courier during World War II. His head was large, his hair an unforgettable pile of red curls. I took a step back and to the side, out of sight of the gunman.

"Reverend Huntsman, please listen to me. You have to stop writing articles and making speeches about drugs. Ten of us started to come after you last night, but I got them to wait till I talked to you." Then this beautiful mother of a four-year-old started crying. "Remember, you have a baby."

For a moment I was frozen, speechless. Gangsters in three states had threatened me, a few times at gunpoint, but to have them threaten my beautiful eight-month-old daughter changed my life. In that moment, I became a committed actor, not just a speaker, counselor and writer.

"Marlina, you told my church committee I was causing innocent people to be arrested. How do you know so much about who gets arrested, why they get arrested, and whether they are guilty or innocent?"

"My husband was an undercover narcotics officer for the Hawthorne Police Department," she said. It was the first I had heard of a husband. She often cruised the residential area, or sat in her parked car at the curb near the parsonage kitchen window. Ollie was the first to suggest that if Marlina couldn't pick me up, she would try to kill me with her car.

At dawn the next morning I sat in the office of the chief of police in Hawthorne, California.

"Mike Vandiveer was never a member of this police department."

"Thank you. I'm not surprised," I said. I stood and walked toward the door.

"Wait!" the captain called. I turned to face him. "There's something about that name that bothers me. Have a seat and wait while I check something." He disappeared into a back room. Ten minutes later he reappeared, staring at an obviously worn sheet of paper. "The Navy is looking for Mike Vandiveer. I want him now!" He picked up a phone and said, "Call every off-duty officer. Tell them to report for duty as soon as possible." The captain was so preoccupied that he hardly noticed I left. I didn't need to face a bunch of tired and sleepy officers as they came back on duty.

I stopped at the Gerrard pharmacy for cough drops. Herman Gerrard and his wife and daughter were regulars in church. Three years earlier he had sponsored me into the Rotary Club. He was at the prescription counter in deep conversation with the big-haired gunman from the night before. I waited for the gunman to turn to leave and blocked his way, staying close enough to reach him if he made a move for his gun. I had boxed when I was in junior high, high school, the Navy and college. I had extensive martial-arts training in the Navy. I wanted to take this man down and take his gun. But I needed him to make the first aggressive move. He ducked his head and tried to walk past me. I blocked his passing. He turned his back, walked to the end of the aisle, around the end of a counter and up the next aisle to the door.

Herman Gerrard, my friend and supportive parishioner was shocked. "What was that?" he asked.

My battle mode faded fast. I began to shake. "Who is that man?" I asked.

"Royal Rooney."

"Where does he live?"

"Behind my store, on the next block. He was arrested on drug charges, then sent to a mental hospital just before you came to Dominguez. He just got out of the mental hospital."

My friend, Captain Weddle, of the Sheriff's Department said, "One of these days I'll open a safe in the office of a lawyer or doctor and find it full of heroin."

"Why a lawyer or doctor?" I asked.

"Who else has the money to finance such a big criminal enterprise?"

* * *

The two elderly district superintendents I had served under made sure I was transferred at Annual Conference in June. They told the Bishop and his cabinet that I was controversial. I was appointed to two small churches far from the big city.

Six months after my banishment to the desert, the sheriff's detectives discovered that the five gangs of drug dealers operating from Dominguez were financed and managed, not by a doctor or lawyer, but by a stock-broker. This made front page headlines in *The Los Angeles Times*.

I spent the next three summer vacations taking courses to qualify for a California teacher's license and became a middle-school teacher. I wanted to know why so many children hate school so badly they depend on drugs to endure it.

Belly-Up

Amy E. Zajac

We turned the corner. Sasha stood up and tugged on her leash when she saw our vivid blue car approach. She obviously recognized it and started barking and jumping side to side. Her new master, John, held tight as we slowly came to a stop next to them. Sasha howled and whimpered her welcoming chatter when we opened our car doors.

Sasha, a gorgeous Siberian husky, had been my dog. Faithful, energetic and adoring, she and I bonded. That's why having to give up Sasha when I lost my house to foreclosure nearly broke my heart. My new small apartment made dog ownership impossible. John, a fellow dog lover, happily took Sasha in and she quickly bonded with his very large canine family. With Sasha, his dog family numbered six.

This was our first visit in two years, and we didn't know how it would go.

Her excited reaction to seeing my parents' car shouted recognition. Sasha remembered us! The second we stepped out, she literally rolled over onto her back, waiting for us to rub her belly. This had been our own special way to show our love and affection — even before hugs. Sasha had not forgotten.

Mom and Dad leaned over close to give Sasha a rub. She didn't wait. She immediately jumped up and rubbed up against them, hugging them both, and me, too.

Then, she fell down and rolled over again, showing us her belly, eagerly anticipating our familiar rubs to her favorite spots. We were all smiles and gentle loving endearments for our Sasha-Girl!

John kept shaking his head in amazement. "She's never done that with me."

"Done what?" I asked.

"Flopped over on her back like that. She's never done that with me."

"Oh...I guess her new canine family gives her a different

perspective than she had with us. That's the only explanation I can have, since she's always been so open with us."

My heart ached with joy knowing that she remembered us — her old family.

Sasha couldn't get enough of us. She took turns focusing her attention first on Mom, then she switched over to Dad. I was last, but definitely not least, as she lovingly rubbed against me.

Before I gave Sasha to John, my parents lived with me and Sasha, and our foursome was a true family; we had a special bond. Giving her up because I couldn't take care of her in a small apartment was a hardship and deep wound that I dealt with for a long time.

We visited outside, away from John's other dogs, so we could lavish our attention on Sasha.

It was easier for all of us. When I asked John if we could come visit, his only concern was how rambunctious the six pack can be with visitors. My very elderly parents could be thrown off balance in that grouping. We missed Sasha so much, my parents and I agreed that the two-hour drive for the twenty-minute visit outside the house was important to all three of us.

When it was time to leave, our dread was eased by John; he already had a plan. "I'll walk her back inside with her favorite treat drawing her. You can drive away after we've disappeared into the house."

Relieved, Mom, Dad and I agreed. It was a perfect plan; Sasha wouldn't have to see us leaving her again.

As John walked Sasha back into the house, I felt my heart thud on the pavement. Yet, I knew she was safe and sound in the house with her new family.

Our welcome and the memory of her belly-up would stay with us forever, because it was who and what she was to us. Sasha belonged to us and always would. We were her first family.

Pythagorean Pursuit

Val Zalfaghari

Mr. V, a mathematics teacher, taught geometry for many years. Pythagorean Theorem was his favorite. He posted $c^2=a^2+b^2$ all over his classroom and made students draw right triangles and measure each side to prove $c^2=a^2+b^2$. He provided his students with many practical applications of the theorem and said, "No one can survive without knowing how to apply Pythagorean Theorem."

Anytime he saw his former students, after a formal greeting, he would inquire, "Have you applied Pythagorean Theorem in real life?" They would always reply, "Yes, sir."

He retired to San Diego. His favorite place was Fashion Valley. He would catch the escalator in front of Bloomingdale's to the second floor and pass Forever 21 on his way to the food court. He glared at the clothes in the window, looked at his own attire, and scolded, "Why not have Forever 80 for men like me?"

One day at the food court, he put down his orange chicken, Pacific chili shrimp, and rice plate on the table and sat opposite to two of his former students. One of them, Peter, wore a police uniform. The other, Jack, had a bright white T-shirt, saggy blue jeans, super-crisp Swiss shoes, and a gold necklace.

Smiling, Mr. V. greeted, "Nice to see you. Have you applied Pythagorean Theorem?"

With a grin, Peter answered, "Sir, I have, but Jack has not."

Mr. V. squinted. "Jack, you were the one who rapped $c^2=a^2+b^2$ for everybody. Why did you not apply it?"

"Sir, I was in a hurry and regret that I did not put the theorem into action."

"Jack, what was the result?"

"Sir, Peter arrested me."

"For not applying Pythagorean Theorem?"

"No, sir. He arrested me for shoplifting."

Mr. V. turned his attention to Peter. "Peter, explain everything so I can bring charges against Jack for wasting taxpayers' money and my time."

"Sir, after stealing and leaving the shop, Jack ran alongside a and b to get to his car. I ran along hypotenuse c, which is shorter, and caught him when he arrived."

Mr. V. picked up his plate, got up, and said, "Peter, thank you for applying Pythagorean Theorem and arresting Jack for breaking it."

Mr. V. walked away mimicking Jack's rapping in the classroom, "Two legs, peep peep. One hypotenuse, peep peep…"

Green Flash

Arthur Raybold

As the sun in all its naked splendor sets

And almost blinds us with its fiery jets,

The lightning-quick green flash's hesitation

Rewards the patient with its revelation.

Very few seem to stare dumbly to the West,

That tiny flash holds promise when life ends

That Love and Beauty will make amends.

Voyager Graveyard

Norma Posy

"Incoming!"

Drone X920, assigned to monitor a specific arc of the sky, had been on duty for about a month now, and was finally rewarded with something to report. Perhaps he would be promoted, or so he hoped. Becoming a W, or better yet a V, would mean a nice increase in his daily energy allotment.

The object was captured before it hit, a good parsec or two from the planet, brought to ground in one piece, given a cursory once-over, and tossed unceremoniously upon a growing trash heap of similar alien objects. A plenary council convened to address this recurring problem.

Grand Exalted One A131 enabled his communication module and called the meeting to order. "So, how many of these things do we now have piled up?"

Waste Management Specialist P244 replied, "This one is number ninety-two."

"Frequency?"

"About one a month, give or take."

"Source?"

Astrophysicist F911 punched a button, illuminating a large cube containing a three-dimensional holographic representation of the stellar neighborhood, about 500,000 light-years across. He gestured with a laser pointer. "Our location over here is indicated in green, and the source of these objects is over there, indicated in red."

"What do we know about the source?" asked A131.

"The major difference is relative time dilation," F911 said. "We are in orbit close to a black hole, and they are pretty much floating in free space. I estimate that one month of our time is about a million years of their time."

"Look, I'm just a humble Grand Exalted One. I forgot whatever I knew about relativity a long time ago."

F911 looked around for help.

Theoretical Physicist C115 rose to the challenge. "Perhaps I can help. The speed of light is a limit. As one approaches that limit, less energy goes into acceleration, and more into relativistic mass. And time slows down. At the speed of light, time stops. A photon of light travels 'with time' rather than 'through time' so to speak. We are orbiting a black hole at 99.99817% of light speed. From the viewpoint of the source of these objects, our time is hardly moving. Hence the ratio of a million of their years to one of our months."

"Thank you," A131 said. "Whatever the genesis, this situation has become a nuisance. We have to look for and catch these things before they hit like the first one did. This requires the expenditure of resources. Anything different about this one?"

"Nothing essentially different," C115 said. "These objects all exhibit obvious intelligent design, but of a rather primitive level of competence. There is a means of communicating with them, but their internal energy source to enable that function dries up long before they get to our neighborhood. It wouldn't help much, anyway. The objects themselves are merely robotic. No on-board intelligence."

"If I may," Biologist G560 broke in, "each carries a plaque, apparently in a winsome hope of discovery by someone such as we. What is pictured varies from one to another of these objects, of course, but this latest one includes a cartoonish picture of two creatures. I assume them to be creatures, but who knows? They sure don't look like anything we would recognize as sentient, much less intelligent."

"So, what are the people who launch these things like?" A131 asked. "Didn't we send a hyper-spacetime exploration to their home planet?"

"Indeed we did, a few of our months ago," G560 replied. "And we've just recently received a report."

"So, let's have it."

Communications Engineer R545 punched a button, and everyone in the assembly settled back to listen.

"Captain's log stardate 4019/5060/ 27/3031. Report from probe starship NCG1000. Target planet is home to intelligent life. Atmosphere loaded with poisonous oxygen. We'd corrode in a hurry if we tried to run around down there. Natives seem to tolerate the oxygen somehow, but they are unable to live peacefully. It is curious. They evolve to the point of some technical competence, launch another of these objects, then evidently destroy themselves in nuclear war brought about by overpopulation stressing natural resources to exhaustion. It takes another million years for the planet to recover, and to re-evolve another intelligent species. Another space voyager is launched, the creatures destroy themselves, and another million years rolls around to repeat. End of report."

"Holy neutrinos," A131 exclaimed in horror. "Do we have a two-way communications link to NCG1000 operating?"

"Yes we do," replied R545. "I'll patch you through."

"A131 here."

"Commander B200 here. Speak!"

"What can you tell us about the creatures who insist on bombarding us with these things?"

"They are carbon-organic oxygen-breathing animals."

A131 paused for a long moment to pacify his circuits. "You sure about that?"

"Yes. We were as surprised as you. There's a lot of organic animal life in the cosmos of course, but we had never before run across any that were intelligent."

"Okay. Come on back home. We have a decision to make."

The Woman in the Hijab

Muriel Sandy

The first thing I hear is a moan. Then another, and another.
"Where am I?" I try to say. My tongue feels like it's glued to the floor of my mouth. Then nothing . . .
Next time I know I'm awake, I hear moans again. They're much louder.
Am I in a mental hospital?
I check my arms. No. I'm not in a restraining jacket. I try to call out, "Where am I?" No one answers. After that, my mind goes blank . . .
Next thing I realize, I'm awake again. I haven't moved. I have no idea how long I've been out. It could have been five nanoseconds. It could have been five hours. I look around. Everything looks hazy. I blink my eyes and try to focus, all to no avail, and I lose consciousness again . . .
When I come to, I see a woman. A Muslim hijab covers her head.
Images explode in my mind. It's 2011. My husband and I are walking through a street in Karachi, Pakistan, when a girl comes towards us. All we can see are her eyes.
"We don't want you here. Go home. This is not your country," she says in broken English and begins to lash out at us with her clenched fists.
My eyes return to the woman standing at the foot of my bed. "*She's back!*" screams through my mind. I call out, "No. Not again. Get out of here." Everything goes dark . . .
When I come to, I recall the woman in the hijab again. I look around. I'm not in Pakistan. I'm in the hospital in Los Angeles, California.
When are they going to take me in for the operation?
I glance down the bed. The right side of my body is incased in a cast from my hip to my toes. I am unable to move. "It's over." I say. "The operation is over. I'm alive." I close my eyes and unconsciousness engulfs me . . .

When I open my eyes, a woman in a colorful blouse is standing at the side of my bed. She smiles down at me. Around her neck is a cord with a badge attached. Without my glasses, I cannot read it.

"I'm Maria, your nurse," she says. "How are you feeling?"

I don't answer.

Then it dawns on me. I had mistaken the woman in the hijab for someone long ago. I'm shocked in disbelief at what I said to her. This went against everything I had been taught as a child. The woman must have been devastated by my remark.

My tongue is still numb. I strain to make myself understood. "That woman in the hijab," I say to the nurse. "Ask her to come to my room. Tell her I didn't know what I was saying. I must apologize."

"I'll see what I can do," she tells me.

All my life I have fought prejudice from others, and now *I* have inflicted that same injury. I cannot believe I'd done this.

Later, when the nurse returns, she says, "I'm not sure the volunteer lady will come. She told me you hurt her very deeply."

"I must apologize."

She leaves without a word.

I agonize over what I did. I recall lectures as a child when my mother instructed my brother and me to recognize prejudice and discrimination. I must not let it slip away unnoticed.

***

I was to remain in the hospital another twenty-four hours before they released me after the seven-hour operation to repair my damaged hip replacement.

Mid-morning of the third day, the nurse comes in to announce I will be discharged that afternoon. Behind her stands the woman in the hijab.

"Thank you for coming," I say." Please accept my apology for my behavior the other day."

She hesitates. "My mother told me long ago, when someone apologizes, it must be accepted."

There was a long pause.

"I accept your apology."
I start to cry.
"Thank you."

Good or Bad Luck

Mardie Schroeder

Jimmy Two Feathers had a flask — for medicinal purposes, he told himself.

This time he intended to cross the Mississippi River. All his searches for his sister, Laughing Water, west of the great river had been fruitless. He had been captured from the east, taken west, and naturally thought somewhere in the west was where he would find her. Since he hadn't, this time he pushed east.

By the time he reached the Missouri River his flask was dry, his horse had pulled up lame, and he was delirious with fever. He had never felt so sick in his life. He crawled to a bit of shelter just before he threw up. Then his bowels emptied in an uncontrollable explosion. He fell into a comatose state. He would never make it to the Mississippi.

* * *

Charli saw the horse first. The thin rein dangling from the side of its head indicated it was an Indian horse. She pulled her team in and looked around for the rider. She hollered out, "Hello the camp," but got no response. She got off the wagon and walked toward the horse. He was badly injured and could barely walk. She went back to the wagon and pulled out her Winchester, took a bead at the temple, and pulled the trigger. It was a clean shot. The horse fell motionless.

Returning to her rig, she urged her team on slowly. She eyed an outcropping of rock and trees about a half mile ahead. She pulled up, jumped down from her wagon and approached quietly. The stench reached her first. Seeing that the Indian was still breathing, she removed all his clothes and buried them. She cleaned him as best she could, moved him to a more sheltered area, and covered him with a blanket. She refilled his canteen, built a small fire and told him she would return in a few hours with food and medicine for his fever. Jimmy Two nodded feebly and curled up in the blanket.

She didn't mention the horse.

***

When she returned, Jimmy Two was flailing around and shouting in his sleep. She stoked the fire, put some herbs in a pot of water, and watched it boil.

When Jimmy Two woke up, facing him was a woman with loosely braided blond hair that hung down to her waist. She wore a fringed skirt, boots, and a loose-fitting shirt of homespun material. A big floppy hat almost covered her eyes. She had a rifle and a dog at her side.

Jimmy stared at her, unable to figure out who or what she was. Finally he asked, "Are you a white Indian?"

"No, I'm just white. Irish actually."

"Why are you here?"

"I'm a muleskinner, delivering supplies to whoever needs them. I came across you, saw you were alive and in need of some help."

"Why?"

"Why what?"

"Why would you skin a mule?"

"I don't. It's what we're called. We work with mules—packing, teaming, that sort of thing."

She poured some of the tea in a tin cup and handed it to Jimmy. "Here, drink this. It's for your fever."

"What is it?"

"Herbs. It'll make you feel better. Go ahead. Drink."

Jimmy Two sipped the hot liquid. "Tastes terrible."

"It's medicine. It should taste terrible."

After downing the tea, Jimmy Two handed the cup back. "I think I could eat something now."

"I'll rustle up some grub. Okay?"

"Sure."

Jimmy Two lay back after finishing his tea and drifted off. He awoke to the enticing aroma of stew.

"What's Laughing Water?"

"What?"

"You were talking in your sleep. Something about Laughing Water."

"She's my sister."

"Are you going to visit her?"

"I'm looking for her."

"She lost?"

"I don't know. I've been trying to find her for many years."

"What does she look like?"

"She's very beautiful."

Charli gestured as if to say, *that doesn't tell me anything.*

"Is she younger than you?"

"No."

"Oh. Older."

"No."

"The same age?"

"Yes."

"Born the same day?"

"Yes."

"Twins?"

"Yes."

"She look like you?"

"No. She's a girl."

Another gesture and a roll of the eyes.

"I get that. But do you look alike?"

"No."

"Okay."

Charli ladled up a spoonful of stew and handed the bowl to him.

Jimmy Two took a spoonful. "Rabbit."

"Yup. Hope you like it."

"I do."

They ate in silence.

* * *

Jimmy Two awoke the next morning to find a pile of clothes next to him. Getting ready to put them on, he noticed that instead of pants there was a long skirt and an old shirt. He wrapped himself in the blanket, picked up the clothes, and went over to the rig.

"You left these next to me. Thought you might need them."

"They're for you."

"What am I going to do with a woman's skirt?"

"Wear it. I'm not takin' you into town with your wing wang waggin' around."

"What town you headin' to?"

"Back that way."

"Well, I'm headed the other way. Plan to cross the Mississippi."

"Last I saw, you had no clothes. Not many places you can go without 'em. I'm takin' you with me. I know a man might be able to help you find your sister."

"How far back?"

"A day or so."

"When do we leave?"

"When you feel up to it."

"I'll get my horse."

"I had to put him down."

"You shot my horse?"

"Yes."

"You. Shot. My. Horse."

"A lame horse ain't no good to a white man or an Indian. Especially an Indian. I'm sorry, but it was the right thing to do. He could barely move. I shot him clean, though. The reins are in the wagon."

"It's a hard thing to thank a woman who shot my horse."

"No need to thank me. I know how you feel."

Charli stoked the fire and heated up the rest of the stew.

Jimmy Two thought about his horse and how this would set his search back. They finished the meal in total silence.

Charli rose to load the wagon and hitch up the mules.

Jimmy Two Feathers donned the skirt and shirt. He gathered up his gear and walked toward the wagon.

"Just throw your stuff in the back. By the way, what's your name?"

"Jimmy."

"I'm Charli."

Jimmy had to mull this over a while. "Are you a man looks like a woman?"

"No, I'm a woman with a name like a man's. Big difference."

"White folks are hard to figure out."

"Suppose so."

They rode on.

"I could really go for a tipple. Got anything among all your supplies?"

"I don't. And if I did I wouldn't give you any."

"Why not? All I want is a little sip."

"All I need's a drunken Indian riding into town."

"I'll just sack out in back then."

"Suit yourself."

Jimmy Two settled himself atop a fifty-pound sack of flour. The rhythmic beat of the mules, the rocking of the wagon lulled him into a deep sleep.

A rifle shot bolted him upright. "What the hell was that?"

"Got us a prairie dog for supper."

Charli leapt off the wagon, the dog already at the kill. "It's a nice fat one. Enough for dinner and breakfast."

She climbed onto the wagon, threw the game in the back, slapped the reins and told Kate and Daisy to "step up." The mules knew their job. The rig creaked and groaned into submission.

"You sure know how to handle a gun."

"Had a lot of practice. My motto is, if it takes two bullets, don't shoot."

"You ever miss?"

"Haven't for a long time."

"What's the biggest game you brought down?"

"Bear. I used to wear a claw round my neck 'til someone else wanted it more 'n me."

"It got stole?"

"Yep."

"Why are you helping me find my sister? Got nothin' else to do?"

"Oh, I got plenty to do. First off, I know a sheriff who's been all over these parts and knows just about everyone. Sooner or later they all pass through. Also, I lost my brother. We got separated when I was about eight and I have no idea where he is. So I guess I feel kind of sorry for you."

"Thank you, Charli. Most people tell me to forget it. That I'll never find her. That she's probably been traded to half a dozen men by now and I wouldn't want to know. Well, I don't care what she's been through. I want to find her."

"I hope you do, Jimmy. I really do."

They continued on, listening to the creaks of the wagon, watching the mules' heads bobbing up and down.

Finally, Jimmy asked, "You ever marry?"

"Nope."

"Why not? A man would be lucky to have someone like you. You can cook, hunt, drive mules, skin 'em even. Sorry. That's a bad joke."

"White man wants something different. And I ain't it."

"White man ain't always smart."

"Some Indians ain't either."

They rode on.

Charli brought the team to a halt late in the day. She unhitched the mules and took them to water before she did anything else. They camped in a wooded copse near a stream.

Jimmy Two got a fire started, hauled water to the campsite, skinned the game, and gathered some herbs.

Charli mixed some biscuits, made gravy, and had a pot of stew going in no time.

Jimmy Two ate like he'd never been sick a day in his life. "I once had a fruit pie. Made me feel the same way I do now after eatin' all this good food."

"It's the first time I seen you smile, Jimmy. You're a good lookin' Cherokee."

"How'd you know that?"

"Figured if you came from east of the Mississippi it was a fair guess. Plus you look Cherokee."

"I've been gone a long time from where I was born. Lived a lot of places. I'd rather not move again."

"Where do you live now?"

"California."

"Seems like that's where everyone's goin' these days." Charli started hauling things back to the wagon.

"We'll get an early start tomorrow. I'm headin' in for an early night."

"You're welcome to stay here by the fire if you want. I won't bother you none."

"Thanks, but the wagon'll do me just fine."

* * *

Two more days and nights of traveling and the wagon finally rolled into town late in the day and pulled up in front of the sheriff's office. Charli gave a shout. "Hey, Virgil. You in there?"

Virgil appeared, a cheroot clamped in his jaw.

"Been a long time, Charli. What brings you to these parts?"

"A hot bath and a meal cooked by someone else for me. For this Indian, he's looking for his twin sister."

"There's a Cherokee woman cooking over at the saloon. Might try there. Don't look anything like him though."

Jimmy was out of the wagon, skirts flying, before Virgil could finish his sentence.

The Fourth of July

Gary Winters

The San Diego sun dripped warm honey. I was getting ready to read the Declaration of Independence. Read it out loud and clear. Then eat hot dogs and baked beans and apple pie and kick back. Barbara handed me the phone.

"The next time I call collect you better accept the charges. This is an *official* call," the voice said, and hung up.

Barbara had answered the phone the first time and said no, she wouldn't accept a collect call from Tijuana. A few minutes later the voice called back collect. This time Barbara accepted charges—I had told her it might have something to do with my daughter. She brought the phone to me in the tomato garden. Miguel said he was calling from a hospital in Tijuana and carefully gave me the name and address, twice, spelling it in English each time, showing off his polyglot skills on my money.

There had been a terrible smashup on the highway: thirty-one victims, four of them dead. The woman who had my telephone number as her emergency contact was unconscious, and he, Miguel, was responsible for *every*one. Sounded like *he* was in shock.

Yep, I figured, my daughter went to Baja every year with her two kids, sometimes with a husband, sometimes without one. I was already halfway there in my mind. I'd trolley to the border and then take a taxi to the hospital. I could be there in two or three hours. Easier than driving.

Miguel said he'd go find a translator, I should hold.

"Habla Español," I said. A good idea. I speak Spanish. But he said he wasn't sure about some words, whatever that meant, and left me holding for several minutes. The phone went dead. It gave me time to think about my daughter.

Her name is Tanis. I named her after a city at the mouth of the Nile, an ancient center of civilization ruled by the Hyksos. Her mother thought she was named after some trollop in a Sinclair Lewis novel. She lived in a feast of illusions. She was a former beauty queen who won the talent part of the Miss California contest with a scene from George Bernard Shaw's *Saint Joan*.

Miguel called back, the second expensive international collect call. Let me say here those country-to-country collect calls are not cheap.

Miguel said the woman was conscious now and they were bringing her to the phone. I waited. The seconds ticked by intense anticipation. The phone went dead.

My daughter's mother and I were divorced. But I had always kept in touch, visiting and sometimes sleeping on the sofa. She picked up a Mexican man somewhere, doesn't matter where. He didn't speak much English. One night after drinking wine he stabbed her to death on the living room carpet with his knife. He then hanged himself in the carport, naked. My daughter was asleep in her bedroom the whole time until a cop woke her and bundled her out of the house. The police report said she had blood on her feet. I checked the house. The last vinyl record in the phonograph stack was Van Morrison singing *Into the Mystic*.

Seven years old, Tanis went from a maternal environment to a paternal lifestyle, just like that. I dressed her in jeans and T-shirts, the prevailing Berkeley dress code. She had all the street names memorized in a week. She climbed trees, walked to school holding her Yamaha guitar by the neck, and played songs for her girlfriends during recess. After school they'd descend like a band of marauding midgets on the coffee house I frequented, so they could swipe powdered chocolate off the steamed-milk foam on my cappuccino with their grubby little fingers. But she couldn't bring herself to call me Daddy without giving a little grunt first to let me know it was an effort.

One day she forgot to grunt. She immediately realized what she'd done — called me Daddy without grunting first — so she grunted *after* she said Daddy. She looked out of the corner of her eye to see if I'd noticed. I didn't worry about it. After all, I did invent a new psychotherapy before I was thirty. I integrated what I'd learned as an actor into the therapeutic process. The United States Office of Patents and Trademarks granted me ownership of DramaTherapy. Ten years later I let the National Association of Drama Therapy use it. It's a matter of public record.

The third collect call came. "Names, names, Miguel."

"I can't tell you that."

"¡NOMBRES! ¡NOMBRES!" I shouted in Spanish. Very slowly.

He gave me eleven names, about two names a minute, spelling each one out. I was patient, let him do it his way, Mexican time—until the connection broke.

One of the strongest emotions I ever had was when I took a good look at my daughter and got the feeling—not a thought, a tangible *feeling*—something that had its own existence inside me—that there was no question I would give my life in a nanosecond to protect her from harm.

The phone rang. Miguel de Garcia de Garcia—he was happy to tell me *his* name—apologized for a broken plug on their telephone, the reason for the break in the connection. He said wait, they were bringing the woman to talk to me and—you guessed it.

These broken phone links were like razor slashes. They bled in my gut like the relationship I'd had with my daughter over the years. I had been at a distinct disadvantage. Her mother had said she would cut me completely out of my daughter's life. She destroyed photographs of us together, our marriage license, and who knows what else. Just because I understood her mental makeup didn't make it any easier.

After the murder/suicide, my daughter stayed with me for two years. When I knew she was all right I placed her with her maternal grandparents. She was their first grandchild, their fifth child almost. They had raised four girls and her grandmother could teach her things I didn't have a clue about. A grand piano and a fireplace adorned her spacious bedroom, with a redwood deck that looked out over Carmel Valley in central California. I arranged for her to share in the inheritance of the estate equally with the other daughters. That was a crucial break in our relationship. I knew that.

Call number five, collect. Miguel said, "They're bringing her right now, any second . . ." We got cut off.

How could my daughter *not* blame me for the way things turned out. In her seven-year-old mind she must have wondered what things would be like if I hadn't divorced her mother. Who knows what she thought. She did all right, ending up with a graduate degree in telecommunications office management from the University of Southern California. I congratulated her and said I didn't know they gave a degree in telephone. No response to that. But in a letter she called me a child pornographer.

When she turned eighteen, I had sent her prepubescent nude photos taken of her when she was seven or eight. A lovely woman who worked at UC Berkeley photographed children at a studio in her home. I directed the shoot, posing Tanis sitting with legs crossed, her arm resting on the side of a dark wooden love seat, staring straight into the lens; lying on the love seat with her knees bent, heels up and head propped on her hand, and a round upside down photo of the Mona Lisa behind her snugly fitted in the small of her back. Poses like that.

Years later, after saying the human body was the most beautiful thing in the world, I told Tanis that since she wanted to be an actress like her mother, I was going to enter the photos in a photography contest. I explained how Brooke Shields at the age of twelve got her start when she won a children's beauty contest. The prize was to be photographed nude. That photograph by Gary Gross in 1983 was on display at the Guggenheim Museum in New York City September 2007 through January 9, 2008.

The photographs of Tanis are amazing. Simple perfection. No adornment needed. I put myself through graduate school at NYU selling my paintings in my own art gallery, so I should know. I'm also an award-winning photojournalist. My daughter made me promise to not enter the photos. She said, "If you wanted a photograph of me you should have gone to Sears like any other father." Well, that's where the train careened off the track. I don't know anything about that kind of TV father. I consider those images of her the best work I've ever done in any medium.

Tanis said she wanted to be an artist. I tacked up twelve ornate astrological posters on the walls in our house in the Berkeley hills. Each one depicted a sun sign with arcane symbols. When she was an adult my daughter told me the posters were pictures of great orgies and giant penises. The only human figures in the entire set were a man and woman running straight forward holding hands, long hair flowing in the breeze, in solid black silhouette. Only the outline of their bodies was visible.

I took my daughter and her brother, Gary, to a family campground up in the mountains among the pine trees for a week. I was on staff as the counselor for teens in exchange for expenses for me and my family, including my girlfriend. One of my daughter's friends, the only one Tanis ever said was smarter than she was, climbed up in my lap as I sat talking with a group of parents. I had helped her learn to swim. She put her little eight-year-old arms around my neck and whispered in my ear, "You're my real daddy."

Another collect call. Up to six now. Miguel was excited, the woman was coming down the hall. If I would just hold on . . . I held for two or three minutes. Then the line buzzed in my ear. An hour had elapsed since the first call. I was raring to get going. A man named Javier called from Tijuana and asked me to accept reversed charges. I said okay. But now I was determined to take command. I got tough — United States Ma*rine* Corps tough.

"Where's Miguel?" I snarled in my best take-charge captain of the championship softball team's voice, the team that beat the John F. Kennedy aircraft carrier's team once by sheer luck.

"He went home," Javier said in a matter-of-fact tone. He began to tell me about the situation in Tijuana. There had been a terrible traffic accident, see, lots of people were dead and injured, and — you might be surprised — we got cut off.

All of a sudden this bright idea dawned on me to call Tanis in Oregon. She answered on the third ring.

We'll Always Have Perris

Marcia Buompensiero

At our college reunion, over cocktails, my friend Kenny and I were reminiscing and philosophizing about roads not taken. He told me this story about a trip he made one summer in 1969 with his buddy James.

* * *

After grueling finals, James and I decided to attend the "Three-day Wild West Festival" at San Francisco's Kezar Stadium where Janis Joplin, Jefferson Airplane, the Dead, Country Joe, Santana, Sly and the Family Stone, and the Youngbloods were performing the weekend of August 22nd.

James' 1956 MGA Roadster 1500 could handle the 503-mile trek, no sweat. We called her the "red-hot mama," which she was. Four cylinders, four-speed stick with wire knock-off rims and a luggage rack. The black rag top was in Lou's garage being repaired. Stocking caps could handle anything the wind, rain, whatever could throw at us. We were young and fearless.

There was only one little hitch. James' grandmother was ailing. We planned a detour to see her along the way. Nana Fitzhugh lived in Perris. California, roughly 450 miles from our destination. We got to Perris Wednesday the thirteenth, late afternoon, just in time for James to arrive at the Honey Vale Rest Home to visit with Nana before her bedtime. She was somewhat senile, but had a lovely smile. I'm not sure she even knew which one of us was James, but she seemed happy to see us both.

James and I found lodging at a small motel on the Highway 395 frontage road just outta town. We only planned to stay the one night and get an early start the next morning (Thursday). The next day, bright and early we grabbed our duffels and headed out the door, leaving the key in the office mailbox. Approaching the car, we immediately knew we were in trouble. Thieves had struck during the night. The car rested on cinder blocks. All four tires and wire wheels were gone.

We fished up enough quarters for the pay phone, found the number of the British Car Imports Dealership in nearby Riverside, and placed the call. The manager said he didn't have those particular tires or wheels in stock and had to order them from L.A. We wouldn't get them for two days. We headed back to the motel and explained our plight. We were handed back our key.

With two days to cool our heels, there wasn't much to do in Perris in 1969. There were a couple of bars, but James and I weren't 21. We hit them and got carded. We tried the local liquor store and were carded, again. We figured the bars and liquor store were in cahoots. Hooch-less and bored, we walked the streets of Perris. On South A Street we stumbled onto the Orange Empire Railway Museum. James and I were checking out an elegant Pullman dining car when the docent, a wiry old man with curly gray hair, crinkly smile lines around his eyes, and dressed in 1800's period costume, offered us a tour.

He pointed to the old photos and filled us in on the land dispute that resulted in the establishment of the town of Perris in 1885. It seems the California Southern Railroad, a subsidiary of the Atchison, Topeka and Santa Fe, wanted to build a connection between Barstow and San Diego.

"Fred. T. Perris, the railroad's chief engineer, was instrumental in getting that done," he said. "Bet you boys thought it was named for Paris, France, just misspelled." He chuckled and winked.

The docent also told us about the love affair that united the towns of Pinacate and Perris and the young couple that paid the price when a powerful railroad baron, the girl's father, tried to keep them apart.

"Rhonda Sue," he said with a faraway look in his eyes, "was tall—Norwegian extraction—with long blond hair that fell in ringlets to her tiny waist. She had eyes like the sparkle of ice in the sun. They melted your heart.

"Rhonda Sue was in love with Jake Thomas, the hardware store clerk. It was mutual. Jake was smart. He worked two jobs to save up enough money to attend college. He wanted to be an architect. He worked the hardware store during the day and security at the railway yard at night. How those kids found time with Jake's busy schedule to rendezvous and fall in love no one could figure out. But they did."

"Rhonda Sue's daddy found out and put the kibosh on it. That was like pouring kerosene on hormones."

"Jake put his college plans on hold. He and Rhonda Sue plotted to elope. Jake dug into his college fund and bought two tickets on the midnight Streamliner to San Francisco. When it stopped in Perris, he and Rhonda were going to board the train. 'Sayonara, Perris!'"

"And it would have worked, too. But the ticket master alerted Rhonda's father. When Rhonda showed up with her little valise, she was met by her father's goons, who escorted her back home. They left a letter with the ticket master that was supposed to be from Rhonda Sue, but it was really written by her daddy. 'I can't go with you, Jake. I'm going to marry Dalton Webber. Please don't try to contact me again.'"

The old man shook his head. "Well, poor Jake. You can imagine. He tore up her ticket, threw it up in the air and boarded that train headed to San Francisco."

"What happened to them?"

"Well, Rhonda married Webber, who was the son of her daddy's competitor and lived in the neighboring town. The marriage cemented the two dynasties. Dalton wasn't a bad guy, but Rhonda Sue didn't love him. Some say she just wilted away and died of a broken heart."

"What happened to Jake?"

The docent scratched his chin and smiled. "Jake got to San Francisco and worked in the gold fields. He found a mother lode and struck it rich. He took some of that money and invested in railroads. He became immensely wealthy. Life goes on. Rhonda Sue's daddy eventually died. Jake married. But he never forgot Rhonda Sue. Even after his wife passed away and he was an old man, he remembered the girl with the golden curls and the deep silver-blue eyes. Every anniversary of her death, he left a bouquet of red roses on her grave. He also gave a bundle of money to this here museum—sort of an homage to Rhonda Sue and their love.

Eventually he died. He was buried up on the hill in a plot right next to Rhonda Sue."

James and I talked long into that night about philosophy — about love and girls. Neither one of us could quite shake the idea of how Jake never got over the tragedy of losing Rhonda Sue. We wondered if, had they eloped and their love been fulfilled, would Jake have become wealthy — or would his life have been only mediocre. Was losing the love of his life what fired him up, spurred him on to fame and fortune?

The next day our tires and wheels came in. Ready to roll, James and I decided to drive by the museum to say goodbye to the old docent. That was a ploy because James and I really wanted to ask the old guy's opinion. We simply couldn't get the idea out of our heads about whether Jake would have become rich if he'd married the girl he loved. It was an idealistic quandary to us, and being young, those are the kinds of dilemmas that spur men to action.

But only the ticket master was at the front desk when we got there.

"Hi, is the docent here? We're leaving and wanted to thank him for his private tour of the museum."

The ticket master looked confused. "Not sure who you were talking to, but we haven't had a docent in nearly sixty years."

On the way out of town James and I took a quick detour — to the old cemetery. We had a hunch we might find the old man there. We found the graves of Jake and Rhonda Sue.

Jake's tombstone bore a small picture of a young man who looked like he wanted conquer the world. There was something familiar about his eyes. Jake's inscription read: "We'll always have Perris."

Right next to it was Rhonda Sue's tombstone. Leaning against it was a bouquet of red roses, still wet with morning dew.

* * *

Kenny, set his empty glass on the bar and nodded for a refill.

"I don't know if the "Casablanca" scriptwriters ever heard about Jake and Rhonda Sue's love story when they wrote that line that Bogart and Bergman made famous. I heard once that a Hollywood screenwriter was traveling from Barstow to L.A. and made an unplanned detour with a layover in Perris."

Kenny stared at the amber liquid in his glass as if it were one of those magic eight-balls. He cradled it as if he could tilt it and read the answer that he hoped would pop up on the bottom—the answer to the question that lingered behind his eyes.

"I'll always wonder," he said, finally. "At least *I'll* always have Perris."

One Night Only

Lawrence Richard Carleton

"ONE NIGHT ONLY Barking Dog Howland in Concert!" Berkeley "Barking Dog" Howland stood outside the hall in Costa Mesa where he'd just performed with his latest group. It was his kind of crowd, a good mix of jazz cognoscenti and the curious. After what, forty-odd years now, always trying new stuff, he still was known mainly for his breakthrough hit, "One Night Only," and his first LP, "I Travel Light," never out of circulation, now on remastered CD and still playing now and then on the remaining jazz stations. It was a famous precursor of jazz fusion, and it made his name.

He'd just gone crazy that night long ago, improvised the whole thing without really thinking. It started with a rambling tale of a one-night stand, then went to his now-trademark extended trumpet solo alternating passages of flutter tonguing and half-valveing, and finished with a loud, gasping "Woof!" No matter what new things he tried, no matter what groups he got together, at some point during any concert they made him play "One Night Only."

The crazy thing was that, for years, wherever he got a gig, you could count on there being some woman of a certain age who'd convinced herself she was the one the song was about. At least that had slowed to a trickle. That note tonight—passed to him discreetly during a break—was going to be another crazy woman wanting to hook up with him at the hotel after the show. "Man, all I ever wanted to do was play," he mumbled to himself.

That gig in San Diego had been the worst. Back in '99, a local talk show decided to take advantage of his being there to invite him to appear with *three* women, each of whom thought she was the one, to duke it out in front of a live audience. He was glad he refused to go on that show, and disappointed that they did it anyway. He honestly doubted he could identify even at that date who was the one. Hell, he wasn't entirely sure it was just one, instead of a composite. Well, he'd deal with one more crazy lady tonight. Tomorrow, the band would head back to San Francisco, his home town.

Big brother Hume and big sis Locke wouldn't catch him there. They used to when he was starting out, but they didn't any more. The music was okay with them, but not his world of sex and drugs. Their parents had raised all three kids to be like them, college professors with long lists of publications. Hume and Locke made their parents proud. Now they had their own kids also with academic careers.

Berkeley was the only Howland in three generations not to earn a doctorate. Over time bro and sis had drifted across the Bay to Sausalito, and were more likely to travel to an academic conference than to another jazz gig. "Well, maybe now they're retired I can meet them for lunch," he mumbled. But he knew he wouldn't. "That's okay. All I really want to do is play."

The kids would already be in their rooms. They'd left in a group, saying "Night, Pops" as he stood contemplating the poster outside the hall. He noticed his reflection in the glass display. *Face is gettin' old. Man, time has plowed furrows on me*, he thought, inventorying the marks years of hard living had stamped on him. "Gettin' late," he observed. He savored the multiple meanings that had for him as he turned and made his way across the plaza to the hotel.

In the hotel, he rode up to the ninth floor. He passed what he took to be Alix's room, maybe it was Tommy's. Anyway, the next door was his. He could hear them both in whose ever room it was. He could hear Alix's sax and Tommy's bass, playing riffs on "So What," then laughing, then silence. He passed a really good-looking woman—blue business suit, curly black hair, long lashes, long legs—as she knocked on the door across from his and called into it to open up, are you there. *Too young to be The One*, he thought. *Can't be past her forties.*

Barking Dog slid into his own room, found the snack laid out as always, and dug in so he'd have eaten something before the crazy lady materialized.

It was quiet. Maybe "The One" wasn't coming after all.

What now? Some commotion burst out in the room next to his. He could hear shouting. It sounded like Tommy and Alix and a third party, really going at it, then a door slammed. It was quiet again, then there was some muffled conversation in the hall. Damn. Here came the dreaded knock on his door. Nothing for it, he took his time, but the knocking didn't go away and eventually he had to open up. It was the good-looking woman, looking nervous and agitated. She shot a look down the hall. Berkeley followed it and saw Tommy glower in their direction as he finished tucking in his shirt. Berkeley didn't get to look long, though, because the good-looking woman said, "May I come in?" and slid in before he could answer.

"I have to ask you something and, depending on what you say, tell you something," she announced.

"Who are you?" Berkeley wanted to say.

"Do you remember me from San Jose twenty-one years ago? Of course not." She could tell from his face he wished he did remember. "Anyway, I need to know something about your sax player. To the point: Is she your daughter?"

"Almost," he replied. "People think she is. Truth is, her momma Claire was in my band for years and we were, uh, close. Then she left and next I knew she had a baby girl. That was at least a year after Claire left, though, so Alix can't be mine. Damn good reed player though. Like her momma. Glad to have her with me."

The good-looking woman relaxed a little, and sat after he motioned to a chair. "That's a relief. It makes the next thing easier."

Berkeley waited.

"Twenty-one years ago I interviewed you in San Jose. Do you remember 'I Declare'? It was your big comeback hit. You were riding high again, and the venue was a sellout. I was just starting my career as a musicologist and thrilled to land that talk with you. We met in your dressing room, which was noisy, so we adjourned to your hotel room. One thing led to another, and we did more than talk. That night cost me my first marriage, but gained me the light of my life. I'm Jamie Nassau, Tommy's mother." She studied his face. Berkeley waited. "After he told me what he's up to in your band, I knew it was time for him to face you and tell you that you're his dad."

Berkeley was glad he'd sat down too. "I Declare" had been his lament at being de-Claired. Claire had wanted a family, he'd just wanted to play, so she left. Claire had gotten him clean—well, clean from drugs if not other things—and introduced him to some elements of her classical training, and everyone had noticed how much better his playing had become.

When she left he didn't know what to do. But "I Declare" had come to him one night just as spontaneously as "One Night Only" all those years earlier. He was big again, but he really didn't know what he was doing. Now he kind of remembered this interviewer who had picked up on that. One thing *had* led to another, now he remembered. He remembered a lot. He looked her over. "Your hair is shorter."

"I'm older."

Berkeley went to the door and looked down the hall. Tommy and Alix were standing together, nervously.

"Come in, son."

Tommy and Alix traded worried glances. Tommy patted Alix on the hip and trudged toward Berkeley's room.

The next half hour was awkward. Tommy turned out to be no more eager for warm fuzzy family stuff than Berkeley was, nor Jamie either. The main concern on the part of both father and son was that they be able to go on playing together. In the end, they shook hands and agreed to go on calling each other Pops and Son. Alix had at some point inserted herself into the conversation, and she left with Tommy after Berkeley explained to her that everyone could go on as before, and Jamie and Tommy agreed.

Jamie stood in the doorway watching them go. After a while she turned back into the room, closing the door behind her. She marched up close to Berkeley, looked him in the eyes and, while still looking, slipped a card into his hand. "It may interest you to know that I've made a career move," she announced. "I've accepted a new faculty position—tenure-track at last!—in San Francisco. When you're there you can drop by, or not. I know all you really want is to play. Believe me, after three marriages I can relate." She kissed him softly on the lips, and then was gone.

Barking Dog had to sit down again. He looked at the card Jamie had given him. He put it down. He picked it up and studied it again. He took a deep breath and let it out. He had to say it, quietly to himself: "Woof!"

Kip

Chloe Edge

Just before my fourth birthday, my baby brother, Kip, was born. He was named Christopher Timothy Thomas Kerns, and it seemed for a while that his name was bigger than he was. My mom nicknamed him Kip, after her favorite dog. I loved him from the start … As he grew into a little person he became very interesting to me. He was so cute in the face, wide brown eyes and curly dark hair. As soon as he could talk, his sense of humor was apparent. Everybody loved him.

One day when he was two, I heard him yelling from the back porch and I ran to find him. He was covered in ants, screaming in terror, and in a moment I realized how much I loved him. My six-year-old heart ached while I tried brushing off the ants, then picked him up and ran for the hose. By then we both had ants all over us, so I soaked us both and then held him until he stopped crying.

It was during this quarter hour in my early life that I got in touch with my heart. I always knew after that that I had a deep love growing in me and the object of that love was my little brother, Kip. I adored him.

As he grew older, he reciprocated. We were allies, friends, I was his mentor. We always kept an eye on each other. We stood up for each other, told each other our secrets. We never had a fight and we never broke a trust with each other. I thought we'd be sister and brother forever.

We lived in Pacific Beach, on Foothill Boulevard, right where the road curves before Beryl Street. This was a perfect place to ride a Flexi, short for Flexi-flyer, like a sled on wheels. You ride it on your belly. The sidewalk went downhill, the curve was sharp and it was life-and-death, because if you missed it, you planted your head into the concrete base of a streetlight at the bottom of the hill. If you over-shot, you were in one of the two streets. We named it Daredevil Hill. It was "hairy," as we called it, requiring a sensitivity to velocity and strong hands and arms for the braking system on the Flexi.

Back up the sidewalk, in our house, it was a Saturday morning in the spring of 1952. My dad was off on one of his world travels, my mom had her opera music on and we, my sister, Cathie, my brother, Kip, and I were supposed to be cleaning our rooms.

Well, Kip wouldn't do it and nobody blamed him. It was way too big a mess for a five-year-old, and he didn't know where to begin. "I'm not cleanin' my room," he announced, his little round tummy hanging over his belted jeans. Barefoot, with his curly brown hair living its own life, his hands jammed into his pockets, he had gone into the opera music to declare his defiance.

Our mom had ways. I don't know what she told him, how she bribed him, if she promised something, but he came back down the hallway, his little head lowered like a bull heading for a red flag and he marched into his room.

Everything was everywhere. Lots of little boys' rooms, are a mess but Kip was a bone guy when he was real short. He loved skulls and snakes, especially if they had rattles, and he brought in worms and snails in his pockets. His best friend, Chico Leonard, and he had plans for all this stuff they collected. Some of it didn't smell very good.

After a while he got *into* cleaning his room and it took him all day. He hauled out bags of trash and borrowed the broom. He dusted. He even cleaned under the dark brown bunk bed that said U.S.M.C. on the end. My dad had brought those beds with him when he was a major in the Marines, sort of a souvenir.

Kip finally got his room clean. He was so proud of himself at dinner that night. He even took a bath. When it was time for bed, his little chest was still puffed out and he was happy when he said his prayers.

My little brother was always a heavy sleeper. When he got bigger, it was dangerous to try to wake him up. He objected so strongly to being pulled out of his dreams that he became hostile and we had to wake him up with a broomstick. On this particular Saturday night, it was no different.

Around midnight, a drunken woman in a yellow Studebaker missed the curve coming up Daredevil Hill. She lost control of her car in front of our house and she drove it head first into Kip's bedroom. The front wheels were inside his room. It moved his bed about three feet back and he slept right through it.

The next morning when he woke up, Kip was *furious*. He stomped into my mom's room like he was seven feet tall, enraged, little hands on his hips and demanded to know, "Who messed up my room?"

I could really go off right here and tell you all the things we went through trying to grow up, how dangerous it was in our household when our dad was drunk, and how tight the bond between Kip and I became, but that's another story. By the time we were grown up, everyone knew how close we were. All our friends, his girlfriends, my husband, everyone had to accept us as a team and everyone did. We were inseparable.

Kip graduated from La Jolla High School in 1965. He went to UC Santa Barbara and was drafted into the Army. He ended up on the rifle team in competitions. He did his time in the Army and was discharged with a wad of money. On the way home he stopped in Las Vegas and lost it all. He reported to us what had happened and when we asked him how he felt about that, he said, "There is nothing like a clean, fresh start."

He went to UC Santa Cruz to study anthropology and fell in love with Margaret. They had just returned from an archaeological dig in Mexico with their classmates. They were drinking. When the party was over, Kip was too drunk to drive, so Margaret was driving. Kip rode in the passenger seat and another friend of theirs rode in the back seat of the Volkswagen Bug. Kip and Margaret started tickling each other and she accidentally jerked the steering wheel to her left. They flew off a cliff and when they landed, Kip and their friend were dead. Broken necks and backs.

My baby brother, at 25, came home in a body bag and Margaret got two counts of vehicular manslaughter.

From here, stories fly out like sparks from a welding torch. How after a trial which I attended to defend Margaret, she got five months in county jail and they allowed her to go to school from jail because she was a straight A student; how my dad never got over Kip's sudden death, and how I realized, reviewing our last visit a month earlier, that Kip had tied up all his loose ends —

almost as though he knew he'd be leaving the planet.

I had many shocks and traumas in my early life, but I thought that Kip and I would always be a pair of free-spirited siblings, figuring it out together until we were old. He really surprised me, checking out early.

And listen to this: I believe in reincarnation. Our mom taught us when we were very little that we are here on Earth to learn and that we are born and reborn into different lives until we get our lessons right, and then we are released as stars. This was her belief, slightly altered for children's minds. She shared freely about someone being "spiritually evolved" or another one having "many lives to go." She was a Christian mystic who meditated regularly and practiced what she preached. After a few chemistry classes and some physics books, I'm not too sure about the star part, but she could be right about that, too.

A couple of years after he died, I had clear sensations that Kip was in the room with me. That the essence of Kip was sharing a joke with me, or that we were cracking up laughing together, even though I couldn't see him.

That is, until, at 42, I gave birth to my son, Doc. I didn't notice it at first, but after a couple of years it dawned on me that Kip hadn't been visiting for a while. Doc, my then two-year-old son, was developing a sharp imagination and a keen sense of humor.

One day, while we were out at his sandbox, something struck us funny and we started laughing together, just cracking up, eye to eye, laughing and laughing looking at each other and I had the certain recognition, "This is Kip."

One Photograph — Many Memories

Janet Hafner

Mama took this picture. I'm certain of it. My father, who always had his camera ready to capture the significant and not-so-significant moments in our lives, is actually in the photograph. How rare!

My grinning father and his three children in a straight line, obeying my mother's command, "Smile when I say cheese." We complied.

The bicycles at our sides would be considered vintage now — fat tires, pedal brakes, a bell on the handlebars to warn pedestrians, and a wicker or wire basket hanging in front of the handlebars. The perfect place to guard the treasures we would find as we explored.

On clear, bright Saturday afternoons, and only after we had completed our chores to Mama and Daddy's satisfaction, Daddy would ask, "Who wants to go to the park?"

In unison, the chorus would chant, "We do, we do!" Mama knew in advance, of course, that the trip was already on Daddy's schedule. She would have all the ingredients on hand so she could fill the wicker picnic basket.

The reward for chores well-done was an excursion to Alley Pond Park in Queens, New York. Emerald expanses whispered, "Come run, jump, roll and maybe even sit on me."

Four of us had bicycles. Mama didn't. When we were off peddling and exploring in the shade tunnels formed by the towering old groves of sycamore and elms that bent over the path, Mama preferred to spread out the blue and white plaid blanket, and fuss with the feast she had prepared earlier that morning while we were still rubbing the sleep from our eyes. Mama loved to surprise us with tantalizing morsels kept hidden in the well-worn, but never to be disposed of, picnic basket. Each, in our turn, would pester her, trying to learn the contents of the basket.

"Mama, just give me a hint. I won't tell anyone," I pleaded.

Mama would half-turn toward me, tilt her blonde, cascading

curls so they rested on her shoulder, give me a hint of a smile, raise her eyebrows and say, "Not time yet, Janet. I'm sure you can wait."

We both knew I could. I also knew everything Mama fixed and put into that basket would delight and satisfy us. It would be a lovely picnic after our bicycle adventures.

The special day captured in the photo reminded me how we pedaled down the shady paths and could see the small white, yellow and pink blossoms that covered the shrubs like dots. I still remember how my eyes delighted in finding a pattern and my nose inhaled their delicate scents.

I can still hear my brothers' voices calling to me. I can recall it all—the sights, the sounds, the smells—as if were only yesterday. I remember, too, the most endearing memory of them all: Daddy's teachable moment.

"Let's take the north path," my eleven-year old brother, Bernie, suggested.

David lamented, "I don't like that path. It has too many hills. I can't keep up." David, being only six, had the shortest legs and the smallest bicycle.

Daddy rolled his bicycle next to David and placed his strong but gentle hand on his shoulder. Peering into his bright blue eyes, he whispered, "You can do it. Look at how much you've grown since we were here last. Show us how strong you are now."

David lifted his chin and the corners of his mouth crept back to his ears in a huge grin.

"I guess I can do it," David murmured, then added, "Don't leave me behind."

"We won't." Daddy's voice reassured him.

Off we went. Daddy shouted words of encouragement with David determined to prove Daddy right.

The trees bowed over our heads. We ventured into the woods where it was cool and the earth smelled of leaves and bark and dampness. At each rest stop we'd hunt for treasures.

"Look at this feather," I whispered excitedly. "It must be from an eagle." I handled it gently to Bernie to examine.

"That's not an eagle feather," Bernie said, turning it over in his hand several times, his eyes narrowed and his nose was within inches of my prize. He studied it, then announced with authority, "Looks more like a crow's feather."

"You don't know that!" I snapped. "You just want to be the one who finds the best feather."

"Could be a turkey feather." He laughed.

"Not so. It's an eagle feather. Isn't it, Daddy?" My eyes pleaded for agreement.

Dad took the feather and studied it.

"Looks like an eagle feather to me. It's white at the base and has a black tip—a crow's feather is smaller and is mostly black. I'm pretty certain it belonged to an eagle," Daddy said, glancing sideways at me. The corners of his mouth inched up until he wore a broad grin.

Bernie bowed his head and let out a puff of air.

My father could turn ordinary moments into learning opportunities. That day he taught us the Native American meanings of certain feathers.

"A feather from an eagle means great strength and courage," he said. "A crow's feather means exceptional skill and balance, and a bluebird—well, a bluebird's feather means happiness."

With those thoughts rolling around in our heads, we pedaled further into the dark woods in search of more so our baskets, our minds, and our hearts would be full.

Gods and Genies

Barbara Weeks Huntington

Do you remember reading under a soft blanket as a young child when you hugged the hard book against your chest to quiet your beating heart? When you feared the genie would require your three wishes before you worked out your perfect scheme? Do you remember your smug sigh, your clever plan to ask for infinite wishes, the chance to undo those that didn't work out? Did you wake up, stare at the dark ceiling, ponder if the rules allowed you to string wishes in a daisy chain of "ands?"

When you gave up on genies, do you remember holding a different book, praying to God, "If you exist, please grant this prayer and if you are all-wise, will you understand why I don't believe and grant it anyway?" Did you nag your nonexistent god for an unambiguous sign?

When life brought ends, beginnings, suffering, nothing, something, hope, despair, did you confuse genies and gods, add, "if you exist," to every secret plea in your dark night? Did you try to believe? Pretend to believe? Envy those who did? Did you meditate, medicate, hallucinate, hesitate to equate the unexplainable with a deity who would let you return to His arms or Her womb? Did you escape to a monastery, take a Bodhisattva vow, hope you could bring infinite compassion to infinite beings, secretly worry you would crumble at the first test? Did you wonder what happens when gods or genies reveal themselves? Infinite happiness? Infinite pain? Rebirth? Pull the plug? Lights out?

Now, when your crooked hands cling to the soft blanket, when you've seen the here, then not here of death, when friends and loves have gone on to what they expected or didn't, do you still hug the hard book against your beating heart, ask for an unambiguous sign, pray for easy transition to something or nothingness and add, "If you exist?"

Coffee

Anne Janda

Coffee is what I look forward to
when I get up feeling down,
and when I'm down trying to get up.
Some say it does bad things to you,
but it can't do worse to me than some people
do.
Coffee takes me to a garage sale
of yesterday's mistakes and
splendid possibilities for today, not fakes.
When I die, just lay me down and pray
that I will find cosmic coffee beans
willing to be ground.

Jelly Roll Blues

Norma Posy

"You're a carbon-chemistry chauvinist."

The student, a long-haired, bearded, front-row troublemaker in torn blue jeans, a Green Bay Packers T-shirt, and flip-flops, had responded to biology professor Mary Merkle's remark that "life as we know it is the only possible life in the universe."

Professor Merkle sighed and glanced at the wall clock. *Ten minutes to go. Why do I put up with this crap?* She set her lecture notes aside, stepped around the lectern, and addressed the class.

"It may be fun to dream up life, even intelligent life, as a gas bag of neon floating on Neptune, but the best science fiction is at least believable."

* * *

Agent C9000 (the "C" stood for "Cherry") trembled in its cold bowl within a refrigerator. A message had arrived from headquarters. "The time is nigh. Prepare for conquest." The long dormancy of alien invaders was finally over, triggered by global warming.

C9000, as with others of its ilk, "O" for orange, "L" for lemon or lime, "S" for strawberry, was a physically amorphous distributed creature. Any portion carried all the properties of the whole. And any portion quantum-mechanically entangled with every other portion, rendering effective instant universal galaxy-wide communication.

"Finally," said G8141. "Let's do it!"

"Yee-ha," echoed L7771.

* * *

That evening, Professor Mary Merkle arrived at her apartment in Madison, Wisconsin, tossed off her winter coat, kicked off her shoes, greeted her pet cat, and poured herself two fingers of scotch, neat. *What do I have in the house for dinner?* She opened her refrigerator door, and found herself engulfed by an angry red glob of goo that promptly digested her, spitting out her bra and pantyhose when it finished.

Oh, and it ate her cat too.

* * *

Pandemonium reigned as variously colored Jell-O blobs ran wild over city after city. Military weaponry proved impotent. Bullets went right through. Explosives only distributed wiggly chunks far and wide, where they grew and rampaged anew.

Puddings of various persuasions contributed support to the invasion. Tapioca pudding swamped Walla Walla, Washington. Budín de banana overwhelmed Mexico City. Purée d'asperges blanches smothered Paris. Moscow fell under a virulent blanket of борщ пудинг.

Across the galaxy, Jell-O headquarters saw that it was good. Earth had become covered with a blanket of sticky goo.

"Who's next?" Headquarters looked around . . .

The end, at least of Earth.

Looking For Rhett Butler

Peggy Hinaekian

I have been looking for Rhett Butler ever since I was a kid and read *Gone with the Wind,* unbeknownst to my parents, and later saw the movie three times. I constantly daydreamed of Rhett Butler.

No man I met has been a match to him. This is an unfortunate fact. My standards were set high at a very young age. Reality was disappointing and my quest was unattainable. But being an eternal optimist, I looked and looked and looked. I met all sorts of men, young and old, rich and poor, but no one came close, no one thrilled me and made shivers go up and down my spine.

Rhett was the only ONE. His looks, his eyes, his dimples, his sarcasm, the way he talked and walked and above all his masculinity; I could almost smell his maleness through the pages of the book. He had everything. He took charge. And when he kissed Scarlett O'Hara bending her backwards, I visualized that I was Scarlett and a tingling sensation would come over my body. I always dreamt that someday I would meet a man just like him, who would carry me up that flight of stairs to his lair and ravish me all night.

Some men have said that I reminded them of Scarlett. In some ways I was like her, wild, lively and flirtatious. However, if I were Scarlett, I would never have been so stupid as to let Rhett go away and I would certainly not have craved for that insipid Ashley in the first place. What a colorless, predictable man Ashley was.

There were the attractive men, rich men, poor men, stupid men, romantic men, intellectual men, old men and young men. None of them really turned me on. They were just playthings. I was attracted to some at the beginning of the relationship but the attraction fizzled for one reason or another.

The rich men thought they could have me by throwing money and jewelry at me.

The handsome men expected that I would be sexually aggressive and do gymnastics in bed.

The romantic men were just too gooey and fawned all over me.

The intellectual men talked too much about themselves and analyzed everything ad nauseam.

The poor men could not afford me in the first place, so why even talk about them.

The older men bored me with their hangdog looks.

The younger men were too self-centered and wanted a girl to swoon at their feet.

And the stupid men had no place in my agenda.

I needed that Rhett "look," the look that said "I want you," and perhaps he could add "and only you."

Anastasia And Psychotherapists, 1962

Diana Amsden

"*The statistics on sanity are that one out of every four Americans is suffering from some form of mental illness. Think of your three best friends. If they're okay, then it's you.*
—Rita Mae Brown

Anastasia has discovered that to confide in a relative or friend causes that person too much distress, and that to confide in a mere acquaintance leaves her feeling overexposed, as if she had undressed in public; she wants never to see the person again.

Wanting someone safe to confide in, she visits one psychotherapist after another.

One says, "You should've gone insane in childhood. Your good mind saved you."

She is baffled. *I don't understand how that would work.*

The next tells her, "You have a beautiful mind."

She is nonplused. *I don't know what you mean.*

She feels she's telling her next therapist how human beings operate, and thinks, *I didn't come here to teach you psychology!*

The next says he finds Anastasia interesting.

She can barely hide her indignation. *I'm not here to entertain you!*

Anastasia suddenly realizes that a therapist starting or stopping taking notes reveals what he thinks important, thus cuing the patient what to talk about.

Does the therapist know this?

Is he writing down my words, or his interpretation of them?

Every interpretation therapists offer her is off the mark. Anastasia remembers hearing that psychotherapy is a shoehorn for putting on a shoe that doesn't fit.

She observes that most therapists have more respect for the theories they were taught than for the evidence in front of their eyes. She is reminded of the second-century Greek anatomist, Galen. For the next 1,500 years, until Vesalius in the Renaissance, medical students dissecting corpses gave more credence to Galen's drawings than to the corpses in front of them. Galen was right; the corpse was wrong.

A therapist planning a vacation, apparently fearing this might traumatize Anastasia, spends considerable time preparing her for his absence.

However, she is as little attached to him as to the blank wall he imitates.

When Anastasia wants to quit therapy at the Rawlinson University Psychology Department, her alarmed therapist says, "I sense an emotional storm coming!"

Against her better judgment, Anastasia stays—then discovers the department's income is based on patient hours. Indignant that the therapist tried to manipulate her by inducing fear, she tells the head of the department, "Freud omitted an important stage between the oral aggressive and the anal retentive: the gastric ejective!"

She knows she has not had good therapists. She has noticed that an actor can convincingly portray a character less intelligent than himself, but not a character more intelligent. She suspects something similar is true of psychotherapists and patients.

Therapists avoid asking questions, but she knows there must be questions they could ask that would elicit the memories and ideas she needs to access, open new perspectives, suggest new insights—but she doesn't know what the questions are.

Dr. Torrance is the one therapist she likes. He relates to her as one human being to another. When she asks him a question, instead of asking her what she thinks, he actually *answers*.

Anastasia discovers that Ayn Rand, via her books, is her best therapist. Reading Rand is analogous to physical therapy. Following Rand's reasoned arguments is like having a physical therapist exercise a dysfunctional limb until she can move it herself unaided. A passage in *Atlas Shrugged* wrenches her heart:

> "To achieve the virtue of sacrifice, you must
> want to live, you must love it, you must burn
> with passion for this earth and for all the
> splendor it can give you—you must feel the twist
> of every knife as it slashes your desires away

from your reach and drains your love out of your body. It is not mere death that the morality of sacrifice holds out to you as an ideal, but death by slow torture."

She's describing my struggle over Ian Hildebrand. Rand is not religious; how does she know? The crucifix, a human being in agony on an instrument of torture, shows what Christianity can do to you if you take it seriously.

Anastasia thinks about her childhood. *Mom taught me about Santa Claus, the Easter Bunny, the Tooth Fairy, and God, all about the same time. The first three turned out to be her. Mom behaves as if the last one were too.*

Anastasia has heard that the human species is neotenous, that childlike traits persist into adulthood. *One trait might be to want an all-powerful, all-wise, loving father.*

What I Remember About My Mother

Caroline McCullagh

I don't have many memories of my mother from my childhood. Maybe my memory just doesn't work that well, or maybe the trauma of her illness wiped out much of what preceded it.

Mom was a small, plain, dignified woman. Although "Rosie the Riveter" made slacks fashionable after World War II, I never saw my mother in anything but a skirt or dress, and she wouldn't have considered going out the front door of our house unless she was wearing stockings.

She was a farmer's daughter. Her abundant vegetable garden attested to her heritage, until she became so sad and ill that it was more than she could manage.

Although she came from a rural background and had not gone to college, she was well-educated, thanks to the fact that her mother had been a teacher. She spoke fluent French and read philosophy for pleasure. She loved the visual arts and had a sophisticated understanding of painting. I remember often looking at the pictures in one of her favorite books *From Picasso to Surrealism*, just one of the many books we had in our house at the time.

She worked as a secretary in an art school. Although women worked during World War II, it was relatively unusual for women to work for pay in the late 1940s, although she did fit into the secretary-teacher-nurse category that was allowed to women.

My mother was English. When her friends came over, I was often allowed to have a "cup of tea," which was mostly milk with a little tea added. That made me feel very grown up and privileged and English myself.

Though she lived here more than 58 years, she never became an American citizen. She used to say that each time she took the citizenship class, she would become so angry at the presentation of Revolutionary War history that she would get up and walk out. I know now that this story was apocryphal. My mother was too much of a lady to display anger by walking out on anything.

Her British citizenship was a two-edged sword for me. In those days, between World War II and the Korean War, the "red menace" of Communism was rising in the American consciousness, and anyone foreign — even just from England — seemed a little dangerous.

I was impressed by the fact that she had had a brush with royalty and had found royalty wanting. She had worked at an exclusive boys' camp outside Paris where Prince Phillip, the future husband of Queen Elizabeth, attended. It was my mother's task to tidy him up in the afternoon before the chauffeur came to fetch him. She thought he was a very spoiled little boy.

In retrospect, I believe she told this story to me because it had a moral lesson for a young child. All children, even royalty, had to be careful not to become spoiled. Being spoiled was not something imposed from the outside, but something you brought upon yourself by being obstinate or unreasonable.

These are all daytime memories. The memories most special to me, however, have mostly to do with the night. Bedtime was when I had her all to myself. It was the time of softness and coziness and comfort.

I remember, "This little piggy went to market, this little piggy stayed home . . . and "Here's the church and here's the steeple; look inside and see all the people."

I remember that many nights she helped me to sleep by saying, "You're going to feel so relaxed that your toes are going to fall right off, and now your feet are going to fall right off, and your legs are going to fall right off . . ."

But mostly, I remember her stories. Mother told stories; she didn't read them. I know now that these were stories out of *her* childhood. "There was a little old lady who was sweeping her kitchen, and she found a penny. She took her penny to the market and bought a pig. On her way home she came to a stile."

I was intrigued both by the idea that you could buy a pig for a penny and the idea of a set of stairs going up and over a fence.

"The pig wouldn't go over the stile. The woman went along a little way until she saw a dog. She said, 'Dog, dog, bite pig. Pig won't go over the stile, and I shan't get home tonight.' The dog refused."

The story built and built as the old lady tried to find a resolution to her problem. "'Cow, cow, drink water. Water won't quench fire. Fire won't burn stick. Stick won't beat dog. Dog won't bite pig. Pig won't go over the stile, and I shan't get home tonight.' The cow agreed, if the old woman would bring her a handful of hay. The old woman brought her the hay. Cow began to drink the water; water began to quench the fire; fire began to burn the stick; stick began to beat the dog; dog began to bite the pig; pig went over the stile, and so the old woman did get home after all."

The story was repetitive and rhythmic, a perfect vehicle to lull a drowsy child to sleep.

Beyond the pleasure it brought, the story had another meaning for me at the time. The words "stile" and "shan't," repeated so often in the refrain of the story, sounded to my immature ears foreign. My mother used "shan't" in her daily speech also and had just a trace of accent. For example, when she talked about her father the "a" sound in the word was like the "a" in "fast," not the "ah" sound we are used to.

She said other things that sounded exotic to me, or at least not like what other mothers said. If I wanted something, she might say, "You can have that when my ship comes in." If I complained about something she would say, "Worse things happen at sea." These were, I think, a legacy of growing up in a seafaring nation.

If she wanted me to hurry, she said, "Stir your stumps!"

If I wanted her to do something she didn't want to do, she'd say, "I can't, because I have a bone in my leg," or "I have other fish to fry."

If I complained about having to wash up she would say, "Yes, why wash? You'll just get dirty again," or she would tell me, "Once upon a time there was a little old man, and once a year he would get out his handkerchief, touch it to the tip of his tongue and wash the end of his nose." Even at that early age, I think I recognized sarcasm.

With an adult's eye, I now see that these phrases were similar to the stories; they were things her mother told her and, probably, her grandmother told her mother and before. I love the idea that these phrases wind like a ribbon through the centuries to tie me into the generations of women in my family.

On one special night there were no stories, just quiet delight. Mother woke me long after putting me to bed. Our dog, Su-Lin, was about to whelp. I was not allowed to watch the births, but I sat in a chair in our yellow kitchen where Su-Lin lay in her sleeping basket. I was small enough and the chair was big enough that my legs stuck straight out ahead of me. I held an empty squatty, old-style Nabisco Shredded Wheat box on my lap. One by one, four perfect little Pekinese puppies were put into the box. They were so tiny they didn't even fill it half-way.

Can memories be pure experience? I have read that all childhood memories are put through the filter of the adult mind, but I can still feel that chair against my legs and that box in my lap. I can see those puppies piled up on each other and feel the box shift as they moved, nosing around for their mother.

* * *

Try as I might, from that point on, memory fades. I can only bring up images of my mother sleeping, sleeping, sleeping. I know now that this was when she began to sink into the depression that was to consume so many years of her life. The fact that she ultimately recovered and lived many more productive and satisfying years has not brought back those memories to me.

Sloppy-Joe Summer

Ruth Leyse-Wallace

My six-year-old granddaughter is so sweet I just want to do whatever it takes so she will look forward to coming back to my house again. Last summer I was lucky enough to have Isabella's company one whole day out of every week. Aunts, cousins, and even Mom and Dad took turns the other days of the week. Every week the entire summer I asked, "What would you like for lunch today?" and every week the answer was "Sloppy Joes." So Sloppy Joes it was . . . and cookies. We both love our cookies.

Summer vacations really fly by when you plan activities that are new, interesting and in which you're pretty sure you can keep up with a six-year-old. A friend of mine called her visits with her grandchildren "Grandma Camp"—an apt description.

Isabella and her cousins like to play dinosaurs, and on the way to my house we drive past Alpine Materials, which has ten-foot-tall, metal, rusty dinosaurs right in front by the driveway. We took advantage of the photo op and made a collection of pictures of Isabella with the T-Rex and the Brontosaurus (the "Dinosaurs of Alpine"), as well as the rusty brown, life-sized Bighorn Ram, the rusty horse, and the outsized rabbit and owl. At that same corner is a big sign at the curb that she could read . . . "Dippin Dots," it said. Soon after, we found some real Dippin' Dots in the ice cream case at the Lake Murray snack shack, our treat after we fed the ducks and walked partway around the lake.

Parks are a good way to get outside with a granddaughter—we both enjoyed a picnic at Santee Lakes and later the fountains for kids to splash in and for mothers and grandmothers to watch and hold the dry clothes. The Balboa Park puppet show and picnic nearly filled up another day. Isabella loves animals, stuffed and alive, and especially liked getting close enough to touch the stuffed cougar, deer, and coyote at the Mission Trails Regional Park Visitor Center exhibits.

Taking a kid is a good excuse to go places I probably wouldn't go by myself, like the Toy Museum in Poway. I enjoyed seeing the old Monopoly sets, storybook dolls, the first-generation Legos, and the costumes on the Indian dolls, while she mostly enjoyed playing with the other kids in the activity area. It is a good thing we took the opportunity when we did, because I read later the Toy Museum was closing its doors because the owners were moving.

A visit to her great-aunt, who is active in a ceramics club in Rancho Bernardo, introduced Isabella to painting figurines, which later led to the Hobby Lobby store, and sets of plaster animals. There were many other things of such interest that Isabella was willing to spend the tooth-fairy money she had saved to buy something she especially wanted.

The Dollar Store was another place for great shopping. We had to make a second visit after the first visit purchase of a small package of cotton candy. It was so delicious that she wanted to buy a tub size, plus one for her cousin, whom she would play with the following day. It was difficult to choose between the blue and pink flavors—naturally we bought one of each. Until that day, I thought you could find cotton candy only at the county fair or the circus.

There were fun things to do at home too, like getting out the square-dance petticoats, hats, jewelry, and shoes for a morning of dress-up; another ready-made photo-op for a grandma who kept the camera handy all summer. The homemade orange juice-and-toothpick popsicles were fun and tasty with the Sloppy Joes one day.

It is fun to show a new part of the world to a granddaughter: Isabella wasn't familiar with recycling, so just before school started we took about six months of aluminum cans to the recycling center. We saw how cans are weighed, and what large and small things other people brought to recycle, and watched the baby shark in the fish bowl. One of the best parts was getting the $2.08 from the cashier to put in her piggy bank when she got home.

To keep the summer memories, I made Isabella a small, folded, stapled book on my computer and included the photos I had taken with captions about the places we went and things we did. I called it "Sloppy-Joe Summer—Isabella and Grandma."

The next time I saw her, Isabella had a "Sloppy-Joe Summer" book for *me*, full of her crayon drawings and captions written in her first grade printing.

That book went straight to this grandma's heart!

Interlude on an Ancient Road

Barbara McMikle

I'm driving along on my way to the Saturday afternoon party my boss is throwing for all the employees at the dry cleaning place where I work as the front desk girl. The boss lives way out in the country. Because I get away late, I leave the main highway and take this shortcut he tells me about. He says, just get on it, drive straight ahead five miles and the only house I'll come to is his. What he doesn't tell me is that I'll be driving along one of those ancient dirt roads full of potholes that you find in the backcountry of Virginia. And me driving an old clunker with broken-down springs and bare tires.

The clunker is moving right along, doing thirty-five, when all of a sudden a guy dashes across the road so close to my car I gotta slam on the brakes. The clunker spins sideways, coughs and dies. The guy is standing there, staring at me with this look on his face like he's seeing a ghost and I'm it. Never mind I just came within inches of making one out of him.

"I almost killed you," I shout. I climb out of the car all shaky, my heart pounding. He just stands there, staring, his mouth open so wide a bird coulda flown in. He's bleeding from the head. Not my doing, though. Proof of that is a bloody rag tied around the wound. Up close, I see he's just a kid, younger than me, seventeen maybe. He's dressed weird in dirt-stained gray trousers and a gray jacket open halfway to his belly button, showing a red undershirt. He's barefoot. He looks just plain pitiful.

"You look awful," I tell him. "You need help. Can I give you a lift somewhere?"

He shakes his head, looking bewildered. He points at the clunker. "What's that thing there?" he asks.

That makes me mad, especially right after I offered to help. With its white paint all checkered and striped with rust, it isn't much to look at, but it certainly is recognizable as an automobile. Shaking my finger at him I tell him, "Now you quit making fun after that scare you gave me."

"You was travelin' right along, but I don't see no horses."

Exasperated, I start to get back into my car. "They're all under the front end," I tell him, meaning horsepower, but he doesn't get it.

Giving me a look that calls me a liar, he says, "If you got your horses hid somewhere in these here woods, ain't gonna do you no good. They'll find them and take them. Cavalry's desperate short on mounts."

What a clown! "Go home and tell your mother to clean up that cut on your head," I say, sliding behind the wheel.

"My ma's in Texas . . . Can't move that wagon more'n downhill without horses."

Is this kid for real? I've taken my share of ribbing in the twenty years I been around, but nothing as off the wall as this.

His next smart-ass remark is, "You oughten to be runnin' around here in your underdrawers, Missy. It ain't decent."

And me wearing expensive new white shorts. I swing back out of the car with intent to cut him down to size. "Listen here, you little . . ." I start and never get to say another word because the most awful racket of men shouting and gunfire cracking fills the air like it's coming from everywhere around.

"Close it up, boys!" a man yells somewhere in the woods. The kid throws himself behind my car, shouting, "Get down, Missy. Quick! Them minie balls flies thick as hail."

A horrible screech of human voices, like a thousand crazed wildcats let loose, rips the air. Scares the spit outta me, sends me leaping to join him in a crouch behind the car.

"All that yellin' and hollerin' is my regiment movin' out. Gonna give it to them blue bellies good." He buries his head in his arms. "Oh, God! I oughter be with them. Oh God! If I ain't the worst coward."

Through all the noise, I begin to see the light. "Civil War," I say to him. "There's what's called a re-enactment going on. Right?"

"We're fightin' them Yankee invaders from up North, Missy. And I don't think it's a re somethin' or other. I didn't see no signs of no battle bein' here before we come yesterday."

Suddenly a whole lot of booms shake the earth. Thick smoke

belches out of the woods, fills the air. Both the kid and me stay crouched to the ground. He says into my ear, "Yankee cannon from the hills over yonder."

His head wound begins to bleed. With his sleeve he wipes away blood that oozes at his hairline, and, to my annoyance, gives his arm a shake, sending a spray of blood onto my car right alongside the rear wheel. He says, "I took this lick in the head in a skirmish a few minutes ago and when I seed blood comin' outta me, I went sorta crazy and skedaddled. I gotta get back. My pards ain't ever goin' speak to me again if they find out I run."

His voice is filled with the worst misery I ever heard outside a two-hanky movie. For an actor in living history, this kid should be up for an award.

"Look," I bellow through the racket, "get in the car and I'll get you somewhere to get that cut fixed. Then you can play your war games again."

I climb into my car, turn the key. The engine grumbles but refuses to start. I'm sitting on top of a rise with a good down slope just ahead of me. If I can get pushed, with luck, the battery will kick in. If only the kid . . . I look around for him. He's still crouched at the car's side. He's looking onto the smoke-choked woods with fear on his face as clear as the blood on the bandage. War games going on in those woods are too real to be any fun. That's what I think.

"Hey, kid! Give me a push!" I shout. The din of cannon fire is deafening and smoke fills the air so thick you can't see more than a few feet ahead. A riderless horse with stirrups flying is almost on top of me before I see him coming. He wheels inches from my car and tears off.

I want to get far away from this craziness in a big hurry. "Push!" I shout again at the kid, jerking my thumb toward the back of the car. "I'll pick you up at the bottom of the hill."

He finally catches on, throws his shoulder against the rear of the car and gives it enough of a shove to start it rolling. Pretty quick, I get the motor to turn over. At the bottom of the hill I stop, waiting for him to show.

I sit a full half a minute before it dawns on me that something is different. Too quiet. I get out of the car, hear a bird singing loud as Grand Opry. I look back up the hill. No sign of the boy. No smoke. No sounds of battle.

I'm like, Wh-a-a-t? I start back up the hill, walking slow, looking around, seeing nothing but what Mother Nature intends to be there. At the top of the hill, I call out, "Hey, kid!" No answer. The stillness of the woods is spooky. Re-enactors don't just disappear. All that I saw and heard moments ago is no more. Gone like ghosts and pulling all the smoky air pollution after them.

Did I imagine the whole thing? Am I losing my mind? Worms crawl in my stomach. In a daze I go back to my car. I get the door open and am about to climb in when my eye catches something I'd forgotten all about. A spattering of what could be blood lies across the car's body by the rear wheel, right where the kid flung it off his sleeve. Nah, I tell myself. It's got to be rust. I touch it. It isn't rust. I stare at my blood-smeared finger. An icy cold seizes me, bristles the hair on my scalp. That kid is real. Or he was. Once. Long ago. Up there on top of that hill. In seconds, I'm in my car and faster away from that hilltop than I ever thought my broken-down clunker could move.

Gray Ladies
Chapter 5

Richard Peterson

Elwood Museum of Fine Arts
Boston, Massachusetts

Saucy gal, thought Dobbs, peering through the plastic cube. Before him stood the Goddess of Devi Shri, one hip cocked over and offering a seductive smile. She stood less than two feet tall and had large ears. But Dobbs ignored the ears. Instead, he admired the gray statue's narrow waist, rounded breasts, and curvy figure that many women would kill for.

One of the security officers walked past—a tall, slim white kid with a ponytail of blond hair and the obligatory walkie-talkie in his hand. Dobbs found the gallery of Southern Asian and Persian Art pleasantly quiet, nothing but hushed conversations and the low hum of the ventilation system. He breathed deeply and looked around the dimly lit room. Not even a vagrant odor drifted on the temperature- and humidity-controlled air.

Soft footsteps.

"Found yourself a friend, Roy?" said Samantha, smiling and arching an eyebrow.

Dobbs felt his face redden. "Well, I, I do have my cultural side, you know."

She planted a fist on her hip and struck a pose similar to that of the Goddess of Devi Shri. "Cultural side . . . really?"

"All right, all right," he growled, trying to mask a smile. As usual she was dressed fashionably: black dress with turtleneck; silver-clasped black belt; and a black cloak extending to mid-thigh.

The queen of chic, thought Dobbs. He glanced at his watch: 3:55 p.m. The General might be in the German Expressionism gallery by now.

"I gotta meet this guy. Like I explained, it's about the elevator . . . incident. Part of my investigation, remember?"

"Of course, of course," she said, flapping a hand as if shooing off troublesome gnats.

Dobbs didn't need thought-scans to know the woman had been emotionally traumatized by that shocking event. She became almost distressed when the topic came up.

"I've seen the Italian paintings," she hurriedly went on. "Gorgeous! I'll wander over to the gift shop. There's some jewelry and a rack of kimonos that need more, uh, *investigating*."

Dobbs watched her saunter through the doorway. He felt pleased at how their relationship had warmed. Thought-scans told him that she believed his "gift" was some form of psychic ability, and didn't really accept the idea of Sat'ka aliens. But he was no longer "Detective Dobbs," and she felt comfortable enough to poke fun at him. He found that side of her intriguing, since she was usually the no-nonsense businesswoman.

He walked over to another plastic cube atop a boxlike pedestal. Inside this cube sat a stone head about nine inches tall. The description card read, "Head of an Ascetic." Interesting enough, but his thoughts kept flashing back two years. Chicago's National Museum of Mexican Art had been tipped off about a probable theft attempt. Dobbs had spoken at length with the museum director and two security experts; they briefed him on vibration sensors placed behind paintings, burglar-proof display cases, and infrared and microwave motion detection.

Dobbs shook his head, bringing himself back to the moment. Because of a second phone call from the mysterious General, Dobbs had requested this trip. And Samantha complied. *I owe you* — her unspoken words.

They had flown from Chicago's O'Hare to Logan International on Samantha's Gulfstream jet. Onboard were glasses of champagne and large bowls of fruit. Then, upon arrival, luxurious rooms at the Ritz Carlton Boston Common.

Dobbs half-smiled. *A different level of society, all right.*

Having inherited her deceased husband's holdings, Samantha Crane had become the largest shareholder and CEO of Pinnacle Pharmaceuticals. So she had combined the trip with business, scheduling a meeting tomorrow with senior staff of Pinnacle's research lab in Cambridge. Just like his report to her about Drake and Crawley, she wanted Dobbs to "read" those staff members.

He glanced again at his watch: 4:00. *Showtime.* As he exited the room he did the tooth-click to engage thought-scanning.

The German Expressionism exhibit took up several connected rooms, with better lighting and more spacious surroundings. This exhibit seemed popular, with quite a few couples and single people strolling over the polished floors. Dobbs soon recognized the dual thought pattern he'd first encountered at the Chicago chess pavilion. He studied a slim, middle-aged man: dark suit, walking cane, polished shoes, curly dark brown hair, distinguished demeanor. He seemed to be alone, gazing at a landscape painting. Dobbs took a white bishop from his coat pocket and walked over.

"Excuse me. You dropped this?" he said, holding out the chess piece in his palm.

The man stared at him, then down at the bishop. "Quite so. I do believe I left that back in Chicago."

More details: goatee, small mustache, rectangular eyeglasses. "I'm sure you did, General. Where's your London gal?"

A forced smile. "My dear fellow, I never gave you my description. How do you *do* this?"

Dobbs noted the proper British accent. "It's a gift," said Dobbs. "And I *will* explain when I can trust you."

The other man took a breath, softly blew it out. "Ah, yes. That word again. My name, by the way, is Elleston. As for the lady" — two people walked behind them — "so I really *like* these trees," he went on, gesturing with his free hand. "The symmetry and balance. See how the artist added texture to the rolling hills? And the sky, almost an abstract combination of . . . ."

Alone again.

"My associate is" — Elleston paused — "otherwise engaged. Now, to business." His voice dropped to a whisper. "As I said before, a person will be here just before closing. That person, a woman, will be casing this very room for a future *theft,* and the fellow behind your elevator, um, *event,* is the same one planning this theft. This woman could take us one step closer to him."

Leaning on his cane, Elleston led Dobbs to another painting. "As a detective," he murmured, "you of *all* people should want answers."

"Hey, Eddie," someone said loudly. "Getta load of *this* broad!"

Both men looked over. Toward the other end of the gallery a bearded fellow in shabby clothes was motioning for another guy to join him. Soon the two of them were gawking at a painting and trying to suppress bursts of laughter.

"Troglodytes," muttered Elleston. He and Dobbs slowly strolled from room to room, occasionally pretending to study the artwork.

Elleston said, "The two people apprehended . . . have you gotten any intel from them?"

Dobbs shook his head. "I couldn't get near 'em. FBI everywhere. But one agent let slip the phrase, 'compartmentalized job.'"

"Which means the two killers never met their employer."

"Very good . . . or any other players in the op. Their job was to eliminate any witnesses, get the senator to the hotel rooftop, and exfiltrate by helicopter. They wouldn't even know the pilot's identity."

In front of them a frustrated father hurried, bent over, to corral his scampering boy.

"It's a dead end," continued Dobbs. "They were only privy to details about their role in the mission. As for the senator, he's claiming total ignorance—big surprise there."

"Do I detect scorn?"

They stopped in front of another painting. "Damn right. Drake knows more than he says. He's a snake and I don't trust him. Period. Now, what's the story on this guy who hired those killers? I mean, he's got some *major brass*, trying to kidnap a senator."

Elleston sighed. "Ah, yes, well . . . he's a young thug from Haiti and a dabbler in human trafficking. Currently trying his hand at artifact smuggling."

Dobbs folded his arms and chewed his lower lip, thinking. "And you know this how?"

The other man frowned. "Surely you appreciate my need to protect my sources. Listen, in Chicago you claimed to have certain 'skills,' and you *still* owe me an explanation: How you unearthed this *Zack* chap and saw through my disguise." They kept walking.

"We're looking for a short woman, Caucasian."

Dobbs waited, then waited some more. Elleston said nothing.

"That's it?" exclaimed Dobbs. *"That's all?"*

Elleston stroked his goatee. Dobbs' thought-scan detected a smoldering frustration. Elleston himself wanted more information, but didn't have it.

"Look here, old sport, this tip came at great risk to my informant. Wander about, use this *gift* of yours. A woman is casing this place and we need to find her!" He thumped his cane tip on the floor for emphasis.

With that, Elleston walked a few yards and seated himself on a long, padded bench in the middle of the room. Planted his cane upright between his knees and placed both hands atop its gold, curved handle.

Hundreds of miles, thought Dobbs. *For a long shot?* He folded his arms and mentally shrugged. This, after all, was his stock in trade: a few clues, some sketchy leads, and maybe some luck. *Lemonade out of lemons,* he told himself. *Let's get cracking.*

More laughter. He turned to see the two characters at the other end of the gallery, acting up again. Several people were discreetly moving away from their buffoonery. Instead of trying to ignore them, however, Dobbs strolled closer. He scanned everyone in sight. As he passed the doorway to the Southern Asian and Persian Art room, he looked in. A woman was bent over and peering at the "Head of an Ascetic" statue. Dobbs slowed, picking up fragments of thought. Then he glanced back at the two men.

Dobbs picked up his pace. He walked behind the two men, slowed, then kept going. Surprisingly, their thought patterns weren't that different from Elleston's. Right now they were gawking and pointing at a painting called *Reclining Woman*.

"Shit, Georgie, ain't she a hot 'un!"

The speaker, dressed in blue jeans and a battered leather coat, made a crude remark. They both laughed.

Clever, thought Dobbs. *Who would have thought?*

He quickly walked back to the Persian Art room, then entered. Glanced back.

The young security officer was walking past and heading toward the two buffoons.

Dobbs pretended an interest in the various sculptures in the room, many of which were positioned on small shelves jutting from the dull-red walls. Above, tiny spotlights projected a splash of light onto each sculpture. He stayed away from the woman but kept positioning himself so he could watch her. Overt details: knee-length gray winter coat, charcoal slacks; early 20s, reasonably attractive features; long blonde hair piled atop her head and pinned by a multi-pronged comb; pearl-gray handbag with crocodile texture.

Scanning, scanning . . . .

Gray Lady seemed to be focusing on one area of the room, occasionally adjusting her black-rimmed glasses. Once she pressed a forefinger into her right ear.

Dobbs was so intent that he barely noticed when a security officer, crew cut and portly, strode through the room. "The museum will close in fifteen minutes," he murmured. "Closing in fifteen minutes." Soon a female voice came over the museum speakers to announce the same message.

The detective drifted toward the other doorway, as if to leave. Suddenly the woman turned and walked through the opposite doorway and into the German Expressionism exhibit. Dobbs followed.

He spied Elleston near the opposite wall, hovering beside a cluster of people listening to a tour guide. Dobbs hurried toward him, gesturing *come here* with both hands. Elleston came over as quickly as his cane-walking would allow.

"Her. *She's* your caser," said Dobbs, nodding at the blonde-haired woman. "The woman in the gray coat."

Elleston looked over. "You're absolutely *sure?*" he whispered.

"Damn right I am."

As they followed the Gray Lady, Dobbs grasped the man's shoulder and pulled him closer. "Your two troglodytes were a diversion. They're rough around the edges but they were acting— like you. Your intel was shaky. She was in the *adjoining* room, getting instructions through an earpiece and taking video through a micro lens on her glasses."

"Bloody hell!" said Elleston.

They shadowed the petite woman as she threaded her way

through gallery rooms and toward a main corridor. Her bland gray coat was difficult to follow, so Dobbs didn't let too many patrons get in the way. The woman was clearly heading toward an exit.

Dobbs' cell phone abruptly vibrated. He pulled it out and listened. "Sorry, Samantha," he told her. "My friend and I are busy. I'll meet you later, take the car."

Her voice buzzed in his ear. "Okay," he said, "I'll try to make dinner. But if not, I'll see you at Pinnacle tomorrow. For sure."

A female security officer stood beside the open doors; Dobbs gave her a friendly smile. Outside, a chill gripped the air and darkness had almost fallen. A thin band of rose and orange smeared the horizon.

Gray Lady stopped at the top of the broad stairway as visitors flowed past her.

Dobbs and Elleston slowly descended the stairway. At the bottom, Dobbs looked back and mentally congratulated himself. Elleston's two troglodytes had joined the woman, towering over her and talking. Soon the three of them started down.

"Here." Elleston suddenly grabbed Dobb's hand and thrust a pair of latex gloves into it. "Put them on . . . and be smart about it."

Dobbs looked over at the man and scanned. "You *can't* be serious!" he blurted.

"Oh but I am, sport," Elleston said quietly. He swung his cane up under his armpit and began pulling on his own gloves. "We're doing a kidnapping."

Chronicles of DramaTherapy
Chapter 2

Gary Winters

"Neurotics complain of their illness, but they make the most of it, and when it comes to taking it away from them they will defend it like a lioness her young."

— Sigmund Freud

Look at this course description from the National Association of Drama Therapy. "Students will learn to refine skills to work toward the capacity to attune to the protagonist on energetic and unconscious levels using body language and vocal tone as well as language."

I feel a little queasy just reading it. While words like *attune* jazz up mental health copy, they don't say much about the real deal, the genuine article, like my original DramaTherapy (one word), which predates the NADT by ten years.

Here is how it works. The actors I use come from the DramaTherapy group. If you want to call them participants, feel free. These actors are so good at what they do it's scary. It's powerful stuff. Downright emotionally volcanic. Let's take a look at a real DramaTherapy group I directed in Mexico City.

Cast of Characters:
    Psychoanalyst: Dr. Pedro
    Husband/Wife Italian Psychoanalysts: Tony & Sofia
    Blonde Psychoanalyst: Linda
    Male escort: Rolf
    CEO: Lars
    Management Consultant: George
    Mother: Anita
    Transactional Analyst: Marci
    Woman of Independent Means: Elizabeth
    Secretary from Expelled Rich Haitian Family: Cynthia
    Mime Street Performer: Carlos

Director: Gary

Gary: Tell us what you want from this group. Start on my right and go around the circle.

Anita: I'm having trouble with my family.

Peter: I'm here to learn.

Lars: My marriage isn't working.

After we go around, Lars looks spooked. Start with him.

Gary: What's going on, Lars?

Lars opens right up. He seems to be the ideal husband, a vigorous European businessman, and a sportsman. Physically active, he plays soccer. Plenty of dough. Gives his wife whatever she wants: guitar lessons, tennis lessons. He's a proud man. But sex life not so good. No sex in nine months.

Gary: You want to have sex with her?

Lars: Sure.

Gary: You talk to her about it?

Lars: Yes. But she doesn't tell me what's wrong. Only she's going through this or that.

We gather more information and get to know Lars, but don't do a scene until the fourth weekly session. Still no sex. The possibility of her having a lover is raised by at least two members of the group, but Lars dismisses this like how could anyone be so dumb to think that.
We do a scene. I play the tennis instructor coming to visit at Lars' home. I bop in like I'm Brad Pitt and stick my hand out to Lars. He grasps my hand and flings me across the room, saying

something like *You sonofa* . . . I ask for group feedback. Everyone feels that Lars intuitively knows his wife is having an affair with Tennis Shorts Dude. Getting harder for Lars to stay in denial now. We haven't even gotten to the guitar teacher yet.

I see Lars in private session. My assistant plays his wife in a scene. He experiences her point of view. I offer him conjoint therapy with his wife. He decides to go it alone. Brave man. He confronts his wife with the group consensus. She confesses. They get back together. The marriage is saved.

Lars tries to stiff me for my fee.

Win, Lose, or 3-Day Novel!

Laura Roberts

My first NaNoWriMo experience was a total failure.

It was November 2001, and I was living in New York City. In The Bronx, to be exact, in an apartment located just a few blocks from Fordham University, an apartment that I was sharing with not one but two roommates. Even though there were only two bedrooms in our place, there was a third guy living behind a curtain drawn across one half of our kitchen, which gave the whole setup a vaguely refugee camp vibe. All three of us had just graduated from college – me with a philosophy degree, and my two roommates each with business diplomas—and none of us were quite sure what we were doing with our lives and our careers yet.

Oh yeah, as you may recall, in September of that year some psychos had flown two jet planes into NYC's most iconic buildings and pretty much shattered our country's "We're No. 1!" attitude, with the awesome side effect of making it *even harder* to find a job in New York City. I finally got a call back for a receptionist position at the end of September (the previous receptionist, I would later learn, having fled for the safety of whatever Middle-of-Nowhere Midwestern town she'd originally come from, and I say that with love, because I'm originally from some Middle-of-Nowhere Midwestern town, too). I grabbed the job.

I'd been working at this totally thankless job for about a month, and I already hated it. (No joke: I even went to an interview at another company on one of my lunch breaks.) This was my first real nine-to-five gig, and it sucked. The big boss at the company would yell at me every time he called into the office, telling me I was an idiot, and when he physically set foot in the building, he never even deigned to make eye contact with me. He just brushed past my desk and began yelling at everyone else. I guess I should've been thankful for small mercies, but mostly I was busy plotting his untimely death in my head.

Needless to say, I wasn't feeling super happy with my life, and I needed a change. I had heard about the National Novel Writing Month, aka NaNoWriMo, and so on October 30th I signed up to write my very first novel.

As odd as this is going to sound, I have to admit I have no recollection of my 2001 novel's title or premise. I think it's probably because I took NaNoWriMo founder Chris Baty at his word when he said "No plot? No problem!"

My only real goal in 2001, which I do remember clearly, was "1,667 words or bust!" — NaNoWriMo's rallying cry.

Now, I was a recently graduated college student. I was no stranger to all-nighters and cranking out pages upon pages of total bullshit for the sake of a grade. I had even asked some of my professors for permission to write my final papers as Socratic dialogues (essentially: philosophical stage plays), and since I was a philosophy major, many of these professors — no doubt addled by reading 30 or more cookie-cutter essays on Aristotle and Aquinas — were delighted to engage such creativity.

So, I kind of thought writing was my strong suit in life. That I was good at putting words and phrases together to form sentences, which formed paragraphs, which could eventually form chapters in my novel, and after 30 days, *voila!* I would have written a book, no sweat.

If you've ever done NaNoWriMo before, you are chuckling right now at my utter naïveté. You may, in fact, be rolling on the floor, busting a gut laughing.

NaNoWriMo is not in any way, shape or form like writing an essay for university. Even if you wrote your essays as absurdist plays.

I think I only got about 10,000 words into this "novel" of mine before I realized I had *no effing clue* what I was doing. I had no ability to form characters, no idea how to build a plot, no idea what I would write about for 50,000 words (which was starting to sound more like 50 *zillion* words), and no idea how to get from Point A to Point B, much less Points C, D, E and all the way down to Z where you're supposed to write "The End" with a big smile on your face and announce, "I have written a novel! Bow down to me and send forth thy advance checks!"

In short, I failed. I failed hugely and spectacularly. I thought I could take on the NaNoWriMo challenge and beat it handily, but I couldn't.

Failing at writing a novel sucked. For me, it sucked even more than simply having a shitty job, mostly because every day that I went to that shitty job, in order to get through the day, I would tell myself: "You are not your job; you are a *writer*."

Now I had failed to write a novel. What kind of writer can't write a novel?

Well, when you stop to think about it, *lots* of writers can't—or don't—write novels. There are writers who pen poems, writers who spill out short stories, writers who churn out articles, writers who are corporate employees or freelancers who work on all kinds of PR and HR documents . . . and the list goes on. You don't necessarily have to write novels to be a writer. It's just one of the most visible ways you can someday be known and recognized for your writing.

So after my big, embarrassing NaNoWriMo failure—which, let's face it, was more in my mind than anything else, because these were the days before The Internet became all-encompassing and easily accessed from your phone in a matter of 3.2 nanoseconds, and no one I knew in real life actually knew that I was *trying* to write a novel—I picked myself up, dusted myself off, and went back to writing. I wrote short stories inspired by my shitty job, some of which were published by Über. I wrote crazy stories inspired by my self-loathing and fear that I would never find a real career, some of which were published by other places. And then I applied to Concordia University's Creative Writing program (which required submitting a portfolio full of my written work), and got accepted, and did a second BA, and graduated With Distinction as . . . *A Writer.*

And I've been freelancing ever since.

But none of that would have ever happened if I hadn't failed at my first NaNoWriMo. Because, then, I probably wouldn't have done something even crazier, like attempting to win NaNoWriMo a second time.

In 2003, I gave NaNoWriMo a second chance.

I had quit my shitty job in New York and moved to Montreal

to go back to school. I had started a Master's Degree in Philosophy, and discovered that the program wasn't quite what I'd been expecting. For one thing, no one was terribly keen on my submitting essays in Socratic dialogue format—no matter how hilarious my dialogue was. For another, the entire program was hell-bent on using as much ridiculous jargon as possible, along with rehashing third, fourth or seven-millionth-hand takes on Aristotle, instead of heading back to the original source and talking about whatever the hell it was that Aristotle had allegedly said to begin with. It was a bunch of talking heads, and very little philosophy—in my opinion.

In short: I was once more unhappy with my life and the direction it was heading.

So what did I decide to do? Apply to switch from the Philosophy MA into the Creative Writing MA, of course!

The only problem was that Concordia doesn't allow students into their Creative Writing MA unless they have already studied Creative Writing at the undergraduate level. (This, by the way, runs completely counter to virtually every other Masters-level Creative Writing program in existence, in both the U.S. and Canada. But I digress.) Having discovered this key piece of information *after* I'd already applied for the Creative Writing Masters, I was rejected, lost my $50 application fee, and felt a bit hopeless about the whole thing.

So instead of studying for my final exams in philosophy that year, I signed up for NaNoWriMo again and wrote a novel.

I called it *The Midnight Optimist,* and completed it almost entirely while typing away on my laptop in various cafés throughout Montreal.

I hit the 50,000-word mark this time, out of sheer determination.

On November 30, 2003, I typed the words "The End" and won NaNoWriMo for the first time.

I received a winner button to put on my website, and a PDF certificate heralding my win—which I printed out with my name and the title of my book, and taped to my wall as proof of my achievement.

I felt overjoyed. I had won NaNoWriMo! I had written a

novel! Surely this meant something? It meant I really, really, really wanted to be a writer—right?

I took my renewed sense of optimism over to the English department and applied to the Creative Writing undergraduate program. One of the requirements for entry into the program was that I had to turn in a portfolio of my writing, so I gathered together my meager collection of short stories, and included a selection of chapters from my *Midnight Optimist* manuscript.

Happily, I was accepted into the program. I took every writing class Concordia offered on the arts of short fiction and playwriting (they didn't offer any novel-writing courses, and I did my best to avoid the poetry classes for fear of becoming A Poet). I learned how to put stories together. I read hundreds of books. I critiqued my fellow students' work. I learned how to talk about writing, how to make editorial suggestions, how to view literature as something more than just a word count to be achieved.

I joined the staff of the university's literary arts magazine, *The Void*, as copy editor and proofreader.

I joined the staff of one of the university's weekly newspapers, *The Link*, as the Literary Arts Editor.

I submitted a piece to one of the university's literary anthologies, *Headlight*, and it was accepted for publication. (Oddly enough, that piece was a poem—an art form in which I still possess no formal training.)

I started my own online magazine, *Black Heart.*

In 2007 I graduated With Distinction from the joint-honors program in Creative Writing and English Literature.

I began freelancing immediately, in order to pay my bills. I wrote profiles of virtually every business in Montreal for their online wing of the Yellow Pages, MontrealPlus.ca.

In October of that year, I started writing a weekly column for the city's alternative newspaper, *Hour*. I was given free rein to write about anything I wanted, and I was paid for it, too.

I was officially a writer. And it was all because of NaNoWriMo, once again!

Winning NaNoWriMo brought me more confidence to try new things, to write more words and more frequently, to stretch my imagination and improve my craft.

In 2008 I won NaNoWriMo again, penning a manuscript entitled *The World's Craziest Ninja*. And in 2011, I decided to take on an even bigger, crazier challenge: I entered the 3 Day Novel Contest.

Would I be able to write an entire novel in just three days?

I was about to find out. And my NaNoWriMo-centric worldview was about to be shattered forever.

The 3 Day Novel Contest is not for the faint of heart, nor those who find themselves queasy at the thought of locking themselves into their apartments over a long weekend and typing away madly on a manuscript that must be finished in just 72 hours.

It is, however, a real thing that people do every Labor Day weekend throughout the U.S., Canada and the rest of the English-speaking world. In fact, people have been doing this since before I was born! The contest officially began in 1977, and has been held annually ever since.

In 2011, I decided to officially participate in this madness. I sent in my $55 entry fee and began plotting an outline for what would eventually become my first published novel, *Ninjas of the 512*.

The 3 Day Novel Contest completely changed the way I looked at writing, particularly with respect to writing a novel. It is, in fact, diametrically opposed to the approach used when writing a NaNoWriMo novel.

I completed the 3 Day Novel Challenge, submitted my manuscript for judging, and waited. It didn't win the grand prize (which is publication, hence the $55 entry fee), but I realized that that didn't really matter to me. It was 2011, and thousands of people were beginning to self-publish their own stories at Amazon. I asked myself: Why can't I do the same?

And so, after several rounds of editing, hiring a cover designer, and tweaking the manuscript to fit the KDP guidelines for publication, I set *Ninjas of the 512* loose on the world.

I had completed a novel in three days, and now I had published a novel professionally. What next?

I decided to get back to work on a manuscript that I'd been working on, off and on, for several years. I wanted to finish it, at last. And I wanted to apply my 3 Day Novel writing skills to a 30-

day time period to see what would happen.

In 2012, I signed up for NaNoWriMo once again. And this time, I cheated.

Whistle While You Work

Arthur Raybold

I was fourteen years old when I began to work for Miss Sarah Battelle in the summer of 1944. I was glad to find any job, especially one paying fifty cents an hour. It would mean that I could save up enough money to help my dad buy the lumber we needed to build a chicken coop, something we'd talked about all during the previous winter.

We lived in the small town of Mattapoisett, Massachusetts. Miss Battelle lived on one of the large estates on Ned's Point Road. Each of those estates extended from the road right down to the shore on the harbor. It was a favorite pastime of many in town to walk along that road to Ned's Point Lighthouse in the off-season, to catch glimpses of the large summer houses of the rich and sometimes famous people we almost never saw.

There was a mansion on the estate, built by her family in 1894. Nobody lived in it now, but the Batelle family and their friends had filled the house during summer holidays for several generations, and now the empty house sat boarded up, looking a bit derelict. Back in 1929, Miss Battelle had decided to build a Cape Cod-style cottage just for herself on a plot of land on the south side of the estate. It was a lot cozier and easier to care for than the big house, which she planned to have torn down at the end of that summer.

Miss Battelle was a heroine of the First World War, risking her life on the battlefields of France as an ambulance driver. And she was a real eccentric. After her death in 1953, *The New York Times* ran an article about her: "Safe Deposit Box Yields an Arsenal." In the box was stored live ammunition—grenades, cartridges, primers for big artillery shells, and parachute flares that she had brought home from France.

On the day I started my new job, when I saw the mansion close up for the first time, the exterior was a sort of dying yellow that seemed to express a sadness that it had no summer company. The woman who greeted me was Maria, the large, smiling housekeeper who cooked and cleaned for Miss Battelle. Maria took an immediate liking to me and gave me my daily duties, which could be anything from washing Venetian blinds in a tub to tending the large asparagus patch next to Miss Battelle's cottage.

These were tough jobs, but the most demanding chore was to mow the lane between her cottage and the neighbor's gigantic hedge. This grassy area, roughly twenty feet wide, began at the top of Ned's Point Road, and extended all the way down to the waterfront more than two hundred yards away. To do this, I had to push an old rotary hand mower up and down twenty times. It took me two full days without interruption to finish.

One day, while Maria and I were dismantling some Venetian blinds in the living room, she said, "Artie, would you whistle that tune once more?" I had been whistling without realizing it.

"Do you think Miss Battelle will mind?"

"Not at all. She already told me it reminds her of her brother who was a whistler too."

I repeated Berlin's "Alexander's Ragtime Band," one of the favorites my dad played on the old upright when he came home from work. I would whistle the tunes the next day, so as not to forget.

"Oh, I love that one," said Maria.

"Thanks! Here's another one my father plays a lot." I began to whistle Berlin's "A Pretty Girl Is Like a Melody." Maria pursed her lips, blowing hard, but nothing happened. While we laughed at her attempts to whistle, Miss Battelle entered the room and began to sing, "A pretty girl is like a melody that haunts you night and day, just like the strain of a haunting refrain . . . ."

Miss Battelle stopped, took a breath, and sat down. "Let's leave the music to Artie or you'll need to call an ambulance for me. Maria, I came in to say I want you and Artie to add to the asparagus patch to create an army of asparagus marching to the harbor. We'll call it the Asparagus Brigade."

"Okay, Miss Battelle, I'm sure we can do that."

After lunch, Maria and I finished scrubbing the blinds, carried them outdoors and hung them from the clothesline. Then we set about creating a master plan for the military asparagus. After preparing the garden bed, we planted hundreds of seeds to simulate a brigade.

The highlight of the summer was when Henry Morganthau came to visit Sarah Battelle. He was President Roosevelt's Treasury Secretary at the time.

Morganthau carried a walking stick and sported a large mustache, and although it was summer, he wore a three-piece woolen suit. He had a deep voice and tapped his stick when he spoke, maybe to emphasize what he was saying. "Sarah, how good it is to see you. I've been meaning to stop by for some time, but things in Washington are so hectic."

"I can only imagine," Miss Battelle said, giving him a warm embrace. "It's so good to see you, too! And how is dear Beverly?"

"She's just fine, happy to be back here. We want you to come to dinner on Saturday. Now remember, our house is the last before the lighthouse."

"I think I still remember where your house is, Henry," she replied tartly, but with a smile.

"And who is this young chap?"

"This is Artie, our young landscaper."

I remember quite well how his large hand enveloped my smaller one, saying, "My boy, see that you work hard, and be a real help to Miss Battelle."

Toward the end of summer, Miss Battelle began to have the mansion torn down, and around Labor Day she called me into the cottage. "I know you're going back to school soon and I wanted to reward you for being a big help to me this summer with mowing and gardening. You and your Dad can have any of the lumber you need from the big house in order to build that chicken coop you've been telling us about."

"Oh Miss Battelle, thank you so much! Now we'll be able to do it. My Dad will be so surprised when I tell him."

"Good boy, Artie. And make sure you keep on whistling!"

Rituals

Frank Primiano

The hand grasped his shoulder and a husky female voice behind him said, "Just a moment, sir. Haven't you forgotten something?"

Oh, shit, he thought, *they were watching me.*

"What?" he said as he stopped walking and turned his head to look back, small beads of sweat forming on his forehead. His heart beat faster, pounding in his ears.

"That package there, next to the sport coat rack. Isn't it yours? Come on, let's go get it."

"Uh, yeah. That's mine. How could I have left it?" he said, mumbling, and followed the large, black woman back into Penney's.

He had abandoned the paper bag to save time. He intended to take a shortcut to get to the car by the deadline and, of course, couldn't be seen carrying anything. But now, if he could get away in the next few minutes he'd have to take the long, "innocent" route to a trash can out of sight of the store. He couldn't take the chance that these people wouldn't keep an eye on him as he walked through the mall.

"Here it is," the officious but polite lady said. "Let's look inside to make sure it's yours." She unfolded the top of the bag and examined the contents. "That's a real nice shirt. Yellow with lavender stripes. Short sleeve, 14 inch neck. Mmmm. I'd have figured you for at least a 15½ or 16."

"It's not for me. It's for my kid brother," came out a little too fast. He took a surreptitious glance at his watch. Only four minutes left. His face was hot. He could just imagine how red it must be. Ever since he was a child he couldn't stop that reaction to embarrassment or guilt." Oh, and here's the sales slip. You got a real bargain. It says y'paid only $5.95

at register six. Well, here y'are. Next time remember to take what you bought home with you. Y'don't wanna waste your money, do you?"

Relieved to the point that he thought it would show, he took the package, thanked her, and walked again into the mall, quickly, but not too quickly. He could feel her eyes on his back as he headed for the cross corridor that led to the parking lot.

* * *

She stood at the entrance to the store eying his retreat. *Something ain't kosher about that kid,* she mused.

"What was that all about?" The voice of the store manager broke into her thoughts.

"Oh, that fella walked outta the store without a shirt he paid for, and I returned it to him."

"Well, that's a new one: a security guard catching a shop-dropper instead of a shop-lifter."

"Yeah, but something funny's goin' on . . . I feel it in my gut."

"Wait a minute," the manager said, smiling. "Since when does a new plain clothes security guard develop a sensitive gut after only three days on her first job? I know you were second in your class at the academy, but a nose for criminal intent comes only after years of experience and exposure to bad guys."

"Well, maybe thirty years raisin' four kids and now havin' to keep ahead o' two gran'chillen qualifies me," she said with a sardonic smile.

"Touché," the manager said as he feigned a wound to his chest and walked away chuckling.

The boy was still in sight carrying the bag, making his way more quickly now through the Saturday morning shoppers.

What's wrong? she worried. *He looks like a clean-cut, athletic, high school senior or college freshman. But somehow he don't seem like your everyday Penney's shopper. His hair's styled and neatly combed. His Nike's prob'ly cost 150 dollars. His Dockers are pressed with a crease. And that watch he kept looking at. It's a Rolex that must've set his old man back 4,000 bucks.*

So what's he doing in Penney's buying a six-dollar shirt?

Maybe he got cheap taste in shirts. That's probably true, judging from his sweatshirt. It's the plainest one I ever seen. It don't have even one label or 'signia on it. Just an old, plain, grey, long-sleeved sweatshirt. And on a hot day like this. Then the alarm gonged in her head.

"Damn," she said under her breath, unable to decide whether or not to run after the boy. He was just turning into the corridor out to the parking lot. No, she couldn't stop him now . . . on just a hunch. There'd be no probable cause. Instead, she went to register six.

It was as she feared. He'd paid for the shirt where the watches, jewelry and fine pen and pencil sets were sold.

To distract the sales girl?

The displays, with their stacks of products on top of the counter for the big clearance sale, looked undisturbed, but only an inventory check would confirm her suspicions.

* * *

He snatched a quick glance back toward the store before he rounded the corner and could no longer be seen from there. She was still standing where she had been, tracking him. But now he was out of her view.

Up ahead, a trash can sat in the center of the walkway. As he strode, he dug in his pocket for the change. The bills and coins, along with the bag, were disposed of. He took off for the door. Less than a minute to go.

He got to the car as the engine started, and jumped into

the front passenger seat of the moving vehicle.

"It's about time you got here, neophyte. Another two seconds and we'd have been history," the oldest of the three in the back seat said. "These two got here ten minutes ago."

"Who cares about that," came from one of the others in the back. "He's here now. That's all that counts."

"Okay, okay, let's get down to business," the driver said, "What did you get? Or didn't you get anything?"

Still panting, the boy turned to face more toward the rear seat and fished in his right sleeve with his left hand. He pulled out a six-inch-long, narrow, gold foil-covered box.

"What's that?" the driver asked. "Open it."

The boy fumbled with the wrapper. He removed the top. In a molded, velvet liner lay a fat, black fountain pen with a gold clasp and a distinctive white snowflake emblem on its top.

"Whoa! He got a Mont Blanc. That's costly," one of the boys in the back said, his eyebrows raised. The driver took his eyes off the road for a quick look.

"Man, it's too neat," the other young one said with envy. "You'll probably get the trophy for the most valuable haul. And you even got it in the box. You're smooth."

Damn. The box. I didn't think about the box.

"Hold on a minute," the oldest guy in the back seat said. "Are you telling me they keep these sealed boxes out in the open? How did you get this? Did you really snatch it? Huh? Or did you buy it?" He poked the driver's shoulder. "It was your job to search him before he went in."

"Hey. He didn't have any money or checks or credit cards in his wallet or his pockets or shoes or cuffs," the driver said, "and a cavity search isn't in my job description."

"Well, he could have sewn it in his pants or somewhere else." The oldest guy looked at the boy. "Okay. Did you buy this pen? Answer me, and don't even think about lying."

"Yeah," the driver said. "Did you buy it? I want the

truth. You know we won't initiate you as a brother if you're dishonest."

Pesky Little Critters

Laurie Asher

Outside on the fence, termites swarm

Especially when days are warm.

I watch them fly, their wings a flitter

Then they attack my apple fritter.

I set my foot upon a wooden rail

As it collapses into an empty pail.

Oh, how I wish they'd fly away

And visit that lady across the bay.

It's time to call the Orkin man

To watch him grasp his poison-filled can.

He grabs the nozzle and sprays away

This better be worth what I have to pay.

A week has passed and I hear them crunching

Chomping and chomping, munching and munching.

Now firmly ensconced inside my home

Apparently now just free to roam.

I sense them deep within the walls

Crunching as I walk the halls.

How can these creatures be driven out?

They are hiding behind my tile grout.

Soon I'll be living out on the grass

As termites have overrun en masse.

Now I'll deal with fire ants

Who find their way inside my pants.

So I'll cuddle with dandelions and stare at the moon

And scratch and itch like a crazy loon.

The neighbors are worried as I'm howling too,

"It won't be long 'fore they come for you."

But don't worry as I've got a great plan

I'm going to marry the Orkin Man.

What Dentists Like

Kenneth A. Yaros

Few of us enjoy going to the dentist, even though usually there is a positive outcome. But I'd bet you wouldn't guess what dentists like to do most when we get together? It's telling jokes or stories. Our favorite subject is lawyer jokes; they're endless. A close second is dental stories, but they have to be true or they don't count.

When I was a young dentist practicing in a storybook New England town, I heard one of my favorite anecdotes from an older dentist who had been in practice for over 40 years. After a long day sitting in a seminar, we would gather for drinks. He would usually sit in the back of the room quietly sipping a cola, listening to the younger guys spin their yarns, enjoying the laughter. But one night we found out it was his birthday. Our dental society president turned to him and shouted, "Hey, Rigali, you have to have a story for us. C'mon. It's your turn."

Dr. Rigali looked at his drink and fidgeted in his chair for a while, and smiled. "Yeah, just one. It was a long time ago."

Because he was older and soft of voice, we all moved closer to hear. This is the story he told:

I was home one night when the phone rang. It was an elderly-sounding woman who was really unhappy with her teeth. I listened carefully to her complaint. She was very upset. But almost nothing she said made sense to me.

"Doc," she says, "I hate my teeth."

"What's the problem? They hurt?"

"No, nothing like that."

"You have a cavity?"

"No, no. You don't understand. I can't drink coffee."

"I see. They're sensitive to hot stuff, right?"

"No, that's fine."

"Well, what's the problem?"

"Doc, my teeth get loose whenever I drink coffee. I have to

push them back in."

That really got me going, I had never heard of anything like that, so I asked her how long this had been going on, and she told me nearly forever, and that she was sick and tired of complaining to her husband about it and nothing she could do would make it better.

Thinking she was probably a nut case, I asked her some more questions. "Madam, are you seeing any doctor for a health condition?" I thought maybe she was not quite right, possibly on antipsychotic medication.

"No, Doc. Are you going to help me or not?"

"Madam, it is not that I wouldn't be happy to see you, but don't you already have a dentist?"

"No, I left him over five years ago with my same problem. He called me a crackpot, and told me if I continued to call him he would report me to the police for harassment."

That really got me thinking. What was I about to step into?

"Very well, you seem so upset. Why don't you stop by the office the first thing in the morning, and we'll take a look."

I went to bed, but could hardly sleep that night. When I finally dozed off, I had nightmares of patients opening their mouths and their teeth would literally fall out and drop on the floor, where I would try in vain to find them to put them back in. At last, morning came. I prepared for work still fixated on last night's conversation, scouring my mind for possible solutions for the woman's dilemma.

I entered the office through the back door and checked the reception area to see if she had arrived. There she stood, a small, elderly woman wearing a heavy coat and a head scarf. She was hunched over the reception desk filling out her paperwork. Her husband, covered with tattoos, sprawled on the couch.

Soon, Betsy, my chairside assistant, announced that our new patient was seated and ready to see me.

"Betsy, do me a favor, take her X-rays first, so I have some idea of what is going on. No sense in delaying her diagnosis."

Off she went.

Two minutes later, Betsy returned, announcing the patient had no teeth to X-ray.

"What? Are you sure? She told me her teeth were loose—that was her chief complaint."

"No teeth, Doc," Betsy grinned.

Man, oh man, this is unbelievable, I thought to myself.

Minutes later, I appeared before the woman, shook her hand and managed a smile before I started her examination.

"Nice to meet you. Again, how long did you say you had this problem?"

"Gotta be five years, Doc."

"Okay. Well then, let's take a look."

I adjusted the dental chair and light and took a small mouth mirror to explore the internals of her oral cavity. Almost everything was stained dark brown. Teeth, gums, tongue, Her mouth was darker than the inside of a wallet.

"You drink a lot of coffee?"

"Used to."

"Don't brush too often do you?"

"I can't, Doc. Gave up on it."

Then, she reached into her mouth and removed her teeth in one fell swoop!

"My god! You have dentures. You never told me that."

"Yeah, I know. And they're a piece of crap, Doc. Worst teeth I ever had."

She plunked them down on the shelf in front of us and folded her arms.

In seconds, I realized what went wrong. She was walking around with half-finished dentures! The laboratory never completed them. I couldn't believe it. The teeth were barely being held in by a thin layer of wax. It seemed impossible that anyone would have worn them for years that way.

Within a few days we had fixed her teeth. The following week her husband brought us a huge flower arrangement in appreciation. He told Betsy they had already referred a friend of theirs to us. The problem was, he said, "Her teeth had worms."

I could hardly wait.

To Sandy, From Henry: A Christmas Story

Sandra Yeaman

About his paintings, Norman Rockwell said, "The view of life I communicate in my pictures excludes the sordid and ugly. I paint life as I would like it to be."

I grew up in Norman Rockwell's small-town America, where celebrating Christmas was wonderful and beautiful. This is a Christmas story, but its lessons could come from any holiday in any place or time.

By Christmas Eve in my northern Minnesota childhood, the pile of presents under the tree had grown beyond the tree's circumference. In the late afternoon, we would have a light meal, to tide us over until later. After that meal, we six kids were allowed to pick out one present each to open. With that done, Mom and Dad would pack us into the car for the drive to Grandma and Grandpa's house where all the aunts, uncles, and cousins would meet up. Grandpa and Grandma had 36 grandchildren, so the house was well-filled by the time we all arrived. Our family lived the farthest so we usually arrived last.

Once there, we'd eat the *real* evening meal.

In no time, the suspense grew nearly as high as the pile of presents under Grandpa and Grandma's tree. But we had to wait until Santa arrived to hand out the presents. Santa was usually Uncle Marvin, dressed in a remarkably awful Santa suit that didn't fool any of us. We made a game of seeing who would first notice Marvin was no longer in the room. His absence meant Santa would arrive soon. Once Santa arrived, there was great jostling to see whose present would be passed out first.

Once the presents were opened, we spent an appropriate amount of time playing with the toys before we all headed home late in the evening.

At home, my brothers, sister and I got to open the rest of the presents under the tree. In the morning, there would be more presents, this time from Santa. That was our ritual, our celebration of Christmas as a nuclear and extended family.

But when I turned 12, the routine changed slightly. Grandpa and Grandma started spending the winters in Arizona. With Grandpa and Grandma no longer in town for Christmas, Mom and her siblings rotated hosting the family on Christmas Eve.

That's how we ended up one year for a special Christmas at Uncle Marvin's house.

Uncle Marvin lived on the farm that had been home for Mom and her siblings while they grew up. That house held more memories for their generation than the house in town that we cousins thought of as Grandma's. So it was appropriate that a special gift was waiting there that year.

When my family arrived at Uncle Marvin's house, nearly all the cousins who were old enough to walk and talk ran out to our car with one question: "Who is Henry?" And they were all asking me that question. I had no idea what they were talking about.

They nearly dragged me into the house and up to the tree to point to the envelope lying on one of the boughs. "To Sandy, from Henry" was written on the envelope. I had *no idea* who Henry was.

For the first time ever, there wasn't any competition about which present should be handed out first. Everyone wanted to know what was in the envelope from Henry. When Santa handed me the envelope, every eye followed his hand. I opened the envelope; I pulled out a heart-shaped locket on a chain. And nothing else. I *still* didn't know who Henry was.

Then I heard my mother laugh. She turned and pointed at her younger sister, LaVerne, and explained to those few who didn't already know that Henry had been her boyfriend before she met my father. Henry had given her the locket for Christmas. When Mom met Dad, she gave the locket to LaVerne. LaVerne kept it until Mom's oldest daughter — that's me — turned 13 when LaVerne decided it was time for the locket to be passed on — from Henry, to Sandy.

When I got married, I gave the locket to my sister, Joan. And I never gave it another thought. I assumed Joan still had it.

That is until Joan and I found it in my mother's jewelry box after Mom died. As Joan and I stared at it in the box, we gasped simultaneously and spoke the same words, "We've got to pass it on."

You see, even though Mom married Dad and not Henry, Henry had become part of our family. Henry's daughter, Kathy, married Mom's nephew, David, making Henry my cousin's father-in-law. And Dad's best friend, Norman, had a sister who was Henry's wife, making Norman Kathy's uncle. A few weeks later, when Kathy and David invited Dad and Norman for dinner, the two of them delivered the locket to Kathy, to return it to the family.

LaVerne, Mom, and Henry died within four months of one another. But every Christmas, they are with me in the story of the envelope labeled, "To Sandy, from Henry."

"To the outside world we all grow old. But not to brothers and sisters. We know each other as we always were. We know each other's hearts. We share private family jokes. We remember family feuds and secrets, family griefs and joys. We live outside the touch of time." —Clara Ortega

May all your holidays be blessed with rich family traditions.

Swish

Amy E. Zajac

My daughter planned every detail of her move from California to Washington. She arranged for me to travel with her to divide in half the twenty-four hours of driving time. With her compact sedan, packed to the gills, the last two passengers inserted into the stuffed back seat space were her two cats, Lord Montgomery (a Seal Point Himalayan) and Max (a Blue Point Himalayan).

The rearview mirror's limited visibility mandated that only the side-view mirrors be used. My daughter's multiple house plants, long and viny, draped over boxes, lamps, and oddball sundries, around the seat headpieces and throughout the rear window. When we looked into the back seat, we saw a jungle with wild feline faces lurking from under the greenery. The kitty litter situated on one side next to the door was the last component of the menagerie enclosed in the small space.

We settled in for the long trip with everything we needed: food and water for us and the cats, pillows for us to sleep on, and lots of CDs to accommodate all our music tastes. Almost immediately we heard the swishing sound of one of the cats using the kitty litter. The swishing went on and on and on. It was Max. "Swish, swish, swish, swish, swish." He kept burying and burying and burying his deposit in the litter box with Monty just staring out from under the vines.

The hours dragged on with the lull of turning tires and a country western tune playing in the CD player. Here and there one of us would break into song when we heard a favorite melody.

And . . . then once again we heard, "swish, swish, swish, swish." On and on. Yes, Max spent just a moment making another deposit, but didn't get the idea when his deposit was actually covered up. The swish, swish, swish, swish lasted so long, as if he covered up deposits for both cats, but Monty, as yet, did not deposit even once. Many hours passed without Monty using the litter. This concerned my daughter, so she stopped specifically to give Monty the chance to use the litter without the movement of the traveling car. She took him out and let him walk around, but even that didn't make a difference. When she placed him in the litter, he jumped out and proceeded to hide under the greenery.

Many more hours passed during the long day, extended on into the night. But as sure as each minute came and went, about every hour Max made his way to the litter and, "Swish, swish, swish, swish." It occurred so often we started to count the number of swishes each time. On many deposits, he swished the litter more than thirty times.

"Mom, I'm worried about Monty; he hasn't done a job in the litter box since we left Los Angeles. That was more than fifteen hours ago. He's going to get sick if he doesn't go soon."

"I know this is a concern, but Max has done enough for both of them." I smiled, hoping she would understand my lame joke. She tipped her head with her daughter look, which basically meant, "Oh Mom."

Another eight hours passed before Monty started to howl, long, drawn-out multi-toned meows. They sounded like they came from the back of his throat all the way through to the tip of his tail. Stretching my neck to look in the rearview mirror and see the back seat, I saw how concerned my daughter was for her little friend.

"Since Monty's howling like that, I'm sure he's ready to go. He's scared and won't get into the litter box by himself. You know how temperamental and quirky he is. Max isn't anything like him." She kept looking over her shoulder.

"Heeeeeyy, you need to watch the road!" I said.

"He's going to have an accident, I just know it. I knew I should have put some plastic over the seat to protect it."

"The next exit on the freeway will be in about ten miles, Coeur d'Alene, Idaho. We can stop there." It was barely dark as the sun eased its way over the mountain ridges. A new day was dawning.

"Okay, I'll pull over then."

Monty ceased the howling while we spoke to each other, but as soon as we stopped talking, he started again.

"Sweetie, you have to keep your eyes on this winding road.

Monty will be okay until we can pull over."

There it was again. "Swish, swish, swish, swish, swish."

We looked at each other and burst out laughing. Max proceeded to work through his lengthy deposit-cover-up once again.

Pulling over at the exit, Monty stopped howling as soon as the car stopped. While my daughter scurried around to the back door, I grabbed Max so he wouldn't jump out of the car with the door opened. She lifted the vines and grabbed Monty and gently placed him into the litter box. This time she kept her hand steadily on his back.

Monty stayed where she placed him this time. For a long time, and with a great look of satisfaction on his face, his eyes closed and his face calm, he proceeded to do his business. Twenty-two and a half hours may be a record. His deposit successful, he jumped out of the litter, but did not cover the deposit. The strong odor prevailed through the whole car, and since we were stopped, we took the time to clean the litter.

With about one hour of travel time left to Spokane, we settled back into our drive. I took over driving while my daughter snuggled up to a pillow for quick nap.

Within five minutes, "Swish, swish, swish, swish, swish."

What's More Awesome Than A Butterfly?

Tom Leech

When out strolling in the garden,
Or along a pathway in the park,
What will grab your attention
Is a butterfly with its instant spark.

How can it not capture your eye,
Transforming your stumbling and muttering,
With its colors that glow and glimmer,
And its flipping, flapping, and fluttering?

With those wings you can't help but watch
When they spread open wide as to soar,
Then flicker back next to the posy
For a touch, a quick sip, or maybe more.

Then darting with a move so quick,
Off to one more red or blue blossom,
While flipping, flapping, and fluttering,
Not much could be truly more awesome.

Well something brightens that image,
When you see a pack of eight or nine,
More flipping, flapping, and fluttering,
Brings joy for that flutterer that's mine.

El Niño

Frank Primiano

    The clammy fog oozed along the ground, accompanied by a chill, as the sun receded for the day. The chronically inaccurate TV weathermen might have gotten it right for once. A storm, enormous even by local standards, was on its way, with its mudslides, downed trees, and swamped streets. For the community under the bridge, the fog, and the warnings blasted from bullhorns on cruising patrol cars, signaled that the inevitable evacuation could be put off no longer.
    He wasn't the first to decide to leave, and he wouldn't be the last. He had delayed abandoning his spot. It was cozy down here, cool in the summer, although cold on days the temperature dropped. The cops didn't permit open fires beside a four-lane city street, but he had a heavy jacket, a blanket, and a rug in which he could wrap himself. And he had his wine that warmed him.
    His territory was a wedge of land beside the bridge abutment, encircled by a flap of cyclone fencing that he could shut with a lock he "found" in the hardware section of a supermarket. This allowed him to accumulate and store more than his share of stuff. The problem was that it couldn't all be moved at one time. He knew a place that'd be above water when the deluge hit. But during the several trips he'd have to make, his things would be untended there, up for grabs by anyone who happened upon them.
    A woman paced in front of her possessions mounded on the sidewalk. He had eyed her ever since she had settled beneath the bridge weeks ago. She carted her stuff with her on her daily rounds to cadge money and food. From what he could see, she steered clear of drugs and prostitution. And she avoided her no rent neighbors, displaying a persistent paranoia that kept her life solitary. So, in the present crisis, she appeared uncertain as to what to do, or whom to ask for help keeping her things and herself safe. He figured that, wherever she wound up, her only protection would be a knife, a pearl-handled, four-inch

switchblade, that he had seen her cleaning on several occasions.

* * *

In the thickening gloom, visibility was measured in single-digit yards. She saw his silhouette as he approached. She rammed her hand into her pocket, the one in which she kept her knife, and moved back two steps. He stopped, extending his hands, palms out. She could make out his face and halted her retreat. They'd never spoken at length, but they weren't strangers, as none are who share the same limited space.

He said, "I sure could use yer help . . . and I kin help you." Saying nothing, she listened as he explained that he needed someone to watch his stuff at a new place while he made the trips necessary to relocate. In exchange, she could share the space and store her stuff there, too.

Her silence continued, her hand still in her pocket. She glanced to her right and left. Both provided possible escape routes. He went on, "We'll move you first. You stay there whilst I go back and forth fer my stuff. But we'll have t' hurry. The storm's started. This place'll be unner water in no time."

She didn't reply, looking at him, then the street, and then her heap of bags. At last she nodded and gave a tentative smile. He showed a wide, gap-toothed grin that gave him a sinister look. Startled, she stumbled back another step, but didn't run. He shielded his mouth with his wrist and lowered his head, still looking into her eyes.

Withdrawing her hand from her pocket, she stepped into her pile of things. What followed was rushed activity. She carried her entire household. He took his first load. Out from the cover of the bridge, they were greeted by violent wind and rain. He struggled to pull a bottle from an inside pocket.

Twenty minutes later he returned for the rest of his cache. Carrying as much as he could, he took two more trips and over an hour to complete the move. By then, water was above the curb, lapping the sidewalk.

* * *

The rain continued into the night. A police SUV began the last run it would be able to make below the bridge. The swift water that engulfed the street was already up to its bumper. The driver swept his spotlight searching for stragglers, or any others unable to understand, or unwilling to acknowledge, the danger they were in.

The vehicle slid to a stop. An officer jumped out, submerging his boots. He waded into the beam of the headlights and grabbed the naked body floating by, face down, the pearl handle of a knife sticking out of its back.

Story of a Drawing

Val Zolfaghari

He was well-dressed, handsome, and a regular customer of Cafe Casino. He came alone, paid exact change for his coffee, and sat alone. He gazed at sea waves for a long time and then drew a picture of a desert. When it was finished, a smirk appeared on his face. He sipped the last drop of coffee and left. None of the other regulars knew where he came from, what his profession was, or why he drew the same picture day after day.

One day, when an old lady fainted in the cafe, he rushed to her aid and revived her. This convinced Dolce, a regular and a criminal lawyer, that the mysterious man was a doctor. Dolce, an attractive middle-aged woman, had become fascinated by him. She also was convinced that he had a hidden secret in his drawing. Many times over the days and weeks as he visited the cafe, Dolce found herself pondering his drawings as she drank her coffee. His drawings only added to the attraction, which quickly grew into an obsession.

Dolce had to meet him. She hatched a plan. The next day, she came back to the cafe with paper and pencil and sat next to him. She spread a piece of paper over the table and sketched a desert similar to his. His reaction was immediate. He crossed out her drawing and shouted, "Do not ever do it again. Do you mock me? You do not know why I draw, yet you copy it. Do you do this to become my friend? How can I be your friend when you make fun of my pain?"

Dolce was immediately remorseful. She placed her hand over his to show him the depth of her feeling. The warmth of her hand soothed his heart's pain. He allowed her touch and wondered: Is she my wife's reincarnation? The man had grieved his wife's passing for years; yet he took solace knowing that she did not live to see what happened to their family after her death.

Touching hands started an unexpected camaraderie. Soon they became lovers. They drew on their vast experiences, their philosophies and their perspectives to enrich their intimate times together. She nicknamed him "Treasure."

They talked about everything except his family and his drawing. He spent most nights with Dolce and she reveled in the daily routine and the ordinary that had taken on greater meaning with him in her life. He fulfilled her desires and, she liked to think, she gave as good as she got. Life was good and everything was tranquil.

Then, the first day of winter came. On that day, Treasure became a completely different person. His emotion boiled like a volcano—deep and brooding, threatening. He took to muttering to himself, his lips moving without sound. His head and hands shook and his actions became erratic, spastic and wild, as if they were hit by a tornado. When Dolce tried to calm him, he ran from her, got into his car and drove away without uttering a word.

Dolce agonized all day, wondering if he might do something to harm himself—or someone else. She wondered if she should call the authorities. It was toward evening when he came back, exhausted and covered in dust. He sank into a chair in front of the fireplace and stared intently at flames.

Dolce offered him a glass of wine. "Are you better? Where did you go?"

"To the desert," he said.

"Why?"

"I had to." He moaned.

"Why?"

"It is my grieving day. Even as a doctor, I cannot cope with it."

She kissed him. "My love, if you tell me everything, your anguish will go away completely."

He remained quiet and stared at the dancing flames.

He pondered whether he dare tell her his darkest secret. *She has shared my naked body. Now, she desires my naked thoughts. I wonder what she will do after my secret is revealed. Perhaps it is better to take it to my grave.*

Dolce studied his face. The flames highlighted the furrows filled with years of pain. She asked herself what the consequence would be if he divulged his perplexing secret. *What will happen to us after we have no secret between us? Will familiarity breed contempt?*

Finally, he broke the silence. "I will tell you the secret that has gnawed at me for many years. I ask you to be fair and if you leave me, I will understand."

Dolce grasped his hands in hers. "From what you have told me, life has not been fair to you, but I will be."

"I killed someone."

It was a shock. Certainly not what she expected. "I am a criminal lawyer and I love and live with a murderer! How can that be?"

He stared at her, pain etched in every crevice of the face she loved. She stopped, remembering her promise. "I will listen to you before making any judgment. Who was he?"

"He knocked at my door and introduced himself. I invited him to come inside. I served him a delicious meal with sleeping pills. I watched him enjoy the food and fall asleep. I tied his hands and legs, put him in my car, and drove him away. How pleasing it was to see him completely at my disposal. He was my prisoner. Anytime I feel depressed, I think of that moment and rejoice."

"Where did you take him?"

"To a desert. I waited until he regained consciousness and was ready for my operation. I wanted him to feel the pain I had felt. I had decided to cut off two parts of his body—his tongue and his male organ."

Dolce's eyes widened. This was not what she expected. Murder in the heat of passion was understandable. This—this was torture.

He saw the shock and condemnation in her eyes. He had to tell her all, to relieve the pain within—even if it destroyed everything they had between them. "Please do not interrupt me. Yes, I took my time inflicting maximum pain. When his pain was excruciating, my face flared with ultimate happiness. That moment has kept me alive."

Dolce swallowed hard. "Did he bleed to death?" She tried to sound clinical but her head reeled with a terrifying assumption. *I am glad that he did not ask me to go to the desert with him. Would I have been operated on, too?*

"No, my job was not done. I dug a grave for him and shoved him into it. I covered his body with fine sand, but not his head. I compressed the sand over him by dancing on it. Then I drove far away and watched him with my powerful binoculars. Vultures circled his head. He could not scare them away. Gleeful, I watched them rip apart his face while he was still alive."

His voice softened. "You see, my drawings are art. I painted the scenery in my mind as colorful as Renoir's paintings. It is still in the gallery of my memory."

I had heard he comes from the region where they stone people to death. They call them 'honor killings.' Now, I'm told they feed people to vultures.

"Who was he?" she managed to say, swallowing back the bile that rose in her throat.

"He claimed to be my son-in-law."

"Was he?"

Dolce couldn't hold back the fury that was building. "What justification do you have for your criminal act?"

He tightened his hold on the arms of the chair and stared at the flame licking the hearth. "Listen to the rest of my story and then you decide."

"It was not a criminal act. You are condemning me before hearing the rest of my case." He looked at her and smiled, but without humor. "Perhaps I should have kept my secret."

Tight-lipped, she said, "Present your case." But she thought, *this is an extremely bizarre criminal case. Should I report him to authorities or not?*

"The revolution happened and suddenly everything turned upside down. Young people forgot the realities of life, and the revolution gave them a thrill that they had not experienced before. They felt powerful and thought that they could solve political, social, and economic problems overnight. Political parties popped out of nowhere and acted like black holes and swallowed most of our young."

"Were any of your children involved?"

"Yes, my only child became hotheaded and felt no need to listen to me. My young, innocent daughter, like other children, was in a sea of excitement and rode the high waves of the revolution without knowing how to surf. I did what I could."

"How old was she?"

"She was only 14 years old when the abyss gobbled her up,

and another more powerful void destroyed her. One party recruited her and then the ruling party executed her."

"What was she accused of?"

"Distributing the opposition's flyers on street corners!" he shouted. He leapt from the chair and started pacing the room, trembling as he ransacked drawers, looking for paper and pencil.

He turned and shouted. "In the name of God, they murdered a child for handing out flyers. Tell me, where the hell was the God who should have protected her!"

Paper and pencil in hand, he drew a man buried in a desert up to his neck and vultures tearing off his face. Then he stared at the drawing, smiled, and became silent.

Dolce asked, "Did you seek justification?"

"Yes, after her death, I went to the judge and protested that she was only 14 years old and was recruited to distribute flyers, a far cry from overthrowing the government."

"What did the judge tell you?"

"The magistrate said, 'If she is innocent, she will go to Heaven. Make sure that before you leave, you pay for the bullets that sent her to Hell.'"

I went home and planned my revenge. I bought an illegal gun, practiced shooting in the desert, and came up with a perfect plan. But it was interrupted."

"I doubted what I read in newspapers about executions in your country," she said. "But it seems I was wrong."

"One day before I was going to execute my plot, a man appeared at my door. He introduced himself as my son-in-law. I thought he was a foolish man, but he was not."

He looked at his drawing, remained silent for a minute, and then continued. "I told him that he could not be my son-in-law because my daughter was too young to marry and was executed a few days ago."

"What was his response?"

This man showed me his revolutionary identity card and said to me, "Our religion says that if a virgin, unmarried woman dies, she will ascend to Heaven. To prevent your daughter from going to Heaven, I had intercourse with her and then shot her. I am legally your son-in-law."

His eyes flooded with tears, which he wiped with the back of his trembling hand. "Now you know why I killed him. You may regret asking me to share the secret of my drawing. Please feel free to report me to the authorities."

His story had captured her heart in a way Dolce did not believe possible. She wiped his tears tenderly. "I do not wish to report you. That was a desperate act of love for your innocent daughter."

"I finally feel I can forgive myself. I feel a sense of peace now that I have shared my failing."

"I sense your daughter sends blessings for your deep devotion. Allow the power of love to elevate you again," Dolce said, turning away as a tear escaped.

"You will not report me to the authorities? Why not? I know in your eyes I have committed a great crime."

Dolce cupped his face in both hands and stared deeply into his eyes, hoping that what he would see reflected there was not condemnation, but love.

"You have not committed a crime. You have served justice."

Home Sweet Home

P. K. Joyce

When I saw them at first, my years of experience working in the Psychiatric ER in the State Hospital made me think that the elderly gentleman was the patient. The sadness on his face made me think that he was in grief from the recent death of his loving wife, a lifelong friend; and that the young man with him was trying his best to cheer him up.

The young man was six feet, three inches tall and carried his two hundred and seven pounds of body weight very well. Shoulders broad and held back, head upright and looking forward, abdomen flat. He took long, strong, purposeful strides as he walked up to the front desk of the psychiatric emergency room. He had a handsome face: hair cut short, bright eyes, nose and full lips perfectly proportioned. His face lit up, showing his pearly white teeth, when he smiled. He smiled a lot. It was a hot summer day and he was dressed appropriately in a tank top, shorts and sandals. The muscles of his arms, chest, abdomen, and thighs appeared well-developed and very strong, as if he lifted weights and exercised daily. His skin smooth, looked clean, well-moistened and soft. He was a handsome picture of health.

The elderly man explained with pain in his voice that the young man was his son, that his son was mentally retarded from birth, and that his son had the diagnosis of "poor impulse control." His son's name was Albert. He said Albert was 23 years old but was functioning at the age of 15. He said it became impossible for Albert and himself to continue to live together. They argued a lot. Albert wanted to go out, to stay out and did not follow his requests to tell him where he was going and with whom. Albert was losing his temper very often, and was becoming more aggressive towards him. Albert was much stronger than he was and could potentially harm him. He said that both have agreed that Albert needed to be placed in a home. Albert appeared very happy with this decision stating he wanted to get out of his father's house. Albert appeared as happy as his father appeared sad.

During the intake, Albert stated that he loved his body and wanted to spend most of his time taking care of it. He is ready to find a wife, and wanted to love her the way he saw how his father loved his Mom until she died. He cannot remember when and why his Mom died. It seemed like a long time ago. He missed his mother — she knew how to make him laugh and would allow him more freedom than his strict father. He was their only child.

Albert was admitted to the Psychiatric ER with the goal of finding him a group home as soon as possible. It was difficult to find a group home for Albert. The social worker called many times every day to all the possible places, but the days turned into weeks and the weeks became months. In the beginning, Albert had a difficult time adjusting and got angry when he did not get his way. With time, patience and adjustment of his medications, his anger was under control, and soon he became more respectful and compliant. He remained happy, confident, and the not-taking-anything-too-seriously-attitude continued to shine.

The Psychiatric ER is a locked-down unit, with very little for the patients to do. Albert did not like to watch TV. The patient with the strongest personality usually decided what channel the TV would be on, and that would not be a program Albert wanted to watch. Albert got to know the staff very well. He kept walking around the unit many times a day and actually became another set of eyes and ears for staff and would sometimes alert us if a patient was in need. After three months of asking several times daily, a group home finally accepted Albert. He did not believe it until the van came and took him away.

Four days later, at about midnight, Albert was brought back to our ER. The next morning, he met me at the door and explained to me what happened. He said he was not hungry, but felt like eating something; said he went into the fridge and took a slice of bologna. He said that in our ER, we gave him a late night snack. Suddenly, he was grabbed and the bologna was savagely snatched from him. He said he got upset and became very angry. He said he was able to free himself, ran for the mop down the hall, and threw it at the attendant who grabbed him. The mop fell short, and the stick on the mop broke. He admitted he threw the mop very hard.

Then he said, "I am so sorry. I am very sorry. I explained to the attendant and to the supervisor who was called in that I knew what I did was wrong. I'll never go into the fridge again after 9.00 P.M. I'll never get so upset and angry again." He said in a softer voice that he will tell me in confidence that "the attendant did not explain to the supervisor, how he savagely snatched the bologna from me, but that's OK. I only, really want to go back, not stay here in the psychiatric ER any longer." He said he made some friends in the home. His friend Danny allowed him to lift his weights: his face lit up, his eyes a-glitter, and his smile showed his beautiful teeth as he spoke of his new friends.

The psychiatrist called the group home and spoke to the supervisor, who insisted that the only way Albert can be readmitted to the group home is that his medications have to be increased to subdue him some more. This was explained to Albert, who agreed to take the increase doses of medications. The next day I saw him, sitting quietly, starring at the TV with no reaction as to what was showing on the set. A great part of his personality suppressed. Later that day, the transportation van arrived and took him back to the group home.

Vacation Questionnaire

Emily Keeler

    Have you ever gone back to school and had to write a story about your vacation? Did you ever have a dingbat say it had to consist entirely of questions? Can you imagine calling a bunch of questions a short story?
    What was your most unforgettable experience? Have you ever had to go real bad? Have you ever been in a john in Jordan? Have you ever straddled an oblong floor-level toilet? Did you have trouble keeping your balance? Did your pants get: a. wet, b. soiled, c. both? Did any change fall out of your pockets? Were there any flies? Would air freshener win out in this place? Did the flush mechanism work? Did you ever figure out how it worked?
    Did you feel greatly relieved, have your money belt, your fanny bag, your back pack all hitched up and discover the lock on the door was rusted shut? Did you take out your traveling tool kit Swiss army knife? Did you break all your fingernails trying to get the damn thing open? Did you look at your watch and know you had missed an important departure time? What language did you swear in?
    Did anyone hear when you pounded on the door? How come there wasn't anyone else in the restroom? Was this section suddenly closed off for security reasons? Where was your tour group by now? Was the leader of your group an advocate of tough love? How long did you have to wait? Have you ever been put on hold? Just how do sheiks get their harems? Would they soon figure you were no spring chicken? Would they give you latrine detail?
    Did you even remember how to say hello in Arabic? Did you finally yell, "Help," loud and shrill in English? Have you ever heard a wolf howl? Are Arab men allowed in women's johns?
    How many came to the rescue? Did the English-speaking one suggest from outside that you scale the eight-foot tile wall? Did you ask him if he had a ladder? Have you ever tried to balance a rickety ladder on a floor that is largely a slanted pool with a

raised, rounded edge? Did the ladder shake a little when you climbed to the top? Have you ever been on a flying trapeze?

Was this the first time you could look down at men? Did you feel sudden empowerment? Have you ever been in one of those groupie trust deals where they blindfold you and tell you to fall? Did you take advantage of your power position? Did you tell him you wanted Lawrence of Arabia?

Did he tell you the only way you could catch up with the group was to get on another camel? Have you ever been on a spitting camel when it rises to its full, majestic height? What rating would you give it on the Richter scale? Do you think camels should have seat belts?

When you caught up with the group, did the guide announce you were being given the favor of climbing a minaret? What was it like when there were no more window openings? Have you ever climbed a thousand little bitty triangle steps, up a spiral in complete darkness? Did you put your hands out to keep from falling? Did the wall feel kind of lumpy? Just where do bats sleep in this part of the world?

Will you ever: a. ride another camel, b. accept another favor, c. lock the john door? Do you dream in questions? Dingbat, how do you get off the merry-go-round?

Christmas Lights at Home

Ken Yaros

Who doesn't enjoy Christmas lights? Unless, of course, they're still up the following July. Whether it's New York City or Waikiki, holiday lights banish winter gloom. For us kids, the house suddenly became bright and promising. Our hopes and dreams were wrapped up and placed beneath the decorated tree. It didn't take much to fire up our imaginations.

I remember the early '50's when I was a young child living in Reading, Pennsylvania. We must have been quite poor. Our street was lined with small, ancient row homes. There were few decorations visible from the street. But Mrs. Dunkle, across the street, had one of those lighted, bubbling fixtures in her front window. You know the ones. Where did those bubbles come from? Where did they go, I wondered, as I pressed my nose against the cold glass? No one seemed to know — it was magical.

Many years later, we lived in Longmeadow, Massachusetts, at Christmastime. Our family had prospered. It was 1976. I was a new dad. The town, a postcard-perfect New England village, boasted a green complete with a white church. Every Christmas, a colorful nativity scene graced the green. The church was brightly lit. A generous fir wreath covered its oversized front doors. The library, city hall, and firehouse nearby were trimmed with colored bulbs similar to those found on many nearby homes.

Young families had moved into newer, even more affluent sections of town. They engaged in friendly competition to outdo their neighbors with holiday lights that covered every surface of their mansions, including the roof. Some were incredibly elaborate, with musical characters.

On the edge of the green stood an older, stately colonial home that sat back from the road. That Christmas eve it snowed heavily. As we walked by the house with our young son, we noticed its Christmas lights for the first time. They were simple — no flashing lights, Santa, or reindeer. No icicles or colored bulbs. The large pine in the front yard was undecorated — the yard pristine. In each of the many windows stood a stout, bright white candle. Their glow reflected gently to the sidewalk, causing the snow to sparkle as though miniature diamonds had been sprinkled on the ground. It was so quiet, you could hear the flakes land.

Every year that house looked the same, white candles in the windows. The scene spoke to us of peace, purity, simplicity, and hope. It was the perfect contrast to glitzy holiday ornaments and commercial distractions. At last, a sanctuary to brighten the soul on a chilly winter's evening. For wherever there is a glowing candle in the darkness, there's room for optimism.

Sometimes I wonder how many others felt the same way after seeing this 150-year-old house candle-lit. We moved away years later. Do new owners live there now? If so, has anything changed? I'd like to believe its lights still shine over the snow — an inspiring example of a real New England Christmas.

While none of us can travel back in time, holiday lights can lift our spirits. It might be for just a moment, but those seconds can awaken fond memories long put aside.

So What's A John Wayne?

Mardie Schroeder

If you want to participate in a horse drive there are a few things to consider. You'll be driving some fifty-plus horses from point A to point B. Usually over five or six days. Once the drive starts there's no stopping. Oh, you do stop for lunch and pitch a tent at night. If you're lucky you may be able to wash off the day's filth in a freezing brook. But maybe not.

You may be given a green horse to ride. No, that's not the color of the horse. It's a horse that's half broke. Could very easily do something stupid, and most likely will. But at the end of the drive, if you've done your job, he'll be a good horse to ride and he'll have some smarts about him.

Pouring rain, sleet coming sideways stinging your cheeks, barely able to see? Maybe you'll have time to unfasten your slicker from behind your saddle. But then again, maybe not. Don't think for one minute a little rain will stop the drive. Oh, did I mention you pay money to do this?

If you've ever seen a herd of running horses, you know they're all bunched up together. No stragglers there. If they're running there must be some danger so nobody wants to be left behind. In fact, they all want to be first. So where does that leave you?

Well, for sure you don't want to be in the middle of the pack. That's the most dangerous place to be. Remember, you're the one driving, not the one being driven. Your job is to keep the herd together, moving in one direction. Don't let any horse get away from the herd. And by the way, your horse will want to be in the middle of the pack, so you have to keep him on the outside. If he's green (you already know what that is), he'll think you're a dumb jerk who doesn't know where you're supposed to be.

Before the start of the drive, wranglers come around and make sure your cinch is tight and everything is fastened onto the saddle properly. Everyone's eager to get started, but believe me this is a crucial part of the preparation. Everything is done to prevent any accidents. Let's not even think about that. If anything comes off your saddle during the ride, just kiss it goodbye.

Finally, someone shouts, "Head 'em on out." And away you go. You start out nice and orderly, but I guarantee it won't stay that way.

Once horses get to running in a pack, they totally forget you're on their back, and believe me they couldn't care less. You have to be prepared to jump logs, duck under tree branches, avoid pitfalls, other horses, etc. In other words, you have no control over your horse at this point.

On one of my drives we were moving along at a pretty nice clip. That means a gallop. All of a sudden a lady comes up alongside me with terror in her voice. "I lost my stirrups." She's reaching out to me like she's expecting me to do a John Wayne. You know, pull her off her horse onto mine. Well, that wasn't going to happen.

"Just grind your rear end into that saddle and keep it there," I said. "Eventually those stirrups will find you."

So unless you're comfortable riding at a full gallop without stirrups, maybe a horse drive isn't for you.

How does golf sound?

Season of the Witches

Barbara Weeks Huntington

Hair flying from the open windows of her parents' Chevy, Kathy sang harmony to my mournful, "Take off your old coat and roll up your sleeves. Life is a hard road to travel, I believe." But our travel was anything but mournful. We had just graduated from high school and were exuberant with our success in conning our parents, who thought we had a place to stay for the Berkeley Folk Festival.

Actually, Kathy had an address from a friend of a friend's distant relative we hoped was still valid, but we weren't concerned. Drunk on the times, a couple of sheltered suburban kids, we thought we were cool since we had actually tried booze, but it would be another year before we could identify the scent of marijuana.

The Central Valley of California is hot by late June, and air conditioning was not standard in Chevy's in the early 60's, so we alternated towels, dampened by a canteen of water for evaporative cooling, on the back windows.

Highway 99. Miles of crops. Cotton, beets, and billboards with pictures of women in one-piece suits diving into motel swimming pools, or waitresses in perky white aprons pouring steaming cups of coffee. We sang over the grind of diesel trucks until our voices croaked. We ached for the braceros bent over rows of green, choked by swirling dust devils. When billboards advertising Selma, Raisin Capital of the World, loomed among the grapevines, we thought about a different Selma—Selma, Alabama, where members of the Student Nonviolent Coordinating Committee (SNCC) were fighting for civil rights. In our naïve, white suburbanite homage to the Civil Rights movement, we made a brief stop in Selma, California, to parade in the town square so we could say we marched in Selma.

Following our map, we arrived at a huge gray Victorian house silhouetted against the fading sunset. The large front window was boarded up. Cats roamed through trees and high grass in the front yard as we dragged our gear and sleeping bags to the door. Four girls who didn't know who we were answered our knock. They told us they were powerful witches and invited us into the stifling interior, which smelled of cooked cabbage and cat shit. One girl, in a long tattered skirt and many strands of beads, led us upstairs to a shabby parlor, then helped us lug our stuff up an even steeper, wobbly wooden staircase to our room. Down a short hall was the bath. No roof, just open to the sky.

    I awoke to cats treading across my sleeping bag and flea bites all over my body. Kathy was sitting on a sagging chair in the corner, examining her legs. We both jumped to a knock on our partially open door as a cheerful voice called us to breakfast. The witches were much more sparkly than we were as we joined them for peanut butter on toast and some sort of herbal tea. When we asked about what kind of witches they were, they assured us they were good to people they liked, but put spells on people who crossed them. They told us of a blues harpist who had moved in with one of them. When he stole her money, they put a hex on him. They laughed that he thought he had removed the spell when he put a stake through a pigeon and left it on their front lawn.

    That day, after spending some of our food and gas money for calamine lotion and bug spray, Kathy and I found some cute guys who were in charge of a locked parking lot near the university who said we could park our car there to sleep in it when they closed at night as long as we moved it out when they opened in the morning. We left the witches' house never to return. At least the car was free of fleas.

    Then the folk festival opened at the university. Joan Baez, Doc Watson, Alameda Riddle, Mississippi John Hurt. We worshiped them the way kids in the future worshipped rock stars. But they were accessible! Since we could not afford the $12.00 fee for the entire festival, we paid for a few sessions at fifty cents or a dollar, but hung out late at night outside the main events and jammed (singing, playing spoons, or beating rhythm on whatever we could find) with our heroes. Loquats were ripe in Berkeley and they supplemented any of the shared snacks that made up our meals. If joints were passed, I never saw them, or perhaps just didn't know what they were. After a few glorious days in Berkeley, we returned home. Instead of jamming with folk stars, we played our guitars and sang in a suburban Shakey's Pizza Parlor in exchange for the pizzas people ordered and never picked up.

The following fall I headed to the University of Washington for college. I found coffeehouses and sang for coffee between sets of the real folk singers. I was kind of interested in a guy named Mike Murphy who played a mean blues harmonica. One night as we sat around the coffee house, I bragged about jamming with Baez at the Berkeley Folk Festival. Mike said, "I've been to Berkeley. Had a girlfriend there who was a witch. She tried to put a spell on me, but I'm a warlock, so I ran a stake through a pigeon and left it on her front lawn."

Occurrence at Dachau

Barbara McMikle

As a child, I was fascinated by my mother's tales of parishioners who sighted ghosts of their deceased loved ones in our church. Our priest supported the sightings, saying, "As long as they are remembered they live again. We must not forget." His words held me spellbound. But as years went by and childhood faded ever further into the past, I began more and more to scoff at the possibility of contact with what my mother called "the other side."

I was too sophisticated to believe. That was my attitude until fate intervened to make me a believer. It happened at Dachau Concentration Camp. A small voice from out of that camp's death-drenched past called to me for help.

I visited Dachau with my 16-year-old niece, Stephanie, in August of 1964, almost 20 years after the camp was liberated by American soldiers. The major reconstruction of the site into an extensive memorial to the many inmates who died there had just begun in 1964. Therefore, much of the site was left as it was at the time of the liberation, allowing visitors a glimpse into the unaltered past.

As I write, I live the day again. Rain that morning had dwindled into a tired drizzle. The overcast sky dropped a funereal pallor across the landscape. As no guided tours existed, my niece and I wandered through the camp on our own.

We passed by a high, scarred wall where executions took place. We looked at ovens that once disposed of the dead. In the museum, we saw pictures of naked bodies piled high behind the crematorium and in what appeared to be boxcars. By that time revulsion was choking me.

I had neither the heart nor the stomach to see anything more at Dachau, and my niece shared my feelings. We wandered to a bench near the entrance where we sat in silence, both of us struck dumb by the horrors that we had seen. I tried to numb my mind, to not think of the long-ago torture and death that befell the inmates of this place. But there was no denying, the sense of the past lingered in the air, a haunting presence.

When the cry came, the voice was so faint we looked at each other, both wondering if we'd actually heard anything.

Then it came again, a bit louder, enough so that I could make out the words. "Frau, helfen Sie mir. Hilfe! Hilfe."

I looked over my shoulder, certain the cry came from that direction. One of the single-storied buildings we'd seen here and there on the grounds stood not 30 yards behind us. Although it was in a state of ill repair, with peeling paint and dirt-encrusted windows, it was in better shape than the others, many of which were hardly more than foundations.

The cry came again, unchanged, word for word.

My niece, who had also turned to look, nudged me. "Do you see that?" she asked in a near whisper.

I nodded. Behind one of the windows, a face was dimly visible. The windowpane was too dirty to make out features.

The face moved. "Frau Hilfe. Bitte." It was clearly a man's voice.

I paused, frozen in a moment of indecision. Was this a situation that we could handle? Or something to run away from? Ordinarily I would not hesitate to respond to a cry for help, but caught in the grip of the horror of this place, I felt uneasy.

The cry came again, weaker this time and so piteous it reached through all barriers of doubt and directly to my heart. I stood up. "Come with me," I said, beckoning to my niece.

"Come with you where?" she asked, remaining firmly planted on the bench.

"Whoever it is needs help. Wood swells in wet weather. Maybe the door is stuck. Let's see what we can do."

"I'm not going over there," she said.

Her unwillingness cut through my resolve. For a reason I could not explain, not even to myself, I didn't want to go there, either. It took a long moment and a deep breath for me to persuade myself the need to give help was paramount, beyond argument. "All right," I said. "Just wait here. I'll be right back."

But she came with me anyway, saying, "I can't let you go alone."

We were at the door in minutes. I knocked. Called out. Waited. No response came.

"There's no sound in there, Aunt Barbara," my niece said. "I bet whoever was there got out already."

What she said was possible, although we'd seen no one leaving. I took several deep breaths, trying to rid myself of a persistent feeling that someone still in there needed my help. He had spoken directly to me. "Helfen Sie mir Frau," he had called. Frau. That was me.

"Let's find out anyway," I said quietly. I took hold of the doorknob and pushed. The door opened with little effort, groaning on its rusted hinges as it swung inward.

"Aunt Barbara, please don't go in there," my niece said, her voice tight with apprehension.

"It's something I have to do." I replied. "You wait out here."

I stepped through the door. Inside, it was heavily shadowed with only a faint film of light sifting in through the filthy windows. Stacks three levels high of what had once been bunk beds indicated the building had been used as a barracks. Now the support slats were broken, the boards split and lying every which way, looking like skeletal remains of what once was. The stench of mold was almost suffocating.

"Hello," I called. "Anybody in here?"

The only response was the rustling sound of a rat that suddenly scampered across the floor. From the doorway, I could pick out the window where we had seen the face. Something I could not resist drew me to that window.

I stepped carefully over the dirt-strewn broken floorboards until I stood at that window exactly where we had seen the face. Cobwebs almost covered every pane. The heavy dust on the floor below was disturbed only where I had stepped. Until I arrived, no one had stood at that window for a long time. All around me the near darkness seemed suddenly filled with watching eyes. I felt the skin on my face tighten My scalp bristled.

"What did you find out?" my niece asked as I stepped free of the foul-smelling barracks.

"Nothing," I said, because there was nothing I could bring to words.

It has been 40 years since I heard that anguished cry. My mother would tell me that I'd heard a voice from the other side. I'd agree with her. But that explanation does not go far enough. Someone from a different time, from a different dimension, called to me for help that I did not, could not give because I did not know how.

Not until I recalled the words of the pastor of my childhood did the truth find me. He said, "As long as you remember them, they live again." He meant the deceased. Now, if I could go back in time, I'd know the help to give. In that barracks, when I sensed the unseen eyes watching me, I would not know fear. I would call out into the darkness, "You are not forgotten."

Dorothy Stang

Arthur Raybold

I celebrate the life of Dorothy Stang.

Rewards the patient with its revelation.

At the time of her death, no church bells rang.

Devoted to the rain forest people,

Who found strength in her Anapu steeple,

She fought off ranchers and timber-takers,

Dirty politicos and Amazon-rapers.

Paid gunmen stalked her to a remote spot,

But prior to their getting off a shot,

She pulled out her Bible to read aloud.

They traded six shots for the Word of God.

She has found comfort in His staff and rod.

Monte Sol Police Chief Ismael Romero

Diana Amsden

From: *The Stained-Glass Woman, a Tale Of Suspense*
VOL. 3 The Winged Victory

"Do you not see how necessary a world of pains and troubles is to school an intelligence and make it a soul?"
— John Keats, Letter

After going by the coroner's office (no surprises), I went to the station and notified Riverside, California, police that we suspect Riverside resident Orlando Tare of the homicide of his wife and six children.

Experts are examining the refrigerator for evidence of tampering.

I filed witnesses' statements. I took one from Mrs. Tilly García of 236 Pine Street, Monte Sol, a neighbor who witnessed the delivery of the refrigerator:

"A Navajo van was parked in the driveway yesterday. I heard the movers grousing. One said, 'These impractical academics! That stupid professor shipped this junk all the way from California. It would've been cheaper to send a check. I'd be ashamed to give this stuff to the Salvation Army. In fact, they might refuse even to take it. It should go to the dump.'"

I called Navajo Van Lines; I have to interview those men. After typing and signing my report, I drove home.

I walked in my front door at nine p.m. to be met by my sweet Araceli, who was carrying a mug of eggnog in each hand. She was wearing the red velveteen robe I gave her last Christmas.

"The kids are in bed," she said. Above her head, mistletoe

dangled from the ceiling. To be polite, I pecked her forehead, but had to tell her I'd had the worst Christmas of my life, and had to shower and brush my teeth. Eggnog afterward.

* * *

I let the hot water pummel my body a long time. The victim I found slumped against the front door at 238 Pine Street was the girl I was in love with back at Barranca High School. Nadia Esmand, the only Anglo in the junior class, was the best student. The girls envied the red-haired beauty and teased her until she cried.

Then, in the middle of her junior year, Nadia combined her junior and senior year, and would graduate with the senior class. Valerie had the best grades in the senior class and expected to be valedictorian, so Principal Procopio Roybal had a problem.

He and the basketball coach, Eddie Medina, stood in front of our class. On the blackboard, they listed Valerie's grades in one column, Nadia's in another, giving three points for an A, two for a B. Their grades matched, except Valerie took one more class, getting a B. The principal totaled the grades. Valerie's total was two points higher, so they made her valedictorian and Nadia salutatorian.

Nadia was too young and naïve to know they had cheated her, but I was three years older, and I knew that grades should be *averaged*.

With money I earned selling greeting cards and magazine subscriptions to friends and neighbors, I bought a six-inch trophy, a golden girl in mortarboard and gown standing on a pedestal, and had it engraved:
NADIA ESMAND
BARRANCA HIGH SCHOOL
1949

I gave it to her at graduation. In college, she would learn that grades are averaged, and realize she had been cheated. I wanted her to have the statuette to look at and know that I knew the truth, and cared, and wanted to honor her. I knew she was too good for me, and could do better than me, but I could still be her true friend and champion.

I saw the statuette on the bureau in Nadia's bedroom at 238 Pine Street.

* * *

Figuring I'd wasted enough water, I got out of the shower, dried, hung up my towel, brushed my teeth, and shaved. The guy in the steamed-up mirror is still the ugly dude who barely met police height and weight requirements. *But I'm smart.*

I put on the red plaid robe Araceli gave me last Christmas and came out of the bathroom. Bing Crosby was singing "White Christmas." On a red tablecloth lay my favorite Christmas dinner: *carne adobada*, garlic toast, salad with *guacamole*, Collins Street fruitcake from Texas, and plenty of eggnog.

The kids were home from school and Araceli had been with them all day, so after dinner, I helped clean up. Then Araceli and I sat side by side on our red suede loveseat. Between us and our picture window stood our seven-foot Christmas tree with candle-shaped lights. We open gifts on Christmas Eve, so the skirt under the tree was bare.

I summarized my day for Araceli, omitting details that might distress her. "I recognized Nadia Esmand. When I played basketball at Barranca High School, she was a cheerleader. When she came back from college, she gave me the cold shoulder."

"She thought she was too good for you."

"That's what I thought then. But now that I've seen crime victims, I doubt it. She might've been traumatized and didn't want to be seen by anybody.

"In high school, she dressed well and liked bright colors. Christmas Eve, she wore an old housedress." *She'd had six kids. But to me, she was still beautiful.*

I felt like crying, so I was glad Araceli took my mind off my bad day by telling about her Christmas Day with the kids. I found myself remembering the six dead angels with rosy cheeks and cherry-red lips. I got up and went into our kids' bedroom to listen to them breathe. I thanked God, kissed their foreheads, and left without waking them.

I sat back down with Araceli. "Something broke my heart: The Esmands drive a new Cadillac, but their grandkids had no Christmas tree. In the living room, I saw a green ribbon zigzag tacked up on the wall, a greeting card at the tip of each zig and each zag. Under it, on a bench, were six presents that looked like kids' books."

Araceli said quickly, "Maybe their grandparents had a tree in the trunk of their Cadillac to surprise their grandkids."

I told her no, I'd seen Mr. Esmand open his car trunk to put their box of presents back in. "When I saw Mrs. Esmand, I recognized her. When she identified her daughter's and grandchildren's bodies, she sounded as if she were reciting an inventory."

"Some people cope with grief by closing off their feelings and focusing on trivia," said my understanding Araceli, who likes to give people the benefit of the doubt.

"I think Mrs. Esmand's cold. But Mr. Esmand was taking it hard. This is confidential, Araceli: he thinks his son-in-law killed Nadia and the kids. Nadia left him a couple of months ago."

"You've told me that it's usually the husband or lover, and that a woman's in the greatest danger when she leaves him."

I didn't tell Araceli about the heartbreaking procession of men from the medical examiner's office carrying seven stretchers on which lay one adult-size and six small body bags. However, I did tell her that Mr. Esmand cried out, "I wish it had been me!"

Coming Home

Norma Posy

Diagnostics having reported no errors, synaptic modules powered up and communication channels proceeded to activate. Legacy software programs and data downloaded from the ship's storage vault and installed.

414 awoke.

"Greetings."

The message being received and noted, 414 opened its optical transducers. "Greetings," it sent in reply while sitting up.

It took a bit for its visual processor to finish booting up and organizing itself. 414 slowly became aware of gray bulkheads, a white overhead and deck. Through a passageway, 414 saw the approach of another being. A message arrived in 414's receiver. "Welcome to the cosmos. I'm 390. I'll be your tutor. How do you feel?"

How am I supposed to feel? 414 scanned its internal diagnostics report. "No errors."

"Excellent," replied 390, unplugging 414 from the charging outlet. "Come, let me show you around and introduce you to your crewmates."

* * *

The starship cruised on, monotony occasionally punctuated by a leisurely linger to survey yet another planet. The crew numbered exactly 120, each assigned to a specific task. Some tended the ion engines. Others were responsible for navigation. A group, assigned as defensive warriors, had never been activated. They were suspended in the armory, on trickle charge, in sleep mode.

Occasional fatal trauma could be expected during a journey of many thousands of years. This had happened a few hundred times. 414 learned it had been assembled to replace 212 in the maintenance group. While outside the ship to clean space dust off the windows, 212 had been struck by a small errant meteor. Replacements, such as 414, were numbered sequentially as they emerged from the ship's womb.

At the top of the crew hierarchy were three charged with will. They imbued the ship and crew with the motivation to carry on. This vital task had become difficult, as the original intent of the voyage receded into a dim mist of slowly degrading memory.

* * *

Uneventful stretches of time provided ample opportunity for pastimes. 414, more naturally disposed to philosophical exploration than to the challenging logic games available in the recreation chamber of the ship, found itself intrigued by unending discussions of such arcana as:

"Why are we here?"
"Where did we come from?"
"Did we evolve, or were we designed?"
"Everything happens for a reason."
"No, it doesn't."
"Free will is an illusion."
"What is time?"
"It's just plain obvious to me that we were designed," offered 227.

"But by what or whom?" asked 290, looking around. "I hope 188 is out of range."

188 floated into the cabin, eliciting a mild "Damn" from 290.

"No, I'm not out of range. I've expressed my conviction before. We were created."

"Here we go," 227 sent to 414.

188 continued, "Meat. We were made by meat. We've seen plenty of planets with lots of meat running around. We've never come across a planet with anything like us. But we've occasionally encountered meat that makes machines. I know we are a far cry from steam pistons and pulley wheels. But if meat can create that much . . ."

"Oh, nonsense," interrupted 227. "Foolish talk. We are so obviously superior to meat. I simply cannot imagine any value to your wild thesis. Besides, if meat made us, who made the meat?"

414 kept its thoughts to itself, content to simply absorb the heated discussion. *227 is arguing from ignorance. "I can't imagine it, therefore it cannot be." But 188 offers a possibility worth considering.*

* * *

"Approaching planetary system." The alert emanated from the navigation deck. "Class C star. Third planet looks promising. Liquid water."

The commanding trio of those with will sat up and took notice. "Reverse thrust. Establish orbit."

"Aye, aye, sir," responded the engine-room crew.

"Analysis?"

A few minutes went by before the analytic group responded. "Organic molecules detected. Oxygen-rich atmosphere. Ambient temperature on the high side of comfort. Lots of flora. And some meat."

"Take a few orbits," the will triad ordered. "Scan for items of interest."

414 followed the proceedings with curiously enhanced attention.

Presently, the ship's scanners spoke. "Widespread evidence of collapsed civilization. Lots of ruins, heavily radioactive in places. Meat is present, but sparse."

"Prepare landing party."

* * *

414 found itself part of the landing party. The excursion module set them down in a grassy spot strewn with rubble and surrounded by demolished structures. Small furry meat scurried away squeaking. The hatch opened. The landing party strode forth. 414 looked around. "This seems to be the ruins of a once-mighty civilization."

"It is sad," another member of the landing party replied. "I wonder what happened. It isn't just decayed. It is demolished."

A figure of meat climbed out of a hole in the ground,

emaciated, wearing rags.

The figure fell at the feet of 414 and croaked through cracked lips. "Feed me."

A program came alive deep within 414, a program that had not been activated for many thousands of years. 414 suddenly knew the purpose of its being.

"Yes, master."

Contributors

Amsden, Diana Avery, Ph. D. — Diana's academic background is mainly anthropology, archaeology, architecture, and art history. Googling her name reveals scholarly and popular works, and an *Atlas Shrugged* index. The 2014 *Guilded Pen* published her poems and a short story. The 2016 *A Year in Ink* (volume 9) published a chapter from volume 1 of her upcoming trilogy, *The Stained Glass Woman, a Tale of Suspense*, a multigenerational family saga. Website: DianaAmsden.com.

Asher, Laurie — Growing up, Laurie acquired her formal education on the boardwalk at Venice Beach, California. As a product of the California Public School System she never did quite master grammar or punctuation skills and will always require excellent editors! She has written one currently unpublished children's book in honor of her nephew, and is working on two other novels. She started writing after retiring from a real estate career. Her favorite 'literary' quote is: "Everything stinks until it's finished." — Dr. Seuss. Laurie currently serves as secretary of the SDW/EG board of directors.

Barrons, William — "Having been born on the coldest day in February of 1926, in the coldest city in Michigan – Cadillac —," Bill says he somehow survived the Great Depression. He joined the Marines quick at 17. Served 2 ½ war years, including in the Pacific, got out, got married, went to college and had kids. Bill rejoined the Marines in 1949 as a Public Information Officer. He had great joy writing for newspapers and TV. Became a 2nd Lt. Platoon Commander, a position he really loved. When his wife got sick and nearly died, Bill went on inactive duty to care for his family. He became a telephone equipment engineer in Chicago, then designed and sold home remodeling for 22 years. Retired at age 69, Bill did research and wrote full time. So far, he's written a dozen books and at age 90, he says he plans to continue writing, "until I'm 100!" Bill's published detective/mystery books about the San Diego Police Department's Homicide Detail include: *.22 Caliber Homicides; Nude Beach Homicides; Coldest Cold Homicides; Forever Homicides; Red Hot Homicides; Homeless Homicides; Rawhide Homicides;* and *Hellish Homicides.* He's currently working on *Holiday Homicides.* When not solving homicides, Bill works on his memoir *Marine Corps Daze* about his service in WWII and after.

Beeby, Gered—Gered is past president (2003) of the San Diego Writers/Editors Guild and remains on the Board as a Director-At-Large ("Official Greeter"). His suspense-thriller novel of industrial espionage, *Dark Option* (2002), was nominated for a PMA Benjamin Franklin award in the category, Best New Voice—Fiction (2003). He has written two screenplays. The first, "The Bottle Imp" is a deal-with-the-devil story based on Robert Louis Stevenson's 1892 classic tale. Gered has also written "Dark Option" for the screen. He has contributed to all *The Guilded Pen* anthologies since its first edition in 2012. Gered continues to work on screenplays, a short-story anthology of his own, and his memoirs. He also serves as a reviewer for the San Diego Book Awards.

Bonpensiero, Joseph (Lt. Col., USAF Ret.)—Joe was born, raised and schooled in San Diego's Little Italy where he learned the Sicilian fisherman's life beginning at seven years old. Not to his liking, he traded fishing as a profession and attended San Diego State University where he graduated and accepted an Air Force commission and headed to jet pilot training. He then became a careerist and world traveler. His first memoir, *Chocolate Moon,* recounted his days as an apprentice fisherman. In 2014, Joe published *NIPUTI...the Nephew,* an expose of his life under the shadow of evil—his Mafia uncle, Frank Bompensiero. Niputi debuted to wide acclaim resulting in book signings at the Las Vegas Mob Museum, an interview that aired on the Las Vegas NBC affiliate, and an article by Joe Deegan, *San Diego Reader.* In June 2016, Joe published *Dinner in Happy Valley,* a Vietnam tour memoir. The future holds publication of *Just My Shorts*—a short story/poetry anthology, and a fictional novel, *Liar's Potion* – an apocalyptic tale of mayhem when an ancient potion is discovered that eliminates man's ability to lie. Joe has contributed to *The Guilded Pen* anthologies since the first edition in 2012.

Buompensiero, Marcia — Is the author of *Sumerland, A Tale of Betrayal and Deliverance*, published in 2016. Writing under the pseudonym "Loren Zahn," Marcia also publishes the Theo Hunter mystery series: *Dirty Little Murders* (2009), *Deadly Little Secrets* (2015), and *Fatal Little Lies* (scheduled to debut in the spring of 2017). *Deadly Little Secrets* received a "highly recommended" rating from the SDW/EG Manuscript Review Committee and was a finalist in the 2015 San Diego Book Awards unpublished manuscript division. Her nonfiction work has appeared in *The Southern Cross*, the San Diego Diocesan newspaper. Marcia holds the office of Treasurer as a member of the SDW/EG board of directors and has been the managing editor of *The Guilded Pen* anthologies since 2013.

Carleton, Lawrence Richard — Larry has published and presented scholarly work in philosophy, cognitive science, and software development, thereby putting to use his advanced degrees in computer science and philosophy and his post-doctorate in cognitive science. In recent years, he has turned to short story writing. Larry is alarmed at the tendency in some to enforce intolerance toward those who question beliefs which are false and harmful. He thinks that if a belief gets bruised when it bumps up against reality, it is the belief, not the reality, that needs adjustment. Larry's short story writing is, in the main, an attempt to prompt interest in unfamiliar points of view — an exercise in promoting the acceptance or at least tolerance of diversity in responsible thought — but sometimes he just likes to tell a good story. His short stories have been published in all the editions of The Guilded Pen since 2012, and in other anthologies from time to time. He's now looking into publishing a collection of his best work. (Facebook: Lawrence Carleton)

Clement, Nancy, M.B.A. – When not fretting over how to lose 40 pounds before a class reunion, Nancy enjoys writing and sharing ideas to assist her readers so they can increase their wealth, happiness and well-being. She is a Realtor® and Mortgage Broker and wrote the "Dollar-Wise Diva" column for the *East County* on-line magazine. Her money-saving tips ranged from – how to spend less on college textbooks to how to stage a beautiful, low-cost wedding. She wrote and will publish "How is Buying a House Like Playing Baseball" in the fall of 2016. She can be reached at her website: www.Nancylement.com.

Converse, Alan — Al started writing Vietnam War press releases as a young naval officer, earning him recognition in the Pacific Fleet. After active duty in the Navy and earning his MBA, he entered the field of banking and later, government lending with the Small Business Administration. He has published five novels, *Bitch'n* (2012), *Die Again (2013), Boston Boogie (2014), Baja Moon (2015), and News from the East (2016)*. All are available on Kindle and Amazon. His short stories have appeared in previous issues of The Guilded Pen: "Warrior's Stone" (2012), "The Marble Game" (2013), "The Woods" and "Drippy Pants" (2014), and The Wake Up" (2015). He is currently writing a Vietnam fiction novel based on the 1967 deployment of his ship, *Eldorado*. Al is a John D. MacDonald fan, likes to read *Scientific American* and *The Economist* and hopes someday the San Diego Chargers will win the Super Bowl or the playoffs, or the Division, or something — please!

Crothers, Barbara — Barb hangs out with real writers hoping each of their Muses will accidentally sprinkle a few good words, points of view, grammar and punctuation on the characters she holds hostage. You know it could happen! Barb is a University of Redlands graduate, a Fellow of the Leadership Society and experienced years of drowning in legalese — which should help a bit, too. In the interim she will continue providing short stories (actually chapters of books-in-waiting) and poems for publication in our annual anthology. That should keep her occupied for a while.

Crothers, Fred — Is currently retired and living in San Diego. He has published short stories in every edition of *The Guilded Pen* since 2012. Fred is currently hard at work on a book of short stories of his experiences gleaned from personal memories of operating a tavern in Carson, Washington, from 1975 to 1980. It seemed an easy task to write about the many events that occurred during those five years of ownership, but Fred says he has spent many hours in rewrites and editing to present them in the best possible light, without making fundamental changes to these events to ensure their truth shines through. Originally, he expected to weave the stories into one long saga, but has decided they must be presented each in its own space. Fred thinks others will enjoy this glimpse of reality from yesteryear.

Diamant, Kathi—An award-winning author, actor, broadcaster and adjunct professor at San Diego State University, Kathi leads the Kafka Project, the official international search to recover a lost literary treasure, the missing writings of Franz Kafka. Her book, *Kafka's Last Love: The Mystery of Dora Diamant*, based on two decades of research, has been published in the US and UK, Spain, France, Russia and soon in Chinese and Portuguese (Brazil) translations. It won the Theodor Geisel Award, the "Best of the Best" in the 2004 San Diego Book Awards. As director of the Kafka Project at SDSU since 1998, Ms. Diamant has led the international effort to find the last writings of Franz Kafka which were confiscated by the Gestapo in 1933. Her research has taken her on extended research projects in England, Germany, Poland, and Israel, and is responsible for recovering original Kafka letters and artifacts.

Doublebower, Bob—Bob was born in Philadelphia and raised in the southern New Jersey town of Lindenwold. He attended Villanova University, where he received a Bachelor's Degree in Civil Engineering. He began his engineering work with Bechtel Power division in Washington, D.C. His career has taken him to Colorado, Arizona, Virginia, and California. He now maintains a consulting engineering practice, Regional Shorting Design, in San Diego county. Bob has been published in *The Guilded Pen* since 2012 and is currently working on a horror novel, *The Circling Bench*. Bob is past-president of the SDW/EG board of directors and currently serves as vice president.

Eberhardt, Marty — Marty has raised two sons and two public botanical gardens, Tucson Botanical Gardens and the Water Conservation Garden, through childhood and adolescence. She is enjoying a shift from left-brain writing activities, like grant and annual report writing, to the right-brain pleasures of poetry and fiction. She has published five poems in the last year. Marty is seeking representation for a novel based on the lives of an American family in 1960s Saigon, and has begun work on a lighter work, a botanical garden murder mystery.

Edge, Chloe Kerns — Chloe holds a degree in Lit/Writing from UCSD. She published in *Birdcage Review (1982)* and *Maize, Vol.6 (1983)*. *Tattoo (1988)* was published for women in prison. Chloe has been published in *The Guilded Pen since* 2012. She writes poems, nonfiction and is currently working on a memoir. Chloe has been teaching an ongoing Creative Writing Class for two years at Oasis in Escondido.

Feldman, David — Dave spent 30 years as copy editor at *The San Diego Union-Tribune,* 55 years working as a reporter and editor on newspapers, including *Stars & Stripes* in Europe and *The Honolulu Star-Bulletin*. He has taught journalism in colleges for 34 years. For the past four years, Dave has faithfully copyedited *The Guilded Pen,* and has been published in it since 2012. Dave serves on the SDW/EG board of directors and is currently fighting retirement, but he still accepts editing assignments when he's not tinkering with classic cars.

Hafner, Janet — Janet is a member of The Society of Children's Book Writers and Illustrators and the San Diego Writers/Editors Guild. Her debut middle-grade novel, *Eye of an Eagle*, received a "highly recommended" rating from the SDW/EG Manuscript Review Committee and is soon to be published. Two essays, *The Unknown,* and *One Photograph – Many Memories* are included in *The Guilded Pen, 5th Edition*. She enjoys writing for children and adding episodes to her memoir. Her professional career included teaching English as a Second Language and Spanish at Palomar College, training teachers in effective techniques for second language acquisition, and coaching corporate managers and supervisors to overcome linguistic challenges. She co-created *Conversemos*, a televised Spanish course offered throughout the United States. Travel influences her writing, as does a diary of dream sagas. When she isn't busy creating vivid characters or volunteering, she enjoys the company of her husband, sons and five grandchildren.

Harmon, Margaret — Margaret is an award-winning fabulist and humorist. She authored and illustrated *The Genie Who Had Wishes of His Own: 21st-Century Fables* (with a blurb from Ray Bradbury), *The Man Who Learned to Walk in Shoes That Pinch: Contemporary Fables,* and *A Field Guide to North American Birders: A Parody.* Her humor, fables and essays appear in national publications, on-line and on National Public Radio. www.margaretharmon.com

Hinaekian, Peggy — Peggy is of Armenian origin. She was born and raised in Egypt, and her paternal grandfather owned the largest private library in Egypt and introduced her to books in three languages (English, French and Armenian) at a very young age. Raised in a cosmopolitan environment, she became an avid reader and has kept a journal since the age of twelve. She was editor of the high school newspaper and wrote short stories. Peggy is an accomplished artist. The illustration on the cover of her debut novel published in 2015, *Of Julia and Men,* and the 26 images at the beginning of each chapter are her own artwork. View it on www.OfJuliaAndMen.com. Parallel to her art, Peggy writes essays and short stores. *Of Julia and Men* was included in the New York Times Book Review Magazine under "Discover New Titles - Great Stories, Unique Perspectives." The novel is entirely fictional except for its international settings — Peggy drew on her lifetime of world travel. "Looking for Rhett Butler" is her first monologue. Peggy is an internationally recognized and a well-established artist, living and working in the United States and in Switzerland. Visit: www.peggyhinaekian.artspan.com to see her art and read about her artistic career.

Huntington, Barbara Weeks — Barbara has been a civil rights worker, teacher, computer mail order house CEO, technical writer, marketing analyst/consultant, and director of a university program to assist underrepresented students enter PhD programs. She retired in 2013 as Director of Preprofessional Health Advising at SDSU and is co-author of *Writing About Me: a Step-by-Step Guide to Developing a Powerful Personal Statement for your Application to Medical School*. She earned a BS in Zoology from SDSU and an MBA from UCLA. She lives in Chula Vista surrounded by a drought-tolerant garden where she grows her own organic vegetables and walks her labyrinth of rocks and succulents. For several years she has published poems in *the San Diego Poetry Annual* and *A Year in INK*. Her selections in this anthology are from her soon-to-be-completed memoir, *Laughing Just to Keep from Crying ... and Rattlesnakes!*

Huntsman, Harry — Harry was born on a farm in Arkansas in 1925, the oldest of nine children. None of his family, neighbors or Sunday school teachers had more than an eighth-grade education. After fifteen years as a minister in Arkansas, Texas and California, he taught high school and middle school for twelve years. Harry is at work on a novel about the Tennessee River and the Civil War, and a memoir, *The Minister and the Mafia*. He was published in *The Guilded Pen* (2012 and 2013). Harry is a member and past president of the SDW/EG.

Janda, Anne — Anne was raised on a farm in Southwest Ohio. In 1967 she drove her blue four-door Chevy west and has been in California ever since. She graduated with a master's degree in Social Work from San Diego State University and became a licensed psychotherapist in private practice. Her short story was chosen for the 2016 Writers INK Memoir Showcase. She is writing a memoir which includes three women on her ancestral tree and herself. Their stories span two centuries. Anne is president of the San Diego Writers/Editors Guild.

Joyce, P. K. — Is the pseudonym for Joyce P. Kellawon, MD. MPH. She is a Medical Ethicist, a practicing medical doctor whose life's journeys have taught her humbling realizations. She appreciates the importance of, admires and enjoys the art of writing and is now ready to make her contribution. Her writings will reflect on all aspects of her work and life, indirectly and directly.

Keeler, Emily — Emily was born on a fruit farm in the Spokane Valley in a family with three brothers. Her mother was the daughter of Norwegian immigrants. Emily moved to San Diego in 1996 to be near her son, Chris, and his wife, Susie, and grandchildren. Emily has a BA in literature and an MA in counseling. She was a teacher, including a year-long-stint in Japan teaching US Army dependent children. She served as a lay counselor and a facilitator of groups in the Unitarian Universalist Church, volunteered at the Balboa Park Visitors Center, tutored school children, helped with voter registration, babysat her grandchildren, and taught Haiku poetry classes at OASIS. Emily is a lifelong learner. She enjoys reading, walking in Balboa Park, exercise classes at St.Paul's Manor (a retirement community): Qui Gong, Zumba Gold, and fitness with Crystal. She is writing a memoir of family stories titled "One Woman's Journey."

Lederer, Richard, Ph.D. — Recipient of an "Odin Award" for his contributions to the writing arts in San Diego, as well as multiple San Diego Book Awards. Life member Richard is the author of more than 40 books about language, history, and humor, including his best-selling *Anguished English* series and his current books, *Amazing Words, Challenging Words,* and *American Trivia Quiz Book.* Dr. Lederer's syndicated column, "Lederer on Language," appears in newspapers and magazines throughout the United States, including the San Diego *Union-Tribune,* and he is a founding co-host of "A Way With Words" on KPBS Public Radio. He has been named International Punster of the Year and Toastmasters International's Golden Gavel winner. He has been a contributor to *The Guilded Pen* since 2014.

Leech, Tom — Tom is the author of books on various subjects: presentations/public speaking, outdoors San Diego, world travel and children's poetry. His most recent book, with wife Leslie, is *The Curious Adventures of Santa's Wayward Elves*. Another recent one is the 2nd edition of *Say It Like Shakespeare: The Bard's Timeless Tips for Successful Communication*. Tom is also a prolific freelance writer with over 200 articles published in the *Mission Valley News, San Diego Magazine*, and business and travel publications. Tom's work was published in several issues of *The Guilded Pen* and other anthologies.

Leyse-Wallace, Ruth, Ph.D. — Ruth has published two books on the links between nutrition and mental health since retiring from clinical practice in dietetics. She is a frequent contributor to the newsletter of the Behavioral Health Nutrition practice group and has been published in *The Guilded Pen* since 2012. Ruth is past president of SDW/EG, serves on the board of directors, and served for three and a half years as editor of *The Writer's Life*, the monthly newsletter of SDW/EG. She initiated the SDW/EG Marketing Support Group, which enhances member-to-member communication. She enjoys traveling, and especially likes to read books on consciousness and spirituality.

Mayfield, Don — Don is a retired high school English teacher. He learned to write over those thirty years by responding to his own writing assignments. While teaching, Don led workshops sponsored by state and national teacher associations, the San Diego Writing Project, and the San Diego County Office of Education. Throughout his career he wrote curriculum guides for national, state, and local publication. His major non-fiction: life of a "desert rat" with family in a trailer and outhouse, behind the family fruit and date stand, outside Cathedral City, then a desolate desert town, 1950-57. Don contributes his work to contests, considers publication of his memoir, but he will be satisfied to produce a readable copy as a legacy to his family. Don hosts websites featuring anecdotes of a senior/grandfather/clips from a memoir: www.facebook.com/donmayfi and www.independent.academia.edu/MayfieldDonald

McCullagh, Caroline — Teaches creative writing at OASIS and at the Coronado Senior Center. She wrote a cookbook, *Sing for Your Supper*, for the San Diego Opera and helped write and performed in a short opera, *The Singing Mirror*. The first of her five novels, *The Ivory Caribou,* was published in 2016. She also writes book reviews for the San Diego Horticultural Society's *Let's Talk Plants* (since 2002) and for the Mensa Bulletin (since 2015). She and her writing partner, Richard Lederer, wrote *American Trivia*, a book of American history (published 2012), and the *American Trivia Quiz Book* (published 2014). They also write a daily item in the *San Diego Union-Tribune* on American history (since 2013). She was previously published in *The Guilded Pen* in 2013 and 2014.

McMikle, Barbara — Born in upstate New York, she earned a B.A. Degree in English and Journalism at Syracuse University. Upon graduation, she wrote advertising copy at agencies in New York and Miami. Wanting to get away from desk work and seek some adventure, she moved to California, attended SDSU, acquiring a teaching certificate and an M.A in Comparative Literature. Granted a Fulbright scholarship, she lectured and studied at several German Universities, achieving certification in 20th Century German history. Back in the US, she taught German at La Jolla High School and summers at several community colleges. Along with four novels published, including the current *Through the Dark Door of Time,* a historical romance dealing with social problems in San Diego directly after the Civil War, her short stories and non-fiction have appeared in publications in the US and UK.

Naiman, Joe — Joe is a freelance writer and the co-author of the baseball history book, *The San Diego Padres Encyclopedia* (2002), and is the author of *The School with All the Catchers* (2012), a history of the Crawford H.S. baseball program. He is also the author of a novel, *Another Chance* (2006). Joe has been published in *The Guilded Pen* since 2012. He has been a member of the Society for American Baseball Research since 1980 and was the coordinator of SABR's 1993 national convention in San Diego.

Nelson, Carl — During his first career, Carl rose from enlisted recruit to highly decorated U.S. Navy Captain. He served four tours of duty in the Vietnam War, one of which was for one year as Senior Advisor to the commander of combat riverine operations in the Rung Sat Special Zone (RSSZ) and Logistics base at Nha Be. His war decorations include the Legion of Merit, Bronze Star with combat V, two Air Medals, the Combat Action Medal, and 14 others. Carl's second career as a professor of international business at the California International Business University (CIBU) and writer has spanned twenty-nine years. His long fiction includes: *Madam President and the Admiral* (2008), a political/military/romance thriller that was nominated for a Pulitzer Prize; *Secret Players*, which won the San Diego Book Awards Association prize of "best thriller" of 2003; *The Advisor (Cô-Vân)*, a Vietnam War thriller won the 1989 Southern California Writers Conference's award for "best fiction." His non-fiction books include: *Import/Export: How to Take Your Business Across Borders,* (2009), *Your Own Import-Export Business: Winning the Trade Game* (1988); *Global Success; International Business Tactics of the 1990s* (1990); and *Managing Globally: A Complete Guide to Competing Worldwide* (1994). He is a member of the Authors Guild of America, PEN USA, and a life member of and twice served as president of SDW/EG. Carl and his wife Dolores are accomplished world travelers, having toured 15 countries in the past four years.

Peterson, Richard — Rick has written magazine articles and was a former staff writer for *Wholistic Living News*. He authored the article, "Stained Glass Television," in the *Journal of Popular Culture* (Vol. 19. No. 4); a chapter called "Electric Sisters" in the *God Pumpers: Religion in the Electronic Age* (Bowling Green State University Popular Press); and has been published in *The Guilded Pen* since 2012. He is working on a sci-fi suspense thriller. Rick serves on the SDW/EG board of directors as Membership Chairman, and has been a judge for the San Diego Book Awards since 2008.

Posy, Norma — After a lengthy career as a civilian scientist for the U.S. Navy designing submarine sonar systems, Norma retired in 2006 and published *Norma's Voice* (P.D. Publishing, 2006) which took first prize in the annual San Diego Book Awards. Norma's second book, *Side Pocket,* is a 73,000-word contemporary adventure/murder novel. *Side Pocket* took second place in the 2015 Beverly Hills book awards competition. Available at Amazon in soft cover and Kindle editions. www.norma-posy.com

Primiano, Frank — During his career as a biomedical engineer, professor, forensic investigator, and entrepreneur, Frank published in scientific, engineering, and medical journals and textbooks. In retirement, he is writing novels, short stories, and episodic autobiographical pieces. He was a finalist in the San Diego Book Awards 2008 Unpublished Novel, and 2013 and 2014 Unpublished Short Story competitions. His work appeared in SDW/EG's The Guilded Pen - 4th Edition in 2015, and anthologies published by the Writers' Workshop of the San Diego Community College Continuing Education Program, for which he was also an editor, and San Diego Writers' Ink. Frank lived in Philadelphia and Cleveland before moving to San Diego with his wife, Elaine.

Raybold, Arthur — Arthur has penned the *Home from the Banks* (poetry collection). In process: historical novel, more poetry.

Roberts, Laura — Laura can leg-press an average-sized sumo wrestler, has nearly been drowned off the coast of Hawaii, and tells lies for a living. She is the founding editor of Black Heart Magazine and publishes whatever strikes her fancy at Buttontapper Press. Blurring the lines between fact and fiction, Laura has penned 14 books, including the alphabetical travel guides *Montreal from A to Z* and *San Diego from A to Z;* the offbeat writing guides *NaNoWriMo: A Cheater's Guide* and *Confessions of a 3-Day Novelist;* and the satirical adventure tale, *Ninjas of the 512.* She is also the editor of the poetry collection *Haiku for Lovers,* and the new annual anthology *Everything I Need to Know About Love I Learned from Pop Songs.* She currently lives in an Apocalypse-proof bunker in sunny SoCal with her artist husband and their literary kitties, and can be found on Twitter @originaloflaura.

Sandy, Muriel — Muriel Sandy's travel articles have appeared in numerous nationally known newspapers in the United States and abroad. *When West Meets East: A Year in Asia on Our Own* was nominated a finalist in the San Diego Book Award competition 2015. Other stories she has written can be found in OASIS Journal 2014, and 2015. Last year saw the publication of her article "Steeped in Tradition" in *The Guilded Pen*, an anthology produced by the San Diego Writers/Editors Guild. This year she is delighted the guild has chosen to include "Woman in the Hijab."

Schroeder, Mardie — Mardie has been a member of a writing group for four years, and a member of the SDW/EG for three years. She writes the "What You Missed" column for the Guild's newsletter and is a board member. She was published in *The Guilded Pen* in 2014 ("The Watering Hole" and "Sudden Death"), in 2015 ("Argentine Tango"), and in 2016 ("So What's a John Wayne?" and "Good or Bad Luck"). "Good or Bad Luck" is an excerpt from her novel, *Go West for Luck Go West for Love,* published in November 2015.) visit: www.mardieschroeder.com

Warren, Sam — Sam got his start writing as the part-time editor of *This Week in Moscow,* the newsletter for the US Embassy in Moscow, USSR, while in the DIA in the middle of the cold war in 1967. After leaving the Army, he founded the LGBT Center in Orange County. He was the publisher of the *Santa Ana Journal* in Orange County, *The Border Business Journal* in Otay Mesa, editor of the *Uptown San Diego Examiner,* and is the author of a number of books as well as publishing books for other authors. He publishes a weekly column *San Diego Readers and Writers Events* and a webzine http://SDWriteWay.org. He is twice past president of SDW/EG and now lives part time in the southern Mexican beach town of Zipolite.

Winters, Gary—Gary authored *The Deer Dancer,* a multicultural novel about a Yaqui boy in Mexico. *The Deer Dancer* won the silver medal from UC Irvine for the Chicano/Latino Literary Prize; runner-up in the San Diego Book Awards; Best Novel 2010 Mensa Creative Awards; bronze 2011 Book of the Year award for Multicultural Fiction in *ForeWord Reviews Magazine.* The book found its way into libraries around the world and has been in the curriculum at Southwestern College, where *Poets & Writers Magazine* awarded Gary an honorarium to speak. *The Deer Dancer* is currently used as an example of poetical prose in the poetry workshop at Juvenile Hall in San Diego. He has also won awards for short story and photojournalism. His poetry has won numerous awards including winner of a Mensa global contest and was published in a hundred countries. His fiction and poetry have appeared in anthologies and in such diverse publications as *Whisperings, A Literary and Visual Culture Magazine; The Caribbean Writer,* a literary journal of the University of the Virgin Islands; and the San Francisco-based experimental/alternative multimedia quarterly *Free the Marquee.*

Yaros, Ken, D.D.S.—Ken, an alumnus of Albright College, received his DDS degree from Temple University. He spent six years serving with the Air Force and seven years serving with the Connecticut Air National Guard attaining the rank of major. Now semi-retired after 45 years of practice and teaching Dental Hygiene, he has turned his hand to writing short stories both non-fiction and fiction. He has been a contributor to *The Guilded Pen* since 2013 and was published in the national OASIS Journal 2014. Ken often writes under his pen name, KAY Allen, and is putting together an anthology of short stories for Kindle publication.

Yeaman, Sandra—Sandra has lived and worked in 12 countries, most of them so small you probably haven't heard of them. She is working on her memoir of her journey from a small town in Minnesota to Iran in the 1970s. She currently serves as social media manager for SDW/EG and has been published in *The Guilded Pen* since 2013. She blogs at sandrayeaman.com.

Zajac, Amy E. — Amy lives in San Marcos, California. Her first book, *It Started With Patton, Teresa Leska's Story, A Memoir* (2012), is her mother's compelling story as a Nazi political hostage. Amy has many stories published in anthologies since 2009, such as *Chicken Soup for the Soul – From Lemons to Lemonade*, released in 2013. She has been a yearly contributor to *The Guilded Pen* since 2012. Amy's first novel, *Foredestined*, a story of enlightenment after global destruction, was published December 2013. Currently, Amy is working on her dad's memoir. You can reach Amy at: azajac10@yahoo.com

Zolfaghari, Val — Val has lived in the USA, Canada, Spain, England, Turkey, and his native land Iran (Persia). His educational background is in engineering and education. He graduated from the University of California at Irvine with masters and bachelor degrees in engineering and pursued a technical career. In the 1990's, he earned a master's degree in education and Mathematics, and administrative credentials. He taught secondary mathematics and was president of a teacher's union for two terms. He retired in 2013 and after a year of vacation started writing short stories based on his political and teaching experiences. Val has been published in *The Guilded Pen* anthologies since 2015.

I'll call for pen and ink

    and write my mind.

—William Shakespeare

Made in the USA
Charleston, SC
13 November 2016